Original Thirteen Colonies, 1733

New Hampshire

Montreal ■

Massachusetts

Boston ■

Rhode Island

New York

Connecticut

■ **New York**

Pennsylvania

New Jersey

Philadelphia ■

Delaware

Maryland

Virginia

North Carolina

South Carolina

Georgia

North America, 1800-1809

Great Britain

United States

Territories of the United States

Spain

Disputed by Colonial Powers

Lower Canada (1791)

Upper Canada (1791)

Vermont (1791)

Illinois Territory (1809)

Michigan Territory (1805)

Ohio (1803)

Louisiana Territory (1805)

Indiana Territory (1800)

Kentucky (1792)

Tennessee (1796)

Mississippi Territory (1798; 1804 boundaries shown)

Orleans Territory (1804)

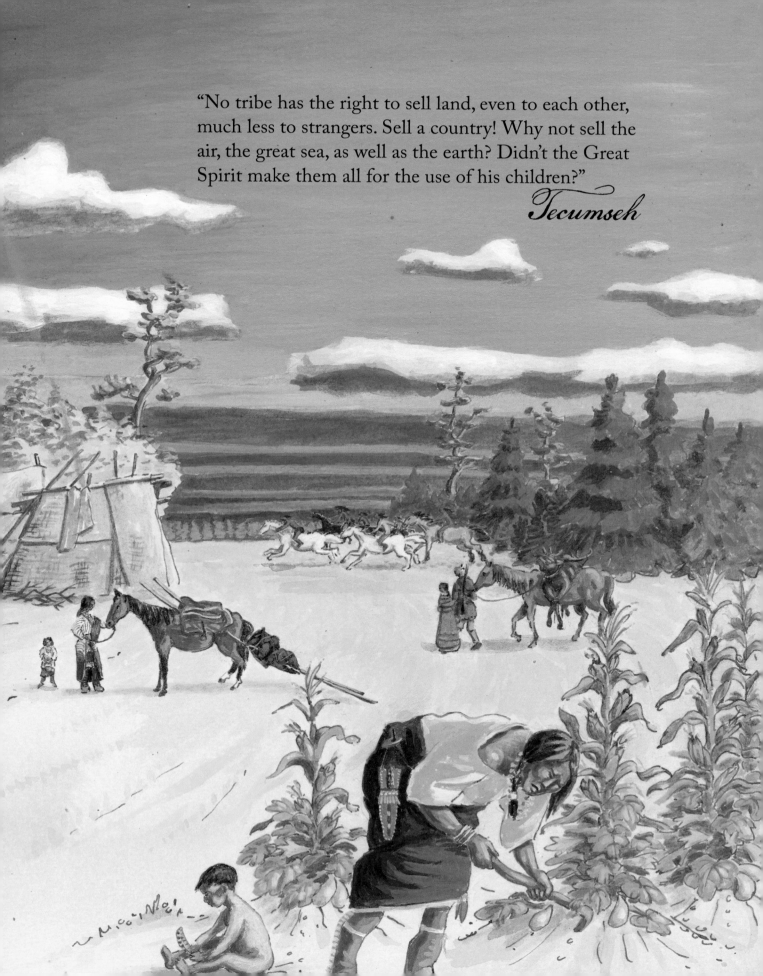

"No tribe has the right to sell land, even to each other, much less to strangers. Sell a country! Why not sell the air, the great sea, as well as the earth? Didn't the Great Spirit make them all for the use of his children?"

Tecumseh

To Nathaniel, Julia, Benjamin
and Robert. — JL

For her loving help and support,
I dedicate this book to my wife,
Susan Tooke. — RR

Acknowledgments
Writing this book has given me the chance to work with people I deeply
admire. At Groundwood, I have had the pleasure of working once more
with Nan Froman, Michael Solomon and my dear friend Patsy Aldana. It
has been an inspiration to collaborate with Richard Rudnicki. Thanks to
Paul-Emile McNab for his skilled research and advice and to my colleague
David T. McNab whose scholarship and published works on indigenous
peoples have been a great source of knowledge and perspective for me.
Again I am grateful to Sandy for her continuing encouragement. — JL

I wish to gratefully acknowledge the stories, enthusiasm and expertise of
Ken Hamilton (Native American culture, customs and history during the
seventeenth and eighteenth centuries) and Kevin Robins (Army Museum,
Halifax Citadel). I am also very thankful for the generous assistance of
Nikki, Neil and Nathan Hamilton; John MacLeod (Fort Malden); Peter
Kirby and Arlene Doucette (Canadian War Museum); and Jennie Silva
(Mt. Mist Farms). — RR

Groundwood Books / House of Anansi Press
110 Spadina Avenue, Suite 801
Toronto, Ontario M5V 2K4
or c/o Publishers Group West
1700 Fourth Street, Berkeley, CA 94710

We acknowledge for their financial support of our publishing program the
Canada Council for the Arts, the Government of Canada through the Canada Book
Fund (CBF) and the Ontario Arts Council.

 Canada Council **Conseil des Arts**
for the Arts **du Canada**

 ONTARIO ARTS COUNCIL
CONSEIL DES ARTS DE L'ONTARIO

Library and Archives Canada Cataloguing in Publication
Laxer, James
    Tecumseh / James Laxer ; illustrations by Richard Rudnicki.
ISBN 978-1-55498-123-6
 1. Tecumseh, 1768?-1813—Juvenile literature. 2. Shawnee
Indians—Kings and rulers—Biography—Juvenile literature.
3. Indians of North America—Wars—Northwest, Old—Juvenile
literature. 4. Indians of North America—Wars—1812-1815—Juvenile
literature. 5. Canada—History—War of 1812—Participation, Indian—
Juvenile literature. I. Rudnicki, Richard II. Title.
E99.S35T16 2012   j974.004'973170092   C2011-907091-X

The paintings in this book are rendered in acrylic on hot press watercolor paper.
Design by Michael Solomon
Printed and bound in Canada

Tecumseh

James Laxer

PICTURES BY Richard Rudnicki

GROUNDWOOD BOOKS

HOUSE OF ANANSI PRESS

TORONTO   BERKELEY

TECUMSEH was a renowned Shawnee chief who was determined to unite native peoples to stop American settlers from seizing their lands. He was a legendary warrior, respected by those who sided with him and even by those who did not. When Tecumseh visited a native village, people paid attention to what he had to say. Even today, two hundred years after his death, he is recognized as one of the most important native leaders of all time.

One way we know about Tecumseh is from the reminiscences written by Stephen Ruddell, a white boy who was raised by the Shawnees. We also know about him from the oral traditions of the Shawnees and other native peoples, and from accounts written by many people who met him over the course of his life, including officials in the United States government and British military officers. Together these accounts create an extraordinary life story...

Early Days

METHOATAASKEE looked into the heavens and saw a meteor shooting across the dark sky. That night, likely in 1768, she gave birth to a baby boy in the Shawnee settlement on the Ohio River.

The family named the baby Tecumethe, which in the Shawnee language means "shooting star" or "blazing comet." English-speaking people have come to call him Tecumseh.

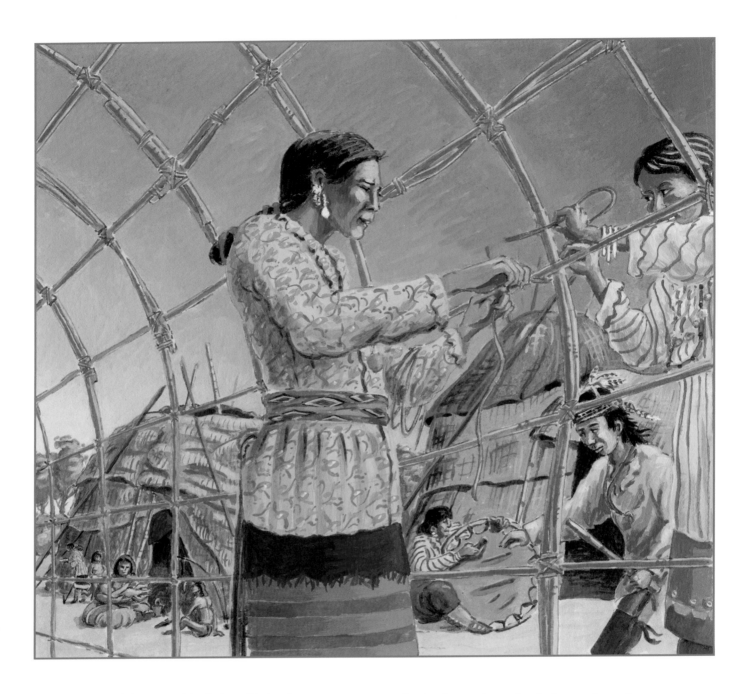

Tecumseh's father, Pukeshinwau, was an admired warrior who belonged to the Kispoko division of the Shawnees. The Kispokos were leaders in war. He was also a member of the panther clan. His name meant "something that falls."

Tecumseh's mother, Methoataaskee, belonged to the Pekowi division of the tribe, which was responsible for preserving traditions. She was a member of the turtle clan, and her name meant "a turtle laying her eggs in the sand."

In the settlement where Tecumseh was born, Methoataaskee and the other women were responsible for building the houses, or wigwams. They were made of bark fastened around wooden posts and built in the shape of a rectangle. Some of them had chimneys and were quite large. Women also made clothes and the other belongings that people had in their homes. They worked in the fields to raise crops, such as corn, beans and pumpkins. In the spring they tapped maple syrup from the trees. They roasted meat and made stews and breadcakes.

Men hunted deer, rabbit, turkey and buffalo, and fished. They made weapons and trained to become warriors who could fight to defend Shawnee settlements from attack.

Children like Tecumseh played near the fields where the women worked. Tecumseh was a mischievous boy, who had to be scolded regularly by his mother.

Settlers Strike

As a child, Tecumseh lived in a time of war and revolution. The settlers in the thirteen colonies in the eastern region of what is now the United States were rebelling against British rule. On July 4, 1776, the colonists issued the Declaration of Independence and established their own country — the United States of America. Led by George Washington, the colonists fought a war against Britain until 1783, when the British finally recognized the independence of the United States.

One cause of the American Revolution was the desire of the colonists to move west to occupy the lands of the native peoples. The colonists were furious at the British for the Proclamation of 1763, which declared that lands west of the Appalachian Mountains should be reserved for native tribes. The Americans wanted the land along the Ohio River where Tecumseh and his family lived. Even before the American Revolution, settlers pushed west into this territory from Pennsylvania, Virginia and other colonies.

The Shawnee people lived in fear of the settlers' attacks. One fall, when Tecumseh was six years old, Pukeshinwau learned that militiamen from Virginia were sweeping down on native settlements all along the Ohio River. They were burning the houses and destroying the crops in the fields. He rallied his warriors to prepare for the attack.

Young Tecumseh watched the men's war dances. Among the warriors was his thirteen-year-old brother, Cheeseekau. Would there be enough of them to stop the Virginians?

The Shawnees fought well, but the militiamen outnumbered them, and the warriors had to retreat. While the battle was still raging, Pukeshinwau was struck by a bullet and fell to the ground. As he lay dying he counseled Cheeseekau one last time: "Preserve unsullied the dignity and honor of the family and lead forth to battle your younger brothers."

In the years after he lost his father, there were times when Tecumseh and his family had to move to a new settlement because militiamen had destroyed the old one. Methoataaskee would pack up any belongings that had survived the fires, and the family would travel on horseback with the rest of their village in search of a new home.

When Tecumseh was nine years old, his family moved to Pekowi, a new settlement on the bank of the Mad River, which flowed into the Great Miami River. The town was not far from the present-day city of Springfield, Ohio.

Tecumseh remembered the land around Pekowi for the rest of his life. South of the river there was a great flat prairie where the women planted corn. North of it were woodlands, high bluffs and marshes. Tecumseh played in the fields and woods and climbed the bluffs. He learned the lay of the land, developing skills that would make him an able hunter and warrior.

But one day an army of men from Kentucky attacked Pekowi. Just before the attack, the women took Tecumseh and the other children to the bluffs above the town. There they watched their warriors lose the fight and then saw their homes burned to the ground.

It was time to move on again.

A Friend and a Guardian Spirit

IN 1780, WHEN Tecumseh was twelve years old,
he met a white boy named Stephen Ruddell.
Shawnee warriors had captured Stephen and
his younger brother Abraham during a war
against the Americans. They brought the
boys back to Tecumseh's village to be
raised as members of a Shawnee
family. Stephen, who was the
same age as Tecumseh, was
named Sinnamatha, which
meant "big fish." The
two boys became

the best of friends and spent their days together playing and learning to hunt.

Tecumseh soon became a skillful hunter. Stephen has told the story of the time the two of them went hunting when they were in their early teens. Stephen shot one buffalo with his musket. Tecumseh shot sixteen buffalo with his bow and a quiver of arrows. Maybe Stephen was exaggerating, but there's no doubt that Tecumseh was capable of providing food for his own family and for others in his settlement.

When Shawnee boys reached their teens, they had to search for a guardian spirit. The spirit might be an animal or a bird. It would give them strength and would be theirs alone.

Tecumseh's older brother Cheeseekau guided him in his search. He told Tecumseh that his guardian spirit might appear to him during dreams or ceremonies, and that once he found it, he should never tell anyone what kind of creature it was. As part of this passage to manhood, Cheeseekau blackened Tecumseh's face and sent him into the woods by himself to fast and pray. Tecumseh made this journey several times, remaining in the woods for three days on the last occasion.

Stephen Ruddell described Tecumseh as an athletic, attractive, friendly and warm-hearted teenager. "He was fond of creating his jokes," Stephen wrote, "but his wit was never aimed to wound the feelings of his comrades."

There were many opportunities for Tecumseh to develop relationships with young women during games and hunting parties. One favorite activity was the "bringing dance." Young men would begin the dance and then young women would join in, each one selecting the man she wanted as her partner. The women often chose Tecumseh. "The women were very fond of him," Stephen recalled, "much more so than he was of them."

Tecumseh and Cheeseekau

THREE YEARS after the end of the American Revolution, war erupted again between the Shawnees and the United States. As before, the war was about who owned the land. The Shawnees were determined to hold onto their settlements and hunting grounds, and the settlers wanted that land for themselves.

Cheeseekau organized the warriors in his village to prepare their weapons and to ride off to counter attackers from Kentucky. Eighteen-year-old Tecumseh was among them.

For the first time he faced men with guns shooting at him from only a short distance away. He was overcome with fear and fled, leaving the other warriors to carry on the fight. In his absence, Cheeseekau was wounded by enemy fire and had to be carried to safety. Tecumseh vowed never to run away from a battle again.

In the autumn of 1788, Cheeseekau and a small group of his warrior followers decided to seek a new life away from the constant wars with the Americans. They set out for the Mississippi River on horseback, hunting for food along the way.

At that time the Mississippi was the western boundary of the United States. Spain controlled the land on the other side of the river. The Spanish government wanted the Shawnees and other native peoples to settle along the Missouri River, even farther west, to prevent the United States from seizing the territory.

Tecumseh joined Cheeseekau's expedition. So did their younger twin brothers, Lalawethika and Kumskaukau, who were about fourteen years old. Their mother Methoataaskee may have gone on the journey as well.

One day Tecumseh joined a party to hunt buffalo. Riding his horse at a gallop, he was suddenly thrown to the ground. He was unable to stand up and lay clutching his leg in agony. He had broken a thighbone.

Cheeseekau and the rest of the group decided that Tecumseh could go no farther until his wound healed. They built a camp where they could spend the winter and hunt for the food they needed.

When spring came, Tecumseh's thigh still ached, and he could only walk with crutches. Cheeseekau urged him to stay where he was with a few warriors while the rest of the party continued the journey. But Tecumseh insisted on staying with the expedition.

Finally, the bone healed and the pain ended. But Tecumseh was left with a slight limp for the rest of his life.

Cheeseekau's party did cross the Mississippi River. But after a short stay on Spanish territory, where they encountered white merchants and other native tribes, they concluded that they had not found the freedom they desired. And so they re-crossed the great river and headed south-east to the rugged land where the present states of Tennessee, Georgia and Alabama meet.

In a mountainous, rocky territory, where rapids on the rivers made travel difficult, the Shawnees joined up with another tribe, the Chicka-mauga Cherokees. The Chickamauga Cherokees were fighting their own war against the Americans. They had been pushed off their land, down the Tennessee River to Lookout Mountain, close to the present city of Chattanooga.

Tecumseh and his brothers fought many battles alongside the Cherokees. They raided boats carrying American settlers down the rivers. They seized goods from the travelers and often held them for ransom before releasing them. Sometimes warriors died in these fights, and sometimes Americans were killed.

Tecumseh hated the idea of prisoners being tortured or put to death. Once he had been with a party of warriors who captured a boat on the Ohio River. Some of them proceeded to put five of the captives to death, burning one of them while he was still alive. According to Stephen Ruddell, Tecumseh "expressed great abhorrence" about what had hap-pened, and "it was concluded among them not to burn any more pris-oners that should afterwards be taken."

Tecumseh was learning how to influence and persuade others, de-veloping the skills that would one day make him a chief and eventually the foremost leader of the native peoples.

American Troops

Artillery unit

General on horseback

Militiaman with musket, canteen, powder horn and haversack

Soldier with musket

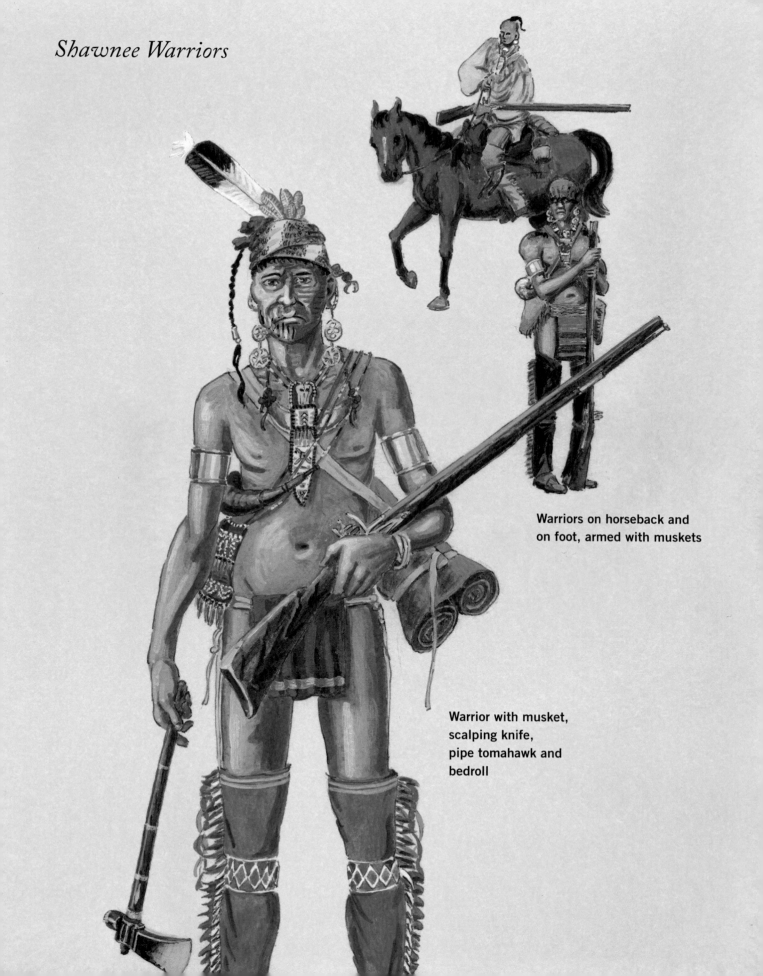

Shawnee Warriors

Warriors on horseback and on foot, armed with muskets

Warrior with musket, scalping knife, pipe tomahawk and bedroll

Chief Tecumseh

IN SEPTEMBER 1792, Tecumseh joined a nighttime raiding party led by Cheeseekau against a small American post close to Nashville. Leaving their horses a short distance away, the warriors crept through the woods under a full moon, planning to surprise the defenders inside the blockhouse. But their rustling in the woods spooked a herd of cattle, and the sounds of the animals brought the Americans to full alert.

One of the soldiers loaded his musket, aimed it through a porthole and fired at the shadowy figures outside. Cheeseekau was shot dead. Tecumseh had now lost both his father and his older brother in battles against the Americans.

In 1795, the Americans forced a treaty on the Shawnees and other native peoples — the Treaty of Greenville — that took two-thirds of the present state of Ohio from the tribes. Tecumseh hated this turn of events, but he was not yet in a position to do much about it.

Even so, by 1795, Tecumseh's skills as a warrior, hunter and leader had attracted enough followers for him to set up his own village on land that remained under the control of the Shawnees in Ohio. About 250 people joined him there. Among them were some of his relatives, including his brother Lalawethika. Tecumseh was now a chief. Soon his leadership would extend far beyond a single village.

Tecumseh thought long and hard about the fact that all of the native peoples, not just his Shawnees, were losing their land to the settlers. And he realized that unless the native peoples came together to form a great confederacy, they could never halt the theft of their land. The tribes would simply be picked off, one by one. But if they dealt with the United States with a single voice, things could be different. Tecumseh saw the land of native peoples as a common meal needed by all to nourish them. He believed they must treat this meal as "a dish with one spoon."

Tecumseh was not the first native leader to have this idea. But he became the most effective leader of his time to act on it.

The Prophet

TECUMSEH's younger brother Lalawethika showed little promise when he was a child. He was lazy, and as a young man he was often drunk. He had lost one eye in an accident and sometimes used a handkerchief to cover the socket.

As he was smoking in his wigwam one day, Lalawethika dropped his pipe and fell into a coma. When he regained consciousness, he told his fellow tribesmen that he had been transported to a place where he had spoken with the Great Spirit. He began to call himself Tenskwatawa, which meant "open door," and he claimed that he was a prophet. The Shawnees had had prophets in the past.

"The Prophet" preached that his people must give up the ways of the white man and return to the traditional path of the Shawnees. He announced that native women must not marry white men. He told the Shawnees that they had to wear the traditional dress of their people. He warned against drunkenness, claiming that when he became a prophet he soared up to the clouds to the dwelling of the devil, where he saw those who had died as drunkards. Flames shot out of the mouths of these poor wretches.

Tenskwatawa believed that he could identify people who were witches and who caused others to fall sick. On a few occasions, different native communities asked him to seek out the witches among them, and then they were put to death.

By 1808, Tenskwatawa and Tecumseh had created a new settlement — Prophetstown — on the Wabash River in the Indiana Territory. Tenskwatawa invited warriors from many tribes to come and live there with him to follow his teachings.

Tecumseh adopted some of the Prophet's ideas. He stopped wearing the shirts and trousers of the white man. Instead, he dressed in a deerskin shirt and leggings and wore moccasins decorated with dyed porcupine quills.

Tecumseh and the Prophet both believed that native peoples should act together to prevent the Americans from taking their lands. For the Prophet this was a spiritual idea, but for Tecumseh it was a political cause. Tecumseh was more broad-minded than his brother. He was willing to work with people from different cultures, including the Americans and the British.

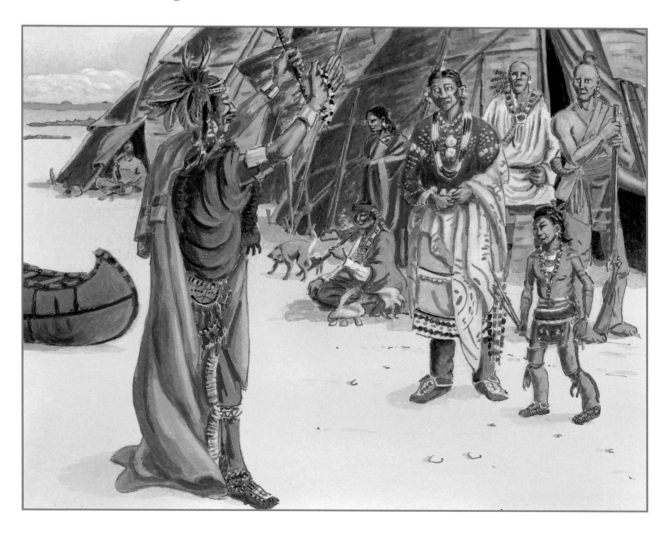

A Warning

BY THIS TIME Tecumseh had gained a wide reputation as a famous warrior and chief. He was organizing the native peoples into a confederacy so that they could talk to the Americans with one voice. He traveled long distances, winning many followers from other tribes to his cause.

As Tecumseh's fame grew, the Americans became aware that he was a leader who could threaten them. One such American was William Henry Harrison, the governor of the Indiana Territory, who was later elected president of the United States. Harrison invited Tecumseh to meet with him to see if the United States could work out a deal with this rising native leader.

In August 1810, the two men met at Vincennes, located in present-day Knox County, Indiana. Tecumseh rode up to the meeting with a party of forty warriors. Governor Harrison had set up chairs and benches outside his house. But speaking through his interpreter Sikaboo, Tecumseh told the governor that he preferred to meet in a nearby grove of trees, and that he would sit on the bosom of his mother, the earth. And with that Tecumseh and his warriors settled themselves on the ground as seats were hastily drawn over for Harrison and his men.

The meeting was tense. Tecumseh told Harrison that the treaties the United States had signed with individual native leaders and tribes were wrong. The treaties must be torn up. The Americans couldn't take away the native peoples' land for the settlers.

When Harrison replied bluntly that the treaties would remain in effect, the warriors raised their tomahawks. Harrison's soldiers shouldered their muskets. For a moment it appeared that violence would erupt, and Harrison ended the meeting.

The next day Tecumseh and Harrison held a final talk. The atmosphere was calmer, but Tecumseh's warning to the United States was clear. If the land was not returned to the native peoples, there would be war.

Tuckhabatchee

ON SEPTEMBER 20, 1811, Tecumseh rode into Tuckhabatchee, the capital of the Muscogee people, located in present-day Alabama, far to the south of the Ohio River. Twenty warriors from the Shawnee, Kickapoo and Winnebago tribes rode into town with him. Thousands of people had gathered there for the meeting of the Muscogee national council. They were anxious to hear what the famous Shawnee chief would say.

Tecumseh and his companions had ridden a long way across the United States to Tuckhabatchee. They had stopped many times so that Tecumseh could talk to different tribes along the way. He was convinced that war was coming between the United States and the native peoples, and he wanted as many warriors on his side as possible.

When he was ready to speak, Tecumseh and his party marched into the crowded council house. They were naked, except for flaps around their waists. Their faces were painted, and they wore eagle feathers on their heads. Bands around their arms held buffalo tails in place.

Tecumseh offered a bag of wampum — sacred beads fashioned from shells — a hatchet and a peace pipe to the head chief, whose name was Big Warrior. Sikaboo stood at Tecumseh's side ready to translate his words from Shawnee to Muscogee.

Tecumseh warned the gathered warriors that there would be war with the United States. He called on them to join the fight, shouting, "Oh, Muscogees! Brethren of my mother! Brush from your eyelids the sleep of slavery, and strike for vengeance and your country!"

A thousand warriors cheered and raised their tomahawks in the air. But all through the speech Big Warrior sat with a disapproving frown.

Seeing this, Tecumseh shouted at him, "Your blood is white: you have taken my talk… and the wampum, and the hatchet, but you do not mean to fight. I know the reason: you do not believe the Great Spirit has sent me. You shall know: I leave Tuckhabatchee directly, and shall go straight to Detroit. When I arrive there, I will stamp the ground with my foot, and shake down every house in Tuckhabatchee."

Tecumseh departed for the north, but the sharp words he had hurled at Big Warrior were not forgotten. Some of the Muscogees were counting the days, calculating how long it would take Tecumseh to reach Detroit.

In the early hours of December 16, the day the Muscogees reckoned he would complete his journey, the earth trembled with the first waves of a powerful earthquake. Every house in Tuckhabatchee was shaken to the ground.

The quake was centered near New Madrid in the present state of Missouri, but it was felt as far away as New York City and southern Canada. For a short time, the mighty shock caused the Mississippi River to flow backwards.

"Tecumseh has reached Detroit!" were the words on the lips of many Muscogees that day. They connected the trembling of the earth with Tecumseh's prophecy and concluded that the Shawnee chief's call to arms must be heeded.

Tribal Chiefs Tecumseh is shown in the middle foreground. Clockwise from Tecumseh are chiefs who supported the native confederacy from the Chippewa, Winnebago, Muscogee, Cherokee, Sac, Potawatomi and Ottawa tribes.

Attack on Prophetstown

WHILE TECUMSEH was on his great journey to win support for the native confederacy, William Henry Harrison led a force of soldiers against Prophetstown.

The Prophet, who was no match for his brother as a warrior, decided to confront the Americans before they reached his settlement. On November 7, 1811, his men launched a pre-dawn surprise attack, but an American sentry spotted them and alerted the Americans.

At the Battle of Tippecanoe, in present-day Indiana, Harrison's soldiers defeated the Prophet's warriors. Then they burned Prophetstown to the ground. The Prophet lost the support of many of his followers as a consequence.

When Tecumseh returned, he was so furious with his brother for attempting a military strike against Harrison that he briefly thought of killing him. Then he calmed down, accepted the disaster and continued to build the native confederacy.

War of 1812

On June 18, 1812, the United States declared war on Great Britain. The Americans had a number of reasons for going to war. They were angry with the British for stopping American trading ships on the high seas and searching them to find British sailors who had deserted from the Royal Navy. The British were in the midst of a great war against the French Empire of Napoleon Bonaparte. They were determined to prevent the U.S. shippers from selling goods to France, and they wanted to stop their sailors from deserting.

A group of American politicians known as the War Hawks, led by Henry Clay and John Calhoun, had their own reasons for favoring war with Britain. The War Hawks supported rapid western settlement on the lands of the native peoples. They accused the British of providing native warriors with weapons, which on occasion was true. Many Americans who were hostile to Britain supported an invasion of Canada, which remained in the British Empire. Former U.S. president Thomas Jefferson declared that seizing Canada would be "a mere matter of marching."

For Tecumseh, this declaration of war was a momentous event. He didn't care why the Americans and the British were going to war. But he was ready to ally with the British if they would help him fight to regain native lands from the United States.

Tecumseh had anticipated the war. For two years he had been traveling throughout the regions on the edge of American settlement, winning native tribes to his confederacy.

In November 1810, Tecumseh had taken more than 130 warriors, 30 women and a small number of children to Fort Malden, the British military post on Lake Erie in Upper Canada (present-day Ontario). Among them, in addition to Shawnees, were Potawatomis, Ottawas, Winnebagos and Sacs.

Tecumseh told the British commanders that war was coming. "We sit at or near the borders where the contest will begin," he said. His plan was to leave many of the old men, women and children near the British fort, while he set out to recruit more native warriors for the battle.

And so when the War of 1812 finally broke out, Tecumseh fought as the ally of the British and as the leader of the native confederacy. His goal was to establish a new native state north of the Ohio River that would lie between the United States and Canada.

Tecumseh and Brock

IN JULY 1812, under the command of General William Hull, American soldiers invaded Upper Canada from Detroit.

"I come to protect, not to injure you," the general proclaimed to the inhabitants of Canada. He warned against any alliance between the British and the Canadians with the native peoples. "No white man found fighting by the side of an Indian will be taken prisoner," he declared. "Instead, death will be his lot."

Tecumseh led warriors from many tribes in the fight against General Hull's invasion. On the evening of August 13, 1812, Major General Isaac Brock, the commander of British troops in Upper Canada, arrived by boat at Fort Malden on Lake Erie. Brock's first request was for a meeting with Tecumseh.

When Tecumseh and Brock met that evening, they struck up an immediate friendship. Brock, who was taller than the Shawnee chief, reached out to shake his hand. Tecumseh wore a large silver medallion of King George III attached to a colorful wampum string around his neck.

"This is a man," Tecumseh declared later, when telling his warriors about Brock. And after Brock had fought side by side with Tecumseh and his men, he wrote in a letter that the native leader who most attracted his attention was "a Shawnee Chief, Tecumseh, brother to the Prophet, who for the last two years has carried on…an active warfare against the United States… a more gallant warrior does not, I believe, exist."

Planning for Battle

Brock and Tecumseh agreed to attack Fort Detroit at once. They planned to cross the Detroit River with British regular soldiers, Canadian militiamen and native warriors.

At a meeting to discuss the details of the attack, the Shawnee chief spread out a long strip of birch bark on the table. He secured the edges with stones, unsheathed his knife and proceeded to create a map with its tip.

Brock was impressed as he watched Tecumseh draw the roads, waterways, valleys and hills of the neighboring terrain. He told Tecumseh that no peace would be made with the Americans until the lands of the native peoples were secure.

The British camp on the eve of battle

As they neared the fort, the attackers used several tricks to alarm General Hull. Tecumseh had his warriors cross in front of the fort several times, sneaking back under cover each time. This made Hull think that there were two or three thousand warriors rather than the real number — six hundred. And Brock dressed the Canadian militiamen in the scarlet uniforms of British regular soldiers, which led Hull to believe that he was up against many more highly trained regulars than was the case.

On August 16, 1812, before an all-out attack, General Hull surrendered Fort Detroit, garrison and all. The American militiamen were set free to return to their homes. The regulars, including Hull, were marched to Montreal. The British later exchanged them for British prisoners held by the Americans.

In celebration of their common victory, Tecumseh presented Brock with a colorful scarf.

Queenston Heights

Two months after the capture of Detroit, American soldiers set out in boats across the swift-flowing Niagara River to invade Upper Canada just below Niagara Falls. The Americans won the first encounter.

But General Brock led his troops in a counterattack. After pausing to allow his men to catch their breath, they charged up the heights at Queenston. Brock urged his men forward, a sword in hand. He was wearing the scarf Tecumseh had given him.

Suddenly, a scout from Ohio fired, striking Brock through the breast and killing him. A few hours later, shouting "Revenge the General!" British regulars, Canadian militiamen and Iroquois warriors rallied and won the battle.

Native warriors were deeply saddened by the death of General Brock. Three days later they lined the route of his funeral procession in his honor.

Retreat

THE SUMMER after Tecumseh and Brock's great victory at Detroit, American ships on Lake Erie, under the command of Commodore Oliver Hazard Perry, defeated a squadron of British ships. With control of the lake in their hands, William Henry Harrison, who had taken command of U.S. troops in the region, led a new invasion of Canada.

Major General Henry Procter, the new commander of British troops in the area, concluded that with the Americans in control of Lake Erie, the British could no longer supply Fort Malden. He decided to give up the fort and to retreat inland up the Thames River.

Tecumseh was disgusted with the British decision to retreat.

"You always told us," he declared to General Procter in front of his officers, "that you would never draw your foot off British ground; but now, father, we see you are drawing back… We must compare our father's conduct to a fat animal, that carries its tail upon its back, but when affrighted, it drops between its legs, and runs off."

The British officers laughed when they heard the translation of Tecumseh's speech. Indeed Procter was no Brock and the British abandoned the fort, setting it on fire so that it wouldn't fall into American hands.

Days later, Tecumseh sat on his horse and watched as the Americans took ground he had defended for over a year.

Moraviantown

Tecumseh decided he had no choice but to continue
the fight. He rallied the native warriors who remained
loyal to him and led them along with British soldiers in
skirmishes against the advancing U.S. troops.

Tecumseh then joined Procter near Moraviantown,
not far from the present city of London, Ontario, where
they prepared their men for an all-out battle against the
Americans.

On October 5, 1813, Tecumseh, dressed in deerskin,
his face painted black and red, walked along the line of
British officers, shaking hands with each of them and
offering a few words of encouragement in Shawnee.

A Warrior's End

EARLY IN THE battle, American soldiers broke
through the British line and forced Procter's
troops to withdraw.

Tecumseh and his men fought on, although
they were now alone against the enemy. On
swampy ground and in dense woods, Tecumseh's
warriors could see their leader firing his musket,
and they drew courage from him. At the high
point of the fight, Tecumseh pushed ahead to lead
his men forward. An American soldier aimed and
fired. His bullet struck the Shawnee chief in the
chest. The news quickly spread among the warriors that their great leader had been killed, and
they retreated from the battlefield into the woods.

Epilogue

THE WAR OF 1812 continued for more than a year after the death of Tecumseh. In April 1813, the Americans burned down the public buildings in York (Toronto). The following summer, in retaliation, the British attacked Washington D.C. and burned the President's House (White House) and the Capitol, the building in which the houses of Congress were located.

Finally, after months of talks between U.S. and British negotiators in Ghent, in present-day Belgium, a peace treaty was signed on December 24, 1814. Under its terms, no territory changed hands. The border between the United States and Canada remained as it was in 1812.

The end of the war opened the way for American settlers to move farther west, taking more land. The British had pledged to side with the native peoples. Brock had told Tecumseh that he would not give up the fight until the tribes had won control of their land. But by the time the war ended, both Brock and Tecumseh were dead.

During the peace negotiations with the Americans, the British did propose the creation of a native state, but when the U.S. representatives strongly opposed this, the British withdrew the idea. Both sides agreed to restore the rights of the native peoples as they had existed before the start of the war. But the Americans largely ignored this agreement.

Under the peace treaty they signed, the British did not live up to the promise they had made to Tecumseh.

During his extraordinary life, Tecumseh fought not only to save his own Shawnees from conquest, but to save all native peoples. In the end, his confederacy did not win. But Tecumseh's courage, eloquence and steadiness of purpose continue to fascinate people in many parts of the world two centuries after his death. He remains a symbol of justice for the native tribes of North America.

EVENTS IN THE LIFE OF TECUMSEH

1768 Tecumseh is born.

1774 Tecumseh's father, Pukeshinwau, dies in the Battle of Point Pleasant.

1776 The Declaration of Independence of the United States is adopted on July 4.

1780 Tecumseh and Stephen Ruddell become friends.

1786 Tecumseh fights in his first battle as a warrior.

1788 Tecumseh, his brother Cheeseekau and a party of warriors depart for the west.

1792 Tecumseh's brother Cheeseekau dies in a raid on John Buchanan's Station, near Nashville, Tennessee.

1795 The United States forces the Shawnees and other native peoples to accept the Treaty of Greenville, taking two-thirds of the present state of Ohio from the tribes.

Tecumseh becomes the chief of a village in what is now the state of Ohio and begins to work toward a native confederacy.

1808 Tecumseh's brother Tenskwatawa creates Prophetstown on the Wabash River.

1810 Tecumseh meets William Henry Harrison, Governor of the Indiana Territory, at Vincennes on August 12.

1811 Tecumseh takes his message to Tuckhabatchee, capital of the Muscogee people, on September 20.

Prophetstown is destroyed in the Battle of Tippecanoe on November 7.

1812 The United States declares war on Great Britain on June 18.

Tecumseh and Major General Isaac Brock capture Fort Detroit on August 16.

On October 13, the Americans invade Canada at Niagara, Brock dies at Queenston Heights, and the British win the battle.

1813 On April 27, U.S. forces attack York (Toronto) and destroy public buildings.

Tecumseh dies in the Battle of Moraviantown, near London, Ontario, on October 5.

GLOSSARY

blockhouse A small fort in a single building to be defended against attackers.

colonist A settler in a colony, such as the settlers in the thirteen British colonies that became the United States.

confederacy An association of states or communities. The native confederacy brought together warriors from a large number of tribes.

garrison A military force stationed in a town or fort to defend it.

Kispoko The warrior division within the Shawnee tribe.

militiamen Military men in a local force that is called into service in a time of emergency, such as an invasion.

Pekowi The division within the Shawnee tribe that maintained traditions. Also the name of a settlement where Tecumseh lived.

regulars Soldiers who have enlisted for permanent service in a country's army.

wampum Sacred shell beads, sometimes woven into a belt, used by native peoples for a variety of purposes. One purpose of a wampum belt was to commemorate a treaty or military alliance.

SOURCES

Page 5 "No tribe…children" Frederick Turner III, ed., *Poetry and Oratory: The Portable North American Indian Reader* (New York: Penguin Books, 1974), 245–246; 12 "Preserve unsullied…brothers" Stephen Ruddell, *Reminiscences of Tecumseh's Youth* (Wisconsin Historical Society, Digital Library and Archives, Document No. AJ-155, 2003), 121; 17 "Stephen has told…arrows", "He was fond…comrades" and "The women…them" Ibid., 124; 21 "expressed great…taken" Ibid., 124; 25 "a dish…spoon" John Sugden, *Tecumseh: A Life* (New York: Henry Holt and Company, 1997), 44–45; 31 "Oh, Muscogees…country!" Sean Michael O'Brien, *In Bitterness and in Tears: Andrew Jackson's Destruction of the Creeks and Seminoles* (Guilford, Connecticut: The Lyons Press, 2005), 23; "Your blood…Tuckhabatchee" Benjamin Drake, *Life of Tecumseh, and of his brother The Prophet, with a Historical Sketch of the Shawanoe Indians* (Cincinnati: E. Morgan and Company, 1841), 144; 36 "a mere…marching" David S. Heidler and Jeanne T. Heidler, eds., *Encyclopedia of the War of 1812* (Annapolis, Maryland: Naval Institute Press, 1997), 266; 37 "We sit…begin" Sugden, 212–213; 38 "I come…you" and "No white man…lot" John Brannan, collected and annotated, *Official Letters of the Military and Naval Officers of the United States during the War with Great Britain in The Years 1812, 13, 14 & 15: with some additional letters and documents elucidating the history of that period* (Washington D.C.: Way and Gideon, 1823), 30–31; "This is a man," A. J. Langguth, *Union 1812: The Americans Who Fought the Second War of Independence* (New York: Simon and Schuster, 2006), 188.; "a Shawnee…exist" Brock to the Earl of Liverpool, York, Upper Canada, 29th August, 1812 (Indian Affairs Canada, RG 10 Volume 10017, Colonial Office Records, Canada Q. 315), 118; 45 "Revenge…General" Adam Shortt and Arthur G. Doughty, *Canada And Its Provinces* (Toronto: Publishers' Association of Canada, 1913), v. III, 234–235; 47 "You always…off" Brannan, 240–241.

FOR FURTHER READING

Reminiscences of Tecumseh's Youth by Stephen Ruddell. Wisconsin Historical Society, Digital Library and Archives, 2003. (To read this work, in Stephen Ruddell's handwriting, go to http://content.wisconsinhistory.org/cdm4/document.php?CISOROOT=/aj&CISOPTR=17916.)

Tecumseh: Shooting Star of the Shawnee by Dwight Jon Zimmerman. New York: Sterling, 2010.

Lands Defended by Tecumseh's Confederacy, c. 1810-1813

CHIPPEWA

LAKE SUPERIOR

CHIPPEWA (OJIBWAY)

OTTAWA

WINNEBAGO

LAKE MICHIGAN

LAKE HURON

CHIPPEWA

WYANDOT

UPPER CANADA

York ■

LAKE ONTARIO

■ Queenston Heights

Moraviantown ■

THAMES RIVER

Detroit ■
Fort Malden ■

LAKE ERIE

SAC

POTAWATOMI

MIAMI

OHIO

KICKAPOO

■ Prophetstown

SHAWNEE

WABASH RIVER

GREAT MIAMI RIVER

■ Pekowi

IROQUOIS

OHIO RIVER

MISSOURI RIVER

■ Vincennes

KENTUCKY

APPALACHIAN MOUNTAINS

SHAWNEE

New Madrid ■

MISSISSIPPI RIVER

TENNESSEE RIVER

LOUISIANA TERRITORY

Nashville ■

TENNESSEE

CHEROKEE

MISSISSIPPI TERRITORY

GEORGIA

Tuckhabatchee ■

MUSCOGEE (CREEK)

ENCYCLOPEDIA
OF GREAT
WRITERS

This edition published by Barnes & Noble, Inc,
by arrangement with Carlton Books Ltd.

1997 Barnes & Noble

ISBN 0 7607 0761 8

M 10 9 8 7 6 5 4 3 2 1

Text and design copyright © Carlton Books Limited 1997

PROJECT EDITOR: Simon Kirrane
PROJECT ART DIRECTION: Zoë Maggs
PICTURE RESEARCH: Charlotte Bush
PRODUCTION: Sarah Schuman

Printed in Dubai

ENCYCLOPEDIA
OF GREAT
WRITERS

TOM PAYNE

BARNES
&NOBLE
BOOKS
NEW YORK

Anouilh

JEAN

born Bordeaux 1910; died 1987

In a tragedy, nothing is in doubt and everyone's destiny is known. That makes for tranquillity. There is a sort of fellow-feeling among characters in a tragedy: he who kills is as innocent as he who gets killed: it's all a matter of what part you are playing.

ANTIGONE, TR. LEWIS GALANTIÈRE

JEAN ANOUILH WAS a versatile and internationally acclaimed playwright. He wrote some 40 dramas, dividing them into different categories, such as "Dark plays", "Pink plays", "Bright plays", "Costume plays", "Grating plays" and "New grating plays".

In his early career, Anouilh wrote jokes for films scripts and worked as an advertising copywriter. Although he was influenced by the dramatist Giraudoux, who was busily trying to revive the classical themes and verse forms of such masters as **Corneille** and **Molière**, this experience as a commercial writer gave Anouilh a unique insight into how modern audiences respond to words.

Consequently, Anouilh's fame rests on plays that take seemingly elevated or aloof themes and make them accessible without impairing their nobility. He adapted the plots of **Euripides** in *Médée* and of **Sophocles** in *Antigone*. In the latter, he tries to place his audience in the Ancient Greek situation of knowing the story before seeing it represented, and uses the device of the chorus to comment on the action and the process of tragedy. Like **Cocteau**, he used innovative techniques to tell mythical stories with a human angle. His writing is full of digressions and cameos, while preserving that unity of time and space in action so admired by Aristotle.

It is a reflection of his dramatic objectivity that *Antigone* appeared in Paris in 1942 without offending the French or the occupying Nazis. The heroine embodies a youthful faith in ideals, while the king merely obeys orders. This duality informs plays dealing with more religious subjects, such as *Becket, or, The Honour of God* and *The Lark*, about Joan of Arc. Both centre on characters embarking upon spiritual crusades in an equally compelling material world.

Apollinaire

GUILLAUME   **born Rome 1880; died Paris 1918**

I leave to the future the story of

    Guillaume Apollinaire

Who was at war and knew how to be

    everywhere

In the happy towns behind the lines

In the whole rest of the universe

THE MARVELS OF WAR

IN HIS SHORT LIFETIME, Apollinaire was at the forefront of every artistic movement pulsing through *fin-de-siècle* Paris. In writing about the Eiffel Tower he was the prophet of modernism: "Here, even the cars look like they're ancient." In writing about art, he was cubism's leading apologist. Writing about his own artistic impulses, he coined the term "surrealist". He found beauty in everything. He wrote plays, stories and art criticism; but the true medium for his all-embracing personality was poetry.

In this he was a ceaseless experimenter. In *Alcools* (1913), he abandoned punctuation. This didn't prevent his verse from making musical or syntactical sense. Many of his poems have become songs, and Poulenc wrote a score for his play *The Breasts of Tiresias* – the first performance of which caused a riot in 1917. His faultlessly lyrical ear bent towards end-stopped lines with rocking internal rhymes, which allowed the content of his stanzas to go wherever it wanted. This let his daring vocabulary loose to unconscious operations through the principle of "automatic" writing. In *Calligrammes* he presented his poetry in pictorial form, so that the reader's eye lands on a cannon or star-shaped poem, with various

MAJOR WORKS

The Decaying Magician
  (1909)

Bestiary (1911)

Alcools (1913)

The Poet Assassinated (1916)

Calligrammes (1918)

The Breasts of Tiresias (1918)

choices of where to begin. Here he slipped in the comment, "I'm also a painter."

He never made these innovations at the expense of sincerity or soul. His capacity for love and vastly generous friendship shines through, such that one can see why he led Paris' artistic community from Montmartre to Montparnasse, and how, when his burial coincided with the Armistice celebrations, his mourners believed the Tricoleurs were draped for him. As a performer, prisoner (falsely accused of stealing the *Mona Lisa*), soldier and socialite, he was all things to an enormous circle of artists.

Auden

W.H.

Our apparatniks will continue making the usual squalid mess called History: all we can pray for is that artists, chefs and saints may still appear to blithe it.

MOON LANDING (AUGUST 1969)

AUDEN WAS PERHAPS England's finest poet of the 20th century. He emerged as a precocious left-wing voice in the 30s, in Alan Bennett's words, "like a student into digs". He was the foremost writer of a coterie that included Cecil Day-Lewis, Stephen Spender and **Christopher Isherwood** – collaborating with the latter on several plays, most notably *The Ascent of F6*.

In his youth, his work and life were overtly political: he witnessed the Spanish Civil War and married **Thomas Mann**'s daughter Erika in 1935 to get her out of Nazi Germany.

The publication of *September 1, 1939* marked the outbreak of war and an important development in Auden's career. By then he was already settled in the United States and was fast turning away from political solutions to the crisis. He later repudiated the poem's most quoted line, "We must love one another or die", as illogical; but it stands as a plea for the most personal kind of understanding.

Much of Auden's work dealt with this kind of love, sometimes with a **Proust**-like search for an explanation, sometimes with a refreshing flippancy. Other motifs include the harshness of time, the abuses of history and the power of music. He collaborated with composers, most notably Britten and Stravinsky, to produce some of the best libretti in opera.

His verse, meanwhile, never lost its own musicality. He would write ballads, sonnets, or in strict metrical patterns of his own devising and was as at home with Anglo-Saxon schemes as with the cadences of **Horace**. He was able to adopt the forms of **Pope** or **Byron** without losing his unique diction, distinguished by compassion and devastating understatement.

He became a US citizen in 1945 and Professor of Poetry at Oxford in 1956. Unlike **Eliot**, his first publisher, he seemed at ease with his public role, and even into his old age was ready with apt or trenchant lines in response to global events. He died in 1973, and is commemorated in Westminster Abbey.

Austen

JANE **born Steventon Hants, 1775; died Winchester, Hants 1817**

Where people wish to attach, they should always be ignorant. To come with a well-informed mind, is to come with an inability of administering to the vanity of others, which a sensible person would wish to avoid. A woman especially, if she should have the misfortune of knowing anything, should conceal it as well as she can.

PERSUASION

THERE IS NO MENTION of Jane Austen's literary achievements on her tomb in Winchester Cathedral, as only four of her novels appeared during her lifetime. This is partly because of the extensive rewriting all her work underwent before reaching the state that many of her readers consider perfection.

She began early, with parody. At 14, she had **Richardson** in her sights: *Love and Friendship* is a skit on his correspondence novels. Another early book, *Northanger Abbey*, plays with the Gothic genre. This accounts not only for her command of style, and her humorous touch, but also the feeling that her books present a world of their own, with rules and characters peculiar to it.

It is a world where practical considerations preside over passionate ones. In *Sense and Sensibility*, for example, Marianne makes an impulsive choice, and errs; while in *Pride and Prejudice*, the independent-minded Elizabeth refuses to marry for convenience, before slowly coming to love Mr Darcy – that he's a wealthy London gentleman helps. It is a world in which all characters, major or minor, are key components, each tipping one way or the other the balance between social acceptability and unfettered self-expression.

Her prose is noted for its understatement and irony, although it is gentle enough to prevent the light treatment of the social types portrayed from descending into ridicule. Even so, some read Austen's work as a sustained satire on her age's conventions. Others more pryingly look for private causes for this view of life, citing her permanently single status (although she was once engaged for a night). Whichever way one reads Austen, one will be aware of a supremely delicate manner rendering a complex kind of living into the subtlest kind of art.

Beaumarchais

PIERRE AUGUSTIN CARON DE **born Paris 1732; died Paris 1799**

In the end, the urge to tell someone, "I love you," becomes so pressing that I say it on my own, running in the park, to your mistress, to you, to the trees, the clouds, to the wind that carries them along with my lost words...

THE MARRIAGE OF FIGARO

IN SPITE OF HIS REPUTATION as one of France's greatest comic dramatists, Beaumarchais' first audience was for his autobiography. He published it from 1774 to 1778, and presented himself as the social underdog in an ongoing inheritance dispute. The public loved it.

His writing for the stage has been called "more journalism than art". If this is true, Beaumarchais was an excellent journalist. Just as his memoirs caught the public mood, so his *Marriage of Figaro* (portraying a household in which a Count pretends to concede his right to sleep with a bride-to-be under his jurisdiction, only to be exposed) showed an unerring sense of where power was going in pre-Revolutionary France. On the one hand, Beaumarchais' vision of a household in which the servants know more than the master seems to come from **Plautus**, and to be harmless enough; on the other, da Ponte's attempts to turn the play into an opera libretto in Vienna a year after its publication met with censorship. The text was considered dangerous.

But this does not diminish Beaumarchais' achievement as an artist. Through all the playful antics of *The Barber of Seville*, just as in the more involved intrigues of *The Marriage of Figaro*, he took immense care over staging details, costumes and characterisation. The successes were immediate and far-reaching. Translations of each play appeared in England within a year of their first French performance; Mozart's and da Ponte's *Figaro* was performed the year after that.

The drama, *Eugénie*, set in London, didn't enjoy the same success and Beaumarchais' fortune declined with the revolution. He was accused of arming counter-revolutionaries and he fled to Holland. He later returned to his native Paris, where he died in a fine house on the boulevard that now bears his name.

Beauvoir

SIMONE DE

born Paris 1908; died Paris 1986

I feel at one with women who have assumed responsibility for their lives and who struggle to succeed. However, this does not prevent me from being interested in that part of failure which is inherent in every life.

INTRODUCTION TO THE BROKEN WOMAN

SIMONE DE BEAUVOIR'S novels and memoirs chronicle the shifts in her thinking throughout her life. For some readers, her first three novels are too obviously the work of a philosopher; for others, her fourth, *The Mandarins*, lacks the clarity and reasoning of those that preceded it.

Despite this, she successfully used the novel to explore and express her philosophy of existentialism. This demands, among other things, that people make "authentic" personal choices and through storytelling de Beauvoir illustrated both circumstances and consequences of this type of thinking. In *All Men are Mortal*, for example, the narrative closely follows the thoughts of a hero in his response to the prospect of death. As in her previous book, *The Blood of Others*, the need for action against authority (in this case, the struggle against the Nazis in France) when one's conscience demands it, finds an expression that goes beyond the theorising that existentialism renders redundant.

In this she followed **Sartre**, whom she met at the École Normale Supérieure and who became her lifelong companion. She seemed so much to rehearse his views that she was dubbed "La Grande Sartreuse", but in her stance on feminism, her own thinking became more clearly distinguished, particularly with the publication of *The Second Sex* in 1949, which made her name. Again, philosophical argument is sustained by personal conviction. In this case the belief that in society the idea of "woman" is a male myth and that male codes force women to adopt fixed roles as mothers and lovers. Her later novels explore these myths (notably in the advertising world of *The Beautiful Images*) and how female characters respond to them.

The fluid nature of her belief system meant that she could reassess her opinion that socialism was necessary for women's equality, and that individuals could act independently of society. Her autobiographical books examine how and when these changes occurred.

Bellow

SAUL

born Lachine, Canada 1915

University presses sent manuscripts for his professional judgment. They lay in bundles, unopened. The sun grew hot, the soil was damp and black, and Herzog looked with despair on the thriving luxuriant life of the plants.

HERZOG

SAUL BELLOW'S WRITINGS aim to retrieve the element of the spiritual that the urban climate of the 20th century often seems to have destroyed. His tales of angst are set against the chaos of the metropolis (usually Chicago) and he strives to pick out the individual from the increasingly blurred crowd.

Throughout his novel-writing career, he has tackled this with a wealth of techniques. His first two novels, *Dangling Man* and *The Victim*, were strictly structured and doggedly realistic. His first big critical success, however, took a very different approach. *The Adventures of Augie March* is a picaresque ramble through the life of its hero, set in '50s America, the style is more relaxed and the work full of wildly contrasting episodes and locations.

Bellow's most celebrated look at a man trying to find peace in a clamorous world is *Herzog*. A middle-aged academic in the Berkshire mountains writes letters to anyone, including dead philosophers and God. His crazed attempts to kill his ex-wife, however, lead him out of his seclusion and his failure to do the deed finally frees him from the need to keep corresponding with the void around him. It is only then that he achieves some sort of peace.

Bellow's most complete examination of the old, refined man contemplating the agonies of his age is perhaps embodied in the hero of *Mr Sammler's Planet*, who has inside knowledge of the Bloomsbury set and of Auschwitz. As well as the individual conscience, the values of an entire culture seem in peril.

Bellow's hope is often placed in preserving memory, which in turn lends purpose to the activity of writing. In *Something to Remember Me By*, his reminiscing persona concludes: "Well, they're all gone now, and I have made my preparations. I haven't left a large estate and this is why I have written this memoir, as a sort of addition to your legacy."

Bennett

ARNOLD

born Hanley, Staffordshire 1867; died London 1931

Down below is Burslem... If it were an old Flemish town, beautiful in detail and antiquely interesting, one would say its situation was ideal. It is not beautiful in detail, but the smoke transforms its ugliness into a beauty transcending the work of architects and of time.

THE MAN FROM THE NORTH

ARNOLD BENNETT'S WRITING owes much to the legacy of **Balzac**, especially his treatment of provincial settings. Most of the action in Bennett's books takes place in his native Five Towns, the area in Staffordshire famous for pottery.

The upsurge of capitalism documented by Balzac was fully developed in industrial Britain by Bennett's time. He wrote of it intimately, taking the reader from individual, thoroughly realised streets, to views of the towns around from neighbouring hills. Throughout, we witness progress and its impact on the landscape and humanity.

He was particularly remarkable for his sympathetic treatment of female characters. He was made assistant editor of *Woman* magazine in 1893, for which he wrote advice columns, and in 1918 he contributed to Marie Stopes' pioneering pamphlet on birth control. These contributions to women's issues were perhaps the reason that his depiction of women was less clouded by romanticism than in the work of most of his male contemporaries.

He was one of the leading exponents of realism in England. George Moore was a mentor, but his technique owes as much to the theory and practice of **Emile Zola**, which he encountered during time in Paris from 1902 to 1912. His narrative and characters share a practical attitude toward the real world. The dialogue in his books is often curt and written in dialect, and comment on the action can be similarly understated.

Bennett's working methods reflected the industrial climate in which he lived. In his journals he occasionally speaks of "producing" novels or even "manufacturing" characters. His apparent lack of themes disappointed **Henry James**, but he found a great admirer in Max Beerbohm.

Boyd

WILLIAM

born Ghana 1952

My first act on entering this world was to kill my mother.

THE NEW CONFESSIONS

WILLIAM BOYD BELONGS to the normally comic tradition of "The Englishman Abroad", except that he's Scottish. He was born in Ghana, West Africa, and his novels are often set in similar countries that sometimes remain nameless The first, *A Good Man in Africa*, about a low-ranking, low-life British diplomat, placed Boyd in **Evelyn Waugh** territory. A subsequent book moved to East Africa, and used a wide range of narrative voices to document the immediate effects of World War One on a remote town.

America is another of Boyd's locales. he continues to document clashing cultures in *Stars and Bars*, in which a young art expert finds himself in New York. As if the glitterati were not bewildering enough for the hero, he is then sent to make an important purchase from a typical Southern family. This book, together with *On Yankee Station*, won praise on both sides of the Atlantic. The author was astute enough to make his naïve British hero every bit as ridiculous as his hosts appear to him.

In his writing, Boyd has experimented with different techniques, angles and models. In *The New Confessions*, the precedent is **Rousseau**, and the thoughts of the narrator wander. For *Brazzaville Beach*, he chooses a woman narrator. Hope Clearwater's story is set in Africa, where she is observing the behaviour of chimpanzees. Digressions and flashbacks describe the circumstances that brought her there: she has left Britain and a failed relationship. She learns from her field study and sudden rootlessness to accept the flux of her life, rather than to strive to find permanence. The book won the James Tait Black Memorial Prize in 1991.

Bradbury

RAY

born Waukegan, Illinois 1920

Man, in his immense tidal motion, is about to flow out toward far new worlds; but man must conquer the seed of his own destruction.

THE MARTIAN CHRONICLES

RAY BRADBURY HAS a special place among science fiction writers. He is admired as much for the poetry and humanity of his work as for its visionary qualities.

In all his work Bradbury is concerned that human values and ethics survive in a society that is becoming increasingly impersonal and technological. *The Martian Chronicles* and *Fahrenheit 451* are early expressions of this and, for many readers, his best books.

In the former, a vision of colonists settling on Mars provided a setting in which the author could address the problems of 50s America. On the new planet, the issues of racism, nuclear power and Cold War politics appear throughout a series of related stories. By treating such themes in isolation, in fable form, Bradbury made his own values more strongly felt.

Even in pessimistic narratives, Bradbury demonstrates hope for the future and faith in literature. This is clearest in his most famous book, *Fahrenheit 451*. It is named after the temperature at which paper burns. Bradbury took his confidence to the limit by envisaging a society that completely bans the written word. The nightmare regime condemns all books to be burned and we meet the man whose job it is to throw them on the fire. The narrative then follows his subversion as he falls in love with a dissident. Although the work belongs in the

"dystopian" tradition of *Brave New World* and *1984*, Bradbury provides a way out.

He remains a prolific and extremely versatile writer. Besides short stories and novels, he has written plays, poems, detective stories and, in 1956, the screenplay for *Moby Dick*. *Fahrenheit 451* has been adapted as an opera. Critical response to his work has varied. Today, new generations of readers are discovering his passionate prose, after a period in which he lapsed in favour, but his earlier work was read avidly by **Graham Greene**, **Christopher Isherwood** and Bertrand Russell. Although his writing has never been confined to science fiction, he is most at home there, writing in the genre he calls "the history of ideas, the history of our civilisation birthing itself".

Brontë

EMILY

born Haworth, Yorkshire 1818; died Haworth 1848

No *coward soul is mine,*

No *trembler in the world's storm-*

troubled sphere:

I *see Heaven's glories shine,*

And *faith shines equal, arming me*

from fear.

LAST LINES

EMILY REMAINS the most enigmatic of the Brontës, an impression deepened by the intimations of mystery and madness that pervade her work.

She was not known to have any good friends; instead she maintained a kind of twinship with her younger sister **Anne**, with whom she invented the kingdom of Gondal as a setting for their stories and poems. It was a while before **Charlotte** discovered that Emily had been writing poems, then suggesting the three of them should publish their verse together. A month after publication, only two copies had been sold, but Emily's work stood out from the rest of the volume.

Her only novel, *Wuthering Heights*, appeared in the same year as her sister Charlotte's *Jane Eyre*, but enjoyed nothing like the same success. Readers were unprepared for either for the levels of violence, the forthright language, or the sheer technical brilliance of the book. The story is narrated by Nellie Dean to our own narrator. Her story has a remarkable balance between passionate engagement and mute witnessing. The result is a drama full of inherent ironies and repeated histories: but that is for the reader, not the teller. For Nellie, the speech and action of her subjects is all. The approach draws on many of the effects that Aristotle divined in Greek tragedy.

The action centres on Heathcliffe, a gypsy orphan who is rescued by Mr Earnshaw from the streets of Liverpool. The "strange bond" between him and his foster-sister is never fulfilled and after her death he spends his days in savage jealousy and vengeful bitterness. The immense power of these emotions is sustained by the force of his rhetoric and the atmosphere of the moors, all the way to a more hopeful conclusion.

Long after Emily's untimely death *Wuthering Heights* finally gained recognition as one of the finest English novels ever written.

Browning

ELIZABETH BARRETT **born County Durham 1806; died Florence 1861**

...But poets should

Exert a double vision; should have eyes

To see near things as comprehensively

As if afar they took their point of sight,

And distant things as infinitely deep

As if they touched them.

AURORA LEIGH

IN HER LIFETIME, Elizabeth Barrett Browning was more famous than her husband **Robert Browning** and in 1850 she was tipped to succeed **Wordsworth** as Poet Laureate. Her complete grasp and free handling of metre, together with the depth and immediacy of the ideas her poetry expresses, secure her place among the best of English poets.

She was educated at home and showed precocious literary talent. She was reading Homer in Greek at age 10 and had written her first epic poem (on the battle of Marathon) by the time she was 19. Her father watched this promising career protectively, paying for the publication of her *Essay on Mind* and translation of **Aeschylus'** *Prometheus Bound*. But he kept her at home and would not allow his children to marry. The situation worsened after ELizabeth's brother drowned, a blow from which she never recovered.

Her elopement with Browning in 1846 left her father unforgiving. The couple fled to Italy, where they championed the cause of Italian unity and independence. In this, as well as poems on social reform and the role of women, especially in literature, her verse was often overtly political.

Although this never diminished the quality of her work, it did lead to a decline in public favour.

Her love-lyrics remain her most popular compositions, above all *Sonnets from the Portuguese*. These are not translations, but love poems to her husband, who dubbed her "the Portuguese". In them she adheres to the rigours of sonnet form without allowing it to cramp her style or constrict her syntax. The same combination of poetic strictures and freedom of expression is evident in her chief work, *Aurora Leigh*, which reads as much like a novel as a blank verse epic. Indeed, the narrator digresses to suggest that contemporary themes are riper for poetic treatment than the dustier myths that, say, **Tennyson** was expounding. She died four years after its publication, a literary celebrity, and her *Last Poems* appeared posthumously, in 1862.

Byron

GEORGE GORDON, LORD   **born London 1788; died Missolonghi 1824**

The fire that on my bosom preys

Is lone as some volcanic isle;

No torch is kindled at its blaze –

A funeral pile.

ON THIS DAY I COMPLETE MY
THIRTY-SIXTH YEAR.
MISSOLONGHI, JANUARY 22, 1824

FOR MANY, Byron was the spirit of the Romantic age. Born shortly before the French Revolution, he made liberal speeches in the House of Lords, wrote lethal anti-Tory satire and finally died for the cause of Greek freedom.

This made him a hero to poets such as **Goethe** and **Pushkin**, composers such as Beethoven and Tchaikovsky, and painters such as Delacroix. But it is possible to see him more as a throwback to the 18th century – an establishment-educated nobleman with voracious reading habits and a strong work ethic, whose output aligned him more with **Pope** than his contemporaries. Indeed, he saved his most savage lines for the likes of **Wordsworth** and **Keats**.

His first published work was *Hours of Idleness*, while his second, *English Bards and Scotch Reviewers*, was an attack on the critics who dismissed the first. But it was the appearance of *Childe Harold's Pilgrimage* in 1812 that drew the literary world to throng him. The verse travelogue reflects the author's roving, while his hero shares his feeling of discomfort with his age. Byron later added two cantos to the work to incorporate Belgium, Italy and Napoleon.

If poetry brought him fame, his looks and lovers preserved it. His beauty was often painted and his romances were a constant source of scandal. Meanwhile, his writing continued to betray his preferences for the near-east over Britain and showed his exhaustive knowledge of the area's history. He even compiled an Armenian dictionary.

Towards the end of his life, he was able to combine the satire of *A Vision of Judgement* with his interest in writing about fate-buffeted young men (such as *Mazeppa*) to produce his masterpiece, *Don Juan*. The stanza form incorporates masterful comic rhymes, sustained side-swipes at Wellington and Southey (then Poet Laureate), as well as shipwreck and domestic tragedy. The joy of it is in its bathos and constant digression: one imagines it could have ended anywhere. Before he could complete the vast project, Byron died at Missolonghi, Greece, where he remains a national hero.

Calderón de la Barca

PEDRO · born Madrid 1600; died Madrid 1681

Who's calling me, such that, from the

  hard core

of this round earth, concealing me

  within,

you see the wings that soar?

Who shows me to myself?

GOD, IN THE MIGRANT LAMB,
TR. BERNI ZANZMER

CALDERÓN WAS THE LAST surviving playwright from that great age of Spanish comedy associated chiefly with **Lope de Vega**. Of all the dramatists of his generation, he was the one who commanded the most respect from audiences, patrons and, perhaps most importantly, the church. In a period when the censor's job was to check the soundness of the theological argument in a play, Calderón's work encountered the fewest problems. His orthodox beliefs and noble poetic diction made him by far the most established (and establishment) author in late 17th-century Spain.

He was poet at the courts of Philip IV and Charles II, where he regularly produced comedies that often dealt with the theme of love. He would frequently present Love and Hate as allegorical figures, involved in intrigues and counter-intrigues. Calderón brought these figures further to life with his very active use of staging. Unlike **Shakespeare**, his production and stage directions are indispensable to the action, calling for vivid sets and intricate hiding places. Although the characters were Classical or Old Testament in origin, they pointed to strictly Christian morals and dramatised debates about atonement or transubstantiation.

Calderón had a monopoly on the *autos sacramentales* (sacred pieces) that were staged in Madrid from 1648 until his death in 1681. This involved writing two plays a year to be performed on carts (sometimes needing as many as four to accommodate all his theatrical devices). The most famous of these is *Life's a Dream*, which is still in the

Spanish repertoire. It is his fullest discussion of the difference between appearance and reality, in which the hero is unsure whether he is awake or asleep. Ultimately, he comes to realise the superiority of eternal truths over ephemeral ones and, along with Calderón's other protagonists (including a Faustian figure), he learns that in this life his only hope is Christ.

Callimachus

born Cyrene c. 305 BC; died Alexandria c. 240 BC

Whatever subtle golden balms I'd place

upon my head with garlands fine to smell

turned into breathless flesh. Whatever fell

to my base belly when I stuffed my face

was gone the next day; but whatever strain

I heard, I kept: those things

alone remain.

CAUSES

WE KNOW CALLIMACHUS was one of the most read and admired of the Greek poets, for **Catullus**, **Horace**, **Virgil**, **Propertius** and **Ovid** are forever paying tribute to him, either with outright praise or studied imitation.

He lived and worked in the Greek colony of Alexandria in Egypt and his work is known as "Alexandrian" – a term embracing any classical poetry that was economical, densely worked and demonstrating wit through arcane allusions. Callimachus could scarcely avoid using such techniques. He worked in his home town's almost legendary library, for which he compiled a catalogue of 120 volumes. This incredible reading list enabled him to write treatises on language, sport, traditions, birds, nymphs, winds, and how months or places got their names. In an age before computers, he was able to identify words that appeared only once in the whole of Greek literature.

His poetry is full of this kind of information. He writes furiously against bards who churn out long heroic epics, especially (and most personally) Apollonius of Rhodes, chronicler of Jason and the Argonauts, and his own motto is best translated as "big book, big bad" and he reckoned it better to "keep the Muse trim". Although we know he composed at length, he crammed in his material and often strayed from large to small themes. When he attempts to describe Hercules killing the Nemean lion, he prefers to dwell on the peasant Molorchus, his problems with rodents and the mythic history of the mousetrap.

This episode appears in his *Aitia* (*Causes*), a work of which – like his hymns, epigrams and scholarly texts – little survives. Much of it was burned when Western crusaders ravaged Constantinople in 1204. But whole poems appear in the work of subsequent Latin poets, which, if not always direct translations, are loving homages and exercises in the kind of scholarly composition he made an aesthetic principle.

Calvino

ITALO   born Santiago de las Vegas, Cuba 1923; died Rome 1985

Lovers' reading of each other's bodies... differs from the reading of written pages ... It starts at any point, skips, repeats itself, goes backward, insists, ramifies in simultaneous and divergent messages, converges again, has moments of irritation, turns the page, finds its place, gets lost.

IF ON A WINTER'S NIGHT A TRAVELLER,
TR. WILLIAM WEAVER

THE ITALIAN NOVELIST, short-story writer and essayist Italo Calvino filled much of his work with an enquiry into what is possible. Throughout his career, he raised this question with a flamboyant intellect, which he deployed with an enormous sense of fun. His learning and ease with the language of research pervades most of his fiction and is most effective when it seems least appropriate.

His first novel, *The Path to a Nest of Spiders*, deals with his experiences in the Italian resistance during World War Two. This, and his subsequent collection of short stories, counted him among the new wave of realist writers appearing in Italy.

He blended this with an historical attention to reality in his trilogy, *Our Ancestors*, such that the impossible, fairy-tale characters seem all the more likely. He shares with **Borges** an interest in probability and alternative worlds and explores it scientifically in several stories, assessing the chances of unusual deaths witha clinical detachment..

He indulged his penchant for mathematics in OuLiPo, a polymaths' literary circle that included **Queneau** and **Perec**. A tale by the latter inspired Calvino's loveliest examination of fiction's possibilities, *If On A Winter's Night A Traveller*. The story becomes a romance between two of its readers, who hunt the book we turn out to be holding. Its mesh of skits and responses show how wildly texts and readers can play with each other.

Carroll

LEWIS   **born Daresbury, Cheshire 1832; died Oxford 1898**

"Contrariwise," continued Tweedledee, "if it was so, it might be; and if it were so, it would be: but as it isn't, it ain't. That's logic."

THROUGH THE LOOKING-GLASS

LEWIS CARROLL WAS the pseudonym of Charles Lutwidge Dodgson, a shy and lonely lecturer in mathematics at Oxford University. He was born in Daresbury in Cheshire, the third of 11 precocious children, with whom he devised endless word-games, board-games and mathematical puzzles.

These inclinations and his academic training, along with a childlike joy in the absurd, explain his ability to tell stories that contort the logical procedures he had mastered. The first was the inspired fantasy *Alice's Adventures in Wonderland*. This has been read as an extemporised story recounted to Alice Liddell, whose father Henry was co-author of the still-definitive Greek dictionary, Dean of Carroll's college, and the subject of **Hardy**'s funniest poem.

Although apparently a nonsense tale for children, some read into it a kind of logic, hidden beneath the seemingly random array of now immortal characters – Tweedledum and Tweedledee, the Mad Hatter and his circle…. Recent research has begun to explore the extent to which these figures were based on public persons and movements of the day, or are caricatures of Carroll's friends and colleagues.

The fantasy continued with *Through the Looking-Glass*, which contained the same blend of apparent lunacy with fine skits on contemporary poets (especially **Browning**). Carroll's ear for comic verse has been the envy of literary figures as diverse as **Auden** and **Belloc** and, in *The Hunting of the Snark*, Carroll so impressed Queen Victoria that she asked the author for a copy of his next work. Three years later she received his treatise on geometry, *Euclid and his Modern Rivals*.

Later work for children, mostly in verse, tried to incorporate Christian teaching – Carroll was ordained in 1861. But these seemed to miss what one reviewer thought was the key ingredient of his popularity with children – his ability to keep their attention while seeming not to teach them anything. After all, "What is the use of a book without pictures or conversations?" John Tenniel's illustrations to Carroll's books have come to be loved as much as the texts they illuminate.

Carver

RAYMOND   **born Clatskanie, Oregon 1938; died Washington 1988**

Breathing evenly and steadily once more, we'll collect ourselves, writers and readers alike, get up, "created of warm blood and nerves", as a Chekhov character puts it, and go onto the next thing: Life. Always life.

INTRODUCTION TO
WHERE I'M CALLING FROM

'ERRAND' IS PERHAPS the least typical of Raymond Carver's short stories. It has fine restaurants, champagne, history and the occasional digression. It was to be his last and concerns the death of **Chekhov**. But from this apparent lushness, the narrative closes in on tiny details and leaves the reader to gauge their emotional charge. It is the truest tribute the American writer could pay to the author who inspired him most.

Carver began by writing poems and found the experience of writing short stories similar. His first story collection, *Will You Please Be Quiet, Please?*, appeared in 1976, towards the end of his long struggle with alcoholism, a problem that affects some of his characters. As he had, they are always struggling for a living, in stories whose words and images are assembled with a care and economy that makes the prosaic poetical.

More books brought acclaim, awards and funding, enabling him to write full-time. Although his stories retained their grittiness, they became longer over the years. His characters became more inclined to hope for change, rather than wait for something else. One of his most praised pieces, 'A Small, Good Thing', has a baker atone in an instant for the menacing calls he has made to a dying boy's mother. Carver's work had often focused on the smaller consequences of life-or-death situations, but this kind of resolution was to come much later.

Towards the end of his short life, Carver came to terms with his imminent death. He made a selection of his best stories and wrote farewell poems to his wife Tess Gallagher, before concluding with his description of Chekhov's passing, which presaged his own. By then the comparison had become commonplace.

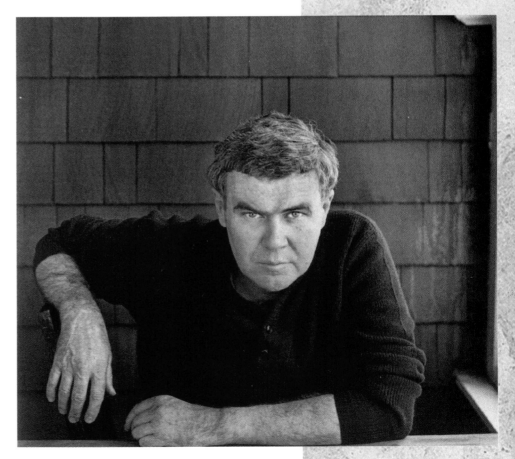

Cavafy

CONSTANTINE   born Alexandria, Egypt 1863; died Alexandria 1933

MAJOR WORKS

Poems (collected and translated
into English, 1951, 1961)

When you undertake your journey to
Ithaca,
pray that the course be long...
and if you find her poor, Ithaca has
not mocked you:
you have become so wise, experienced
so much
that you've already grasped what all
these Ithacas mean.

ITHACA

CAVAFY SEEMS AN UNLIKELY father of modern poetry in Greek. He barely visited Greece – except, most notably, for the award of the Phoenix and for an operation in 1932. He stood emphatically outside the Greek tradition and while his contemporaries Kostis Palamas and the New Greek School were invoking the epic past, Cavafy was finding a voice that was completely his own.

He lived most of his life in Alexandria, where he worked as a civil servant for the water board. His first language was English and he even spent five years in Liverpool. His earliest influences were **Browning,** from whom he learned the dramatic technique of focusing on characters caught up in moments of historical change, and **Baudelaire,** whose model he used to portray the city around him. Many of his poems also share the latter's preoccupation with lost beauty and decline.

His work was born quietly into the world. Only 21 poems appeared in book form during his life, although his brother helped him circulate about another 200. However, they did not go so unnoticed that their open discussion of homosexuality allowed him to walk the streets trouble-free. **E.M. Forster** introduced Cavafy's work to English readers in 1919. But in his day, he was better known as an historian than a poet.

His themes are often historical: never documenting the great moments of Greece's imperial past, but rather those of defeat and decadence. The ambiguous impact of Christianity on the Byzantine Empire and that civilisation's dealings with the outside world provide the ideal setting for all that his characters express. Often, they are coming to terms with regret, guilt, or fleeting sensual pleasures and are unnerved by the presence of anything more spiritual. Cavafy captures this in poems that are almost always short. But they are rounded by echoes and resigned cadences, which, though they seem ironic and understated, go as far as words can to express loss, and then leave off.

Celan

PAUL

born Czernowitz, Bukovina 1920; died Paris 1970

You vary the key, you vary the word
that is free to drift with the flakes.
What snowball will form round the
*   word*
depends on the wind that
*   rebuffs you.*

WITH A VARIABLE KEY,
IN FROM THRESHOLD TO THRESHOLD,
TR. MICHAEL HAMBURGER

AS WELL AS HIS NATIVE Romanian tongue, Paul Celan was fluent in French, English and Russian. He translated poetry from all these into German, the language he used for his verse. His cultural range, which won him a lectureship at Paris' most prestigious university, is spread throughout his *oeuvre*, often imperceptibly. After his parents were deported in 1942, both of whom died in Nazi death camps, he unceasingly addressed the problem summarised by Adorno: "There can be no poetry after Auschwitz."

In his attempts to express the unspeakable, he bent words into a form of music. His first collection contained the much-anthologised *Death Fugue*, whose rhythms force out what might never have been said without them. But he came to resent this poem – it was too direct.

Celan's later books became more obscure. The surreal images and focus on sight in the earlier works yield to a greater concern with language itself. He increasingly broke up the syntax and words of his poems, sometimes in the interests of lyricism, but more often to create new possibilities in German. It was a source of surprise that, after the Holocaust, he chose that language; and it was a sign of healing that most of the honours he was awarded came from Germany.

But healing proved impossible. His work became more concerned with darkness and nothingness. He wrote much-admired love lyrics, but even these seem to come from the shadow of death. George Steiner wrote, "**Dante** and Celan are the great familiars of love's ways in hellishness." In one of his last poems, Celan wrote, "I hear that they call life/our only refuge." It was a refuge he denied himself: he committed suicide in the Seine.

MAJOR WORKS

Poppy and Memory (1952)

From Threshold to Threshold (1955)

Speech-Grille (1959)

The Meridian (1961)

Nobody's Rose (1963)

Threadsuns (1968)

The Force of Light (1970)

Snow-part (1971)

Chateaubriand

FRANÇOIS-RENÉ DE

born St. Malo 1768; died Paris 1848

M. Chateaubriand was not intended by Nature for a statesman. He has too much of the generosity, prodigality, and recklessness of genius.

STENDHAL

CHATEAUBRIAND'S PROSE is the most widely admired in French. He was **Hugo**'s inspiration and **Proust**'s hero – the latter's character Swann was always more interested in a work of art if Chateaubriand had written about it.

Chateaubriand's *oeuvre* cannot be called Classical or Romantic. His forms are strictly the former: much of his output is scholarly, *belle-lettriste* or traditional. He wrote mostly prose, but thought the poet above all other human beings. But for all his reactionary tendencies, demonstrated in his fight against the French Revolution in 1791, and more gradually in his exegesis of Catholicism, his spirit belonged to the Romantic age. He emphasised his personal experiences as an adventurer and as a participant in the epoch's great events.

He left France in 1791 and sailed to America, a land whose desert was the scene of his great novel, *Atala*. Subtitled *The Loves of Two Indians in the Wilds of America*, it takes the avowed view that *les sauvages* are not as noble as **Rousseau** thinks them. Still, Chateaubriand tells their tale as though it were an elevated Greek one, citing **Sophocles** as a model.

After his return to Europe, involvement with the *emigré* army and flight to England, Chateaubriand resettled in France in 1800. His tract *The Genius of Christianity* was vast and impassioned, incorporating fiction as well as theology. Napoleon made him an ambassador to the Vatican, but Chateaubriand resigned when the Emperor had the Duc d'Enghien executed. In 1814 he wrote a pamphlet arguing for the legitimacy of Bourbon rule against the Bonapartes, and Louis XVIII was glad to have him at his side during the regime that followed. When that too was overthrown in 1830, Chateaubriand withdrew from public life to devote himself completely to literature. He translated *Paradise Lost* into French and wrote his extraordinary autobiography, *Memoirs From Beyond the Grave*.

Chaucer

GEOFFREY

born London, c. 1340; died London 1400

Sin I fro Love escaped am so fat,
I never thenk to ben in his prison lene;
Sin I am free, I counte him not a bene.

CHAUCER WAS THE FIRST poet in the strain of English that would come to dominate the British Isles: he remains one of the very best.

Throughout his life he worked as a public servant and was frequently at court. His missions abroad, to France and Italy, account for two distinct styles evident in his early work. During the first trip, he encountered French Romance literature, prompting him to translate *Romaunt of the Rose*. From this period also dates *The Book of the Duchess*, incorporating a French-style dream sequence, (as would his later *House of Fame*) and the poet's own self-deprecating persona, which reappears in *The Canterbury Tales*. In Italy, he quite possibly met **Petrarch** and even **Boccaccio**, many of whose stories Chaucer adapted in his own masterpiece.

The eventual fusion of these styles brought about Chaucer's third phase: the English, which he made his own. Into it he translated Boethius and a treatise on the astrolabe. Such wide reading accounts in part for the diversity of *The Canterbury Tales*; but Chaucer's range of stories recounted in a dramatically coherent sequence by a hotchpotch bunch of pilgrims to the shrine of Thomas à Becket would have been unimaginable without the author's gift for character and satire. The company he presents is more than a cross-section of late medieval society. In the work's general prologue we read of characters we might easily meet tomorrow.

On the journey to Canterbury and back, each pilgrim would tell two stories on the way and two on the way back. Chaucer never realised this massive conception, but in the wild swings in tone, such as from the Knight's Tale of chivalry to the Miller's searingly ribald account of a cuckold's revenge, the author accommodates extremes of behaviour and language, with most of humanity in between.

MAJOR WORKS

The Book of the Duchess
(1369)

The Parliament of Fowls;
The House of Fame;
Troilus and Criseyde
(all 1369–1387)

Anelida and Arcite (c. 1380)

Palamon (1380–1386)

The Canterbury Tales
(1386 onwards)

Treatise on the Astrolabe
(1391, 1392)

Cheever

JOHN

born Massachusetts 1912; died New York State 1982

All my work deals with confinement in one shape or another, and the struggle toward freedom... a sense of boundlessness, the possibility of rejoicing!

INTERVIEW WITH JOHN FRITH

JOHN CHEEVER'S STORIES almost exclusively take place in American suburbia. But the apparent normality of this atmosphere highlights extremes of behaviour and emotion that seem to seep out from the cracks in the tasteful wallpaper.

His heroes are usually male, often with good jobs and well-kept gardens; their journeys to and from these places take them through an America whose countryside is dying under the weight of freeways and supermarkets. But Cheever's questioning of their lifestyle goes much deeper than simply to ask, "Are they happy?" These characters can begin this enquiry themselves, typically by looking beyond their marriages for love, and then buckling under the guilt of even considering it. In this way the most ordinary problems become crises. But the world Cheever creates can bring forth still bigger monsters.

In *A Vision of the World*, a man finds a strange object while digging up his flower-bed. This sets off a hallucinatory narrative, culminating in the subject's inability to hear anything but a gibberish mantra. It is not made explicit here that suburbia can have this effect, but it is in the later work *Bullet Park*, when an express desire to shock a community leads a man to attempt the crucifixion of his neighbour.

Cheever's world is not exclusively macabre or surreal. He is concerned with the boundaries of what is acceptable, an interest that was born when he was expelled from preparatory school for smoking. What finished his education began his career: *Expelled* was a startling debut story for an 18-year-old.

Subsequent collections compounded his fame, especially the *The Enormous Radio* and *The Swimmer*, in which an aging athlete sets out to swim in every pool in Westchester County. The actions of Cheever's characters can be heroic as well as manic and motivated by fairly conventional psychology. In later work, most notably *Falconer*, themes of earthly love and spiritual redemption dominate.

Chekhov

ANTON   born Taganrog 1860; died Badenweiler, Germany 1904

If I give you a professor's ideas, you must not look for Chekhov's ideas in them. If I give you wine, do you try to taste beer?

LETTER TO ALEXEI SUVORIN

CHEKHOV WROTE MORE than 300 short stories besides his five plays. In all these, he strove for a kind of realism but, through an even-handed representation of his characters, and supreme control of his forms, he did something more, managing to engage passionate concern for every event that he shows us.

He practised as a doctor and found time to write many stories, although the journal publishing them could only accommodate very short ones. He was soon allowed more space, however, to expand his treatments of every kind of character. Men and women from all classes and professions people his tales. Although he was much influenced by **Tolstoy**, and especially *Anna Karenina*, his characters were less aristocratic and his treatment of those struggling, less sentimental. Chekhov could not share Tolstoy's spiritualism either.

In the plays, people living apparently tedious lives often wonder what will become of them after death. The end of *Uncle Vanya* has Sonya telling her despairing uncle that "we will see the angels" – but others, like Dr Astrov, or Vershinin in *The Three Sisters*, are more concerned with earth than heaven, speculating on the prospects of happiness in a distant future.

The world he portrays is often one of wasted life with folk doing little to stave off indolence. Boredom menaces the characters, although Chekhov claimed he never found anyone boring, nor created boring people. It is hard to be happy after a Chekhov play or story, but few episodes pass without a joke, and few characters remain unredeemed in the readers' or audience's eyes.

He began his career writing comic tales, and ended it with *The Cherry Orchard*, which he tried calling a farce. It is resonant with his musical dialogue but so full of unreleasable domestic tensions that one could neither call it tragic or comic. Like Beethoven, Chekhov had such unfailing artistic instinct that he created a body of work which eludes categorisation while remaining perfect on its own, unique terms.

Christie

AGATHA   **born Torquay 1890; died Wallingford, Oxon 1976**

The big houses have been sold, and the cottages have been changed and converted. And people just come – and all you know about them is what they say of themselves.

A MURDER IS ANNOUNCED

AGATHA CHRISTIE WAS a poet and authoress of children's books. To posterity, she would have remained so, had her sister not expressed a belief that the writer, nearing 30, could not handle the rules governing the detective mystery. The result was *The Mysterious Affair at Styles*, and some 30 subsequent intrigues followed, involving the Belgian sleuth Hercule Poirot as their unraveller.

A hugely international audience has devoured her novels ever since, with sales especially good overseas. To many, there seems to be much that is absolutely English. There are murders in vicarages involving well-to-do and perfectly polite characters and, with the exception of Poirot, her detectives fit in with this appealing framework, too: Miss Marple is the little old lady from Middleton, Middleshire, who has an unfailing eye, while Tommy and Tuppence Beresford are good-natured amateurs who stumble across clues more by serendipity than deduction. Laws are broken often, but taboos seldom

She took her literary success to the stage, with the excellent *Witness for the Prosecution* and most famously with *The Mousetrap*. The latter has become the longest-running play ever in London's West End theatre district, and its audiences are entreated not to divulge the culprit's identity.

This is the key element of her popularity. Although the murder mystery is a genre which demands strict adherence to convention – a factor which led Christie to describe herself in her autobiography as a "literary sausage-maker" – she is a story-teller *par excellence*. Her increasingly-familiar world of reappearing characters may make seasoned readers think they can crack the whodunit before the end of the story, but Christie's ability to keep the outcome a mystery, by subtly blending in new ingredients, usually keeps them guessing to the end.

Churchill

CARYL

born London 1938

> *We've come a long way. To our courage and the way we've changed our lives and our extraordinary achievements.*
>
> MARLENE'S TOAST IN TOP GIRLS

CARYL CHURCHILL'S ingenious and experimental plays use innovative theatrical techniques to explore political and sexual themes.

She takes on history to examine the moral climate of post-war Britain. Her first major success, *Light Shining in Buckinghamshire*, is set in Cromwell's England, and shows his former supporters rising against him as they feel dispossessed. Subsequent plays bring the past closer to the present: the first half of *Cloud Nine* portrays sexually-repressed Victorian colonists in Africa, while the second brings the same characters (only 25 years older) 90 years forward into the future. Throughout, male characters are played by women, old by young, black by white, and so on. This adds kink to the confusion of a farce-like script, and made Churchill's name. Her next work, *Top Girls*, which used a similar time device, had notable female characters from art, literature and history exchange their survival stories before transforming into businesswomen. Churchill looks at the human cost of female success (especially when achieved by adopting male values) and, in the character of Marlene, points to the rise of Mrs Thatcher.

In *Serious Money*, the past again illuminates the present: the author pays homage to the satirical writings of 17th century playwright Thomas Shadwell in a verse account of the Thatcher-driven 'Big Bang' – London's business transformation. The play was a box-office success, if not a critical one.

Churchill's plays usually rely on invention either in casting or in language. Her latest play, *The Skriker*, takes the verbal tricks of *Serious Money* into a contemporary fairy tale: a woman can transform not only herself but also, by word association, the meaning of what is being said. As elsewhere in her work, the audience is never allowed to become too familiar with what is happening on stage. In all this, Churchill has worked in close collaboration with progressive acting companies and was the first female writer-in-residence at the London's Royal Court Theatre.

MAJOR WORKS

Objections to Sex and Violence (1975)

Light Shining in Buckinghamshire (1976)

Cloud Nine (1979)

Top Girls (1982)

Fen (1983)

The Skriker (1994)

Clare

JOHN   born Helpstone 1793; died Northampton 1841

I love the verse that mild and bland

Breathes of green fields and open sky

I love the muse that in her hand

Bears wreaths of native poesy

Who walks nor skips the pasture brook

In scorn – but by the drinking horse

Leans o'er its little brig to look

How far the sallows lean across

THE FLITTING

IT IS STILL VERY difficult to separate the work of John Clare from the image his contemporaries would project of him. Their view of a barely literate peasant, too sickly to work but touched with genius, sold his first published volume of poems, and made the author the toast of London for a while. The construction remains attractive; but later consideration of Clare's work has been better able to concentrate on the treasures in his subsequent books. By then, his London audience had already grown disenchanted with the novelty.

Still, his first book contained much of the nature poetry valued in the age of **Heaney** and Hughes even more than in his own, for its spontaneity, and its preference for showing rather than telling. But later work impresses still more with its glimpses of his rural England (Northamptonshire) vanishing like Eden: he was to lose his happy seat to the seasons and increasing industrialisation, but his patrons' wish to install him in a larger home unsettled him more. The Paradise of love was to leave him too: of the

many women in his life, he was to miss the first most. Even when Mary Joyce was dead, Clare believed she was his wife. But by now, he was in lunatic asylums. He was allowed to walk in the woods, and continued to capture the fragility of nature and feel himself at one with it – but he had begun developing other selves. He explained how he had written certain **Burns** poems, and his attempts to be **Byron** led to some very unfortunate verse. Still, his pathological sensitivity could manifest itself in his writings as before, and he never lost his ear for song-like stanzas, nor the force of argument that could cohere through unpunctuated sonnets.

Cocteau

JEAN   **born Maisons-Lafitte, nr. Paris 1889; died Paris 1963**

So get it into your head that these victims, which so moved the young girl you took, are nothing but noughts wiped off a blackboard, even if one of those noughts was an open mouth crying for help.

THE INFERNAL MACHINE

APART FROM BEING A POET, novelist and dramatist, Cocteau acted in his own plays, designed the sets (although he collaborated with Raoul Dufy and Picasso on such projects), organised the composers (he is responsible for the grouping of "Les Six", and composed music himself), invented ballet scenarios, executed lively line drawings and directed the films he scripted.

Whether he was guided by classical aesthetics or Dadaist innovation, he showed excellent taste and sardonic wit. As a writer with knowledge of so many other fields, he was always aware of where words stopped and actions began; *The Human Voice* and *Le Bel Indifférent* (written for Edith Piaf) both have women bawling into nothing but silence. In the film *Orphée,* a poet envies a rival who is lionised for producing a book with no writing in it; later, his own poetry reaches him from the underworld through a car radio.

Like **Apollinaire**, Cocteau saw machines as conduits of inspiration: the aeroplane in his poem *The Cape of Good Hope* transports the traveller beyond the world of things, while his view of fate as "The Infernal Machine" gave his great play its title. This latter

shows how Cocteau could bend myth to fit the concerns of his age. By favouring low-key dialogue to the extremes of Giraudoux, he lost no intensity, and prepared the way for **Anouilh.** The drama presents Oedipus on the brink of his terrible discovery as a type of "cursed poet" – a wanderer with strange insights; a figure which had already appeared in Cocteau's novels. Privately, he seems to have led a similar existence; in his public work, its expression gains force to the author's panache and sardonic wit.

Coetzee

J.M.   **born Cape Town, South Africa 1940**

We have all tumbled over the lip into the cauldron of history: only you, following your idiot light, biding your time in an orphanage (who would have thought of that as a hiding place?), evading the peace and the war, skulking in the open where no-one dreamed of looking, have managed to live in the old way, drifting through time, observing the seasons, no more trying to change the course of history than a grain of sand does.

THE LIFE AND TIMES OF MICHAEL K

J.M. COETZEE'S WORK strives to give a voice to the voiceless, and to find words for the disenfranchised or oppressed. He does this in short, sparing novels which are at once compassionate and unsentimental as they present the horrors of war and human evil. They are all the more undaunted in their accounts for being sustained by hope.

He was born in Cape Town and though educated in England and America is now a Professor of English in his homeland. His first book, *Dusklands*, expressed his rage at Imperialism, comparing American activities in Vietnam to the Boers' control over South Africa from the earliest days of colonisation; while a later book has a British magistrate in an unnamed African country yielding to pity for the regime subjects and recognising their inevitable freedom. Its title, *Waiting for the Barbarians*, comes from a poem by **Cavafy**, and Coetzee shares that poet's vision of bureaucracy dwindling into irrelevance. His latest book, *The Master of Petersburg*, set in **Dostoyevsky**'s Russia, shows another search for human values in a collapsing society. Its hero tries to track down a relative who has disappeared in a Kafkaesque city.

Coetzee's treatment of this theme comes out strongest in *The Life and Times of Michael K*, although the author denies that his central character's name has any connection with Joseph K from Kafka's *The Trial*. It is the story of a simple man trying to take his mother across a war zone to her birthplace. His loyalty, and attachment to the earth that responds to him, transcends the causes and campaigns that rage around him. He is retarded, and unfathomable to those around him, but as he rests on his journey, discovers a magical gift for making things grow.

Cohen

LEONARD

born Montreal 1934

Keep looking at that belly-button,

Leonard Cohen. It got angel dust in it.

We are ugly, but we have the music.

CHELSEA HOTEL

OUTSIDE HIS NATIVE CANADA, Leonard Cohen is better known for his songs than the earlier poetry and novels. These are as good an introduction as any, since they combine his lyrical gift with the sensuality and soul that shows throughout; but such a limited look means one misses the rich variety of his work, as well as his humour.

His poetry can swing from controlled rhyme to free-falling satire. In the former, he is metaphysical, using words as icons: his rose is not a rose. In the latter, he is as trenchant as **Ginsberg**, but more concise. His refrain-led verse is less a mantra against government policy than a vision of mad freedom. Seemingly trivial concerns become timeless (the lines on loss, 'Is there anything emptier/ than the drawer where/ you used to store your opium?' are worthy of **Catullus** on towels), while his treatment of Jewish persecution is more harrowing for being balanced with the more ephemeral trappings of love. He expresses his Judaism within the context of Christian and Greek cultures in his first book, *Let Us Compare Mythologies*, and later, in *Flowers for Hitler*, with statements of universal guilt.

His novels continue to explore sexual discovery and spiritual awakening often in a verse-like form. *The Favourite Game* follows a poet in his youthful progress around Montreal. *Beautiful Losers*, meanwhile, reads at once as confession and lament; a scholar pours out his fantasies, invoking both his late wife and the canonised Iroquois martyr, Catherine Tekakwitha. The narrative shifts from internal monologue, to epistolary novel, to third person account; but Cohen executes each with the same spirit and freedom.

He might appear to us now as a cousin to the Beats, once removed; an alternative voice for '50s Canada and '60s London; but even in music, so bound with these temporal links, he transcends the dictates of fashion, sharing his vision with a quiet, unshaking voice.

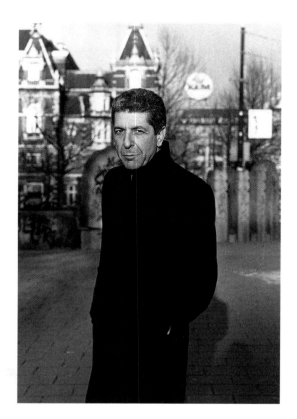

Coleridge

SAMUEL TAYLOR **born Devon 1772; died Highgate, London 1834**

O pure of heart! thou need'st not ask of me

What this strong music in the soul may be!

What, and wherein it doth exist,

This light, this glory, this fair luminous mist,

This beautiful and beauty-making power.

DEJECTION: AN ODE

BOTH IN THEORY AND in practice, Coleridge expresses best in English what a Romantic poet is. His early years were troubled — he fled, disillusioned, from Cambridge and joined the army, only to flee back; then, inspired by the French Revolution, joined in an aborted scheme to establish an egalitarian society in America, which in itself led him to an unhappy marriage.

Coleridge's idea of poetic genius was to feel ideas and shape them within the soul. The feeling most evident in his own early verse is an obsessive guilt. His creation, the Ancient Mariner, has since become the very archetype of remorse. A sailor kills an albatross and must atone for it. His contrition is endless and he is doomed to recount his actions to those he makes listen.

He published this and four other poems with **Wordsworth**'s work in their vital collection, *Lyrical Ballads*. Their friendship affected each other's work and thought enormously, visiting Germany together, where Coleridge began his study of Kant's philosophy. In 1810, however, the two fell out — a blow which came on top of Coleridge's marital problems, unrequited love and increasing addiction to the opium he had been taking medicinally.

His Romantic cast of mind had always rendered his output unpredictable — *Christabel* remains unfinished and a visit from 'a man from Porlock' caused him to abandon the ecstatic *Kubla Kahn* — but from 1810 onwards his work became increasingly fragmentary. He lived with Dr and Mrs. Gillman in Highgate, who helped but never healed his condition. It was here that he began his critical masterpiece, *Biographia Literaria*. Much of it uses Wordsworth to explain the idea of individual genius as opposed to talent. In this book, Coleridge argues that, 'No man was ever yet a great poet, without being at the same time a profound philosopher', a notion supported by his own greatness.

Colette

born Saint-Sauveur-en-Puisaye 1873; died Paris 1954

These women who had been dispossessed of their rightful childhoods and who, as girls, had been more than orphans, were now in maturity the fond instructors of a younger generation. They never looked ridiculous to me. Yet some of them wore a monocle, a white carnation in the buttonhole, took the name of God in vain, and discussed horses competently.

THE PURE AND THE IMPURE,
TR. HERMA BRIFFAULT

COLETTE REVEALS HERSELF throughout her stories and novels which correspond to different times of her life and draw on people around her. Throughout, her writing seeks a kind of self-knowledge, but the one truth her works reveal as really worth knowing – and which transcends any rules of behaviour – is love.

The task of knowing Colette is complicated by the problem of her early work. For a long time, she was renowned chiefly for the *Claudine* novels. These she wrote at the behest of her pornographer husband, who insisted that she record episodes from her school days. He made sure she incorporated shades of domination and sensuality among women. In *Claudine en Ménage*, Colette described more emotional relationships and began to find her own voice – although she still used her husband's pen-name, Willy, yielding the praise to him. She left him in 1906,

proved she was the real author, became a dancer and began writing under her own name.

Her life onstage and new-found freedom prompted more psychological work. *The Vagabond* fictionalises the marriage break-up, as the later memoir *My Apprenticeship* recalls it.

Her style is distinguished by its elegance and compression – like her sensual description, it is the more successful for being sparing. Although she was a deeply personal writer, as prized now for her letters and *Sido*, a reminiscence of her mother, she could express sympathy for all her characters, men as much as women, animals as much as humans. Both are civilised, but only the humans are corrupted by the process. She was the first woman to become President of the Académie Goncourt; she was also a member of the Académie Royale Belge and received a state funeral when she died.

Compton-Burnett

IVY

born London 1892; died London 1969

Families can seldom be explained, and they make better gossip without any explanation. To know all is to forgive all, and that would spoil everything.

DAUGHTERS AND SONS

IVY COMPTON-BURNETT'S NOVELS are all set in the last decade of the 19th Century, and are concerned with large families in old homes. If they are ostensibly well-off, they are nonetheless in a state of decline, morally as in their surroundings. The drama of these books derives from the secrets they keep from one another, and the tensions that emerge between relatives.

In this, she is often compared to the Greek tragedians: her father was eager for her to learn Latin and Greek, and she studied Classics at London University. If the atmosphere of her tales differs from these models, the themes are similar. Strong patriarchs or matriarchs preside, and the characters' actions take ethics to the limit: fraud, murder, theft, suicide and incest are among the subjects they try not to mention at meal time.

But still they talk about them. Compton-Burnett's books are made mostly of dialogue. Her technique is much like **Oscar Wilde**'s, in so much that she takes a cliché and finds an edge to it. Although she can also bring off a similar wit and polish, the effect is more sinister, as the speakers search for handy phrases to fill the silence.

Hilary Spurling's biography tells of Compton-Burnett's own childhood and finds an explanation for the gloom and strangeness that pervades the stories. Bereavement of siblings marked her youth and she always wore black, as though constantly in mourning. The harshest loss was that of her brother Guy at the Battle of the Somme in 1916. Not only did she never speak of the war, but also worked only in an imaginative world that existed before it. Although her style recalls the novels of that period, her irony is one born of hindsight and the knowledge her generation has of the steady fall of the old order into horror and destruction.

Congreve

WILLIAM **born Bardsey, nr. Leeds 1670; died London 1729**

Madmen show themselves most by pretending to a sound understanding, as drunken men do by over-acting sobriety.

LOVE FOR LOVE

CONGREVE WAS THE MOST successful playwright in the London of his day but the influence of his intellect was far reaching. He attended both school and Trinity College, Dublin, with **Swift**, helped **Dryden** in his translation of **Juvenal** and in his own early prose work, *Incognita*, consciously attempted to establish a working definition of the novel.

He was, however, careful not to direct his intelligence merely at his educated friends and the luminaries of William III's court. His comedies enjoyed long runs at Covent Garden (when two weeks on stage constituted a hit), and after a Congreve play, the acting company could afford to rest for the season. So it is all the more surprising that he only wrote four comedies. These are all long and make great demands of the performers. The writing in them shows that he knew his actors' capabilities well, and gave them bizarre characters. These would often be monomanic types, labouring under some delusion, be it that their love is requited, that they are rich, mad or married, or that they can tell the future. Sometimes these figures are cured by the wit Congreve spreads among all his creations, and sometimes not. But their compulsions impel fiendish plots, where rejection in love can lead to schemes of revenge, which themselves can lead to more delusions…

Where the characters seem predictable (Congreve's world is one where most women are of easy virtue, for example), the pace of the dialogue animates them. They are rich in idiolects, with verbal tics or leanings towards certain types of metaphor. Ben in *Love for Love*, for example, can barely open his mouth without a torrent of sea images bursting out.

Besides the comedies, he wrote one tragedy, *The Mournful Bride*, and much verse – including a lament for Queen Mary. He wrote words for the greatest composers of his day too, including Handel, and his *Judgment of Paris* became a text for three composers to set for a competition.

He was highly honoured before his death: **Voltaire** visited him and **Pope** dedicated his translation of the *The Iliad*, and when he did die he was buried in Westminster Abbey.

Conrad

JOSEPH   **born Berdichev, Ukraine 1857; died Ashford, Kent 1924**

To him the meaning of an episode was not inside like a kernel but outside, enveloping the tale which brought it out only as a glow brings out a haze, in the likeness of one of these misty halos that sometimes are made visible by the spectral illumination of moonshine.

HEART OF DARKNESS

PERHAPS WE SHOULD BE less surprised that one of English prose's finest exponents was Polish and spoke no English until he was 20. For Joseph Conrad brought to his adopted language and country a sense of life's strangeness that was lacking in the Victorian tradition.

He left Poland in 1874, after experience of Russian oppression, and joined a ship at Marseilles. Adventures like those that fill his stories led him to England, where he found a precarious kind of stability; the darkness of cosmopolitan London, seething with political tensions, was as close as he could find to a home.

It was here that he wrote his tales of honour and betrayal, focusing on the behaviour of crews in crises. Although tales of sailors' bravado feature in his work (especially *Youth*), he uses the sea as a setting for an enquiry into the effects of extreme stress on his characters' behaviour. He takes recognisable European personalities, like the quixotic Lord Jim or the refined Kurtz of *Heart of Darkness*, and follows them to the limits of morality.

He is concerned with the soul and seldom finds unalloyed goodness there. His sense of the abstract pervades his language, which eschews concrete nouns and tends to describe phenomena negatively. The newspaper report that summarises the happenings of perhaps his finest novel, *The Secret Agent*, concludes, 'An impenetrable mystery will hang forever over this act of madness and despair.' That book is rare in Conrad's corpus for its irony, its glimpses of corruption at all political levels and the tragedy the story reaches through the grimmest farce. Its action centres on the corpulent figure of Mr. Verloc, and his part in a plot to blow up Greenwich Observatory, London's most powerful symbol of global order. Its theme, the fear and love of anarchy, is one the author frequently explored and as with all his themes, he strove to render it timeless.

Cooper

JAMES FENIMORE   born New Jersey 1789; died New York State 1851

The whole party moved swiftly through the narrow path, towards the north, leaving the healing waters to mingle unheeded with the adjacent brook, and the bodies of the dead to fester on the neighbouring mount, without the rites of sepulture – a fate but too common to the warriors of the woods to excite either commiseration or comment.

THE LAST OF THE MOHICANS

WITH HIS STORIES of early American pioneers, Cooper pioneered the American novel.

He was educated at, and expelled from, Yale before exploring his country and the sea, and his later books are full of the latter. He wrote his first novel when challenged by his wife to produce something better than the book they were reading. *Precaution* is in the style of **Jane Austen**, and was a failure. His next, however, *The Spy*, was a bestseller. Its inclusion of General Washington as a character marks the beginning of Cooper's bid to render American history into epic form.

This is the achievement of the 'Leatherstocking' series of novels. They introduce the woodsman, Natty Bumppo, whose popularity obliged Cooper to feature him in a further five books. Bumppo's appeal is that he is alone among the pioneers portrayed as a representative of innocence and simplicity. The only other bearers of such noble attributes are the native Americans and their plight as pawns between the warring factions of white invaders dominates *The Last of the Mohicans*. It is an action-packed escape narrative whose climax, a funeral ceremony, aims at the dignity of *The Iliad*. If Cooper's dialogue should fail to convince, we should bear in mind his epic model.

The success of such books led him to Europe, where he busied himself with democratic movements and became an apologist for the American way of government. But on returning home, his increasingly elitist views, which found their way into the *Littlepage Trilogy*, led to a decline in his popularity. It is as well that he is remembered for his more compassionate works.

Corneille

PIERRE   **born Rouen 1606; died Paris 1684**

… the theatre

is at so high a point, all worship it …

And those whose splendid statesmanship
   preserves

By its illustrious measures all the world

Find in the sweetness of so fine a sight

Means to unbend from such exacting
   tasks.

THE THEATRICAL ILLUSION,
TR. JOHN CAIRNCROSS

PIERRE CORNEILLE WAS the first great French dramatist. He was the first to pen the ennobling tragedies in rhymed pairs of Alexandrines so associated with *le grand siécle*, and which gave Racine such a precedent.

With only his second work, *The Cid*, he broke barely established rules of tragedy. The play's exposition wastes no time in establishing the dilemmas that will bedevil its characters for the ensuing five acts, and all that follows complicates them with subplots, another innovation. The play's vigour thrilled audiences, but divided the French Academy, whose tastes were as up to date as Aristotle's and whose pronouncements were Cardinal Richelieu's.

He was shaken by this disapproval and turned to plays on Roman themes. These better caught the mood of change Richelieu was bringing over France. By setting his action in Rome's periods of transition (the early Republic of **Horace**, or the early Empire

of Cinna), Corneille deftly mirrored shifts in French power, and the increasing onus on kingship.

These pieces brought him a steady income, as well as **Racine**'s opprobrium and **Moliére**'s ridicule. Still, Corneille's earliest and possibly finest achievements were as a comic playwright, where his gift for agonising situations found expression in the tricky spots of farce. This work remains the best known. *The Theatrical Illusion* is a play within a play: a magician allows a man to watch the son he had feared was dead. The usual Cornelian clash between love and duty troubles the characters in the vision, but just as the loose ends are tied, the father watches his son and new wife die a violent death. He is to be comforted, as is the audience, by the knowledge that the characters have become actors and are themselves performing in a play: everyone survives after all. It demonstrates Corneille's feel for the power of theatre, and his own genius for wielding that power.

Crane

HART   **born Garretsville, Ohio 1899; died at sea in the Caribbean 1932**

The imaged Word, it is, that holds

Hushed willows anchored in its glow.

It is the unbetrayable reply

Whose accent no farewell can know.

VOYAGES

THE TRAGEDY OF Hart Crane's early death has long precluded a balanced assessment of his work. Throughout his short life he was an outsider – poor, homosexual and alcoholic – and he ended it all with suicide at the age of 33 when he jumped off a boat while at sea in the Caribbean. Consequently, he left behind a small volume of work, including the beginnings of an epic, *The Bridge*.

In the history of American poetry, *The Bridge* stands out as an example of what might have been. The task of writing a national poem, which so beset Joel Barlow, **Whitman**, **Pound**, **Williams**, **Ginsberg** and **Charles Olson**, seemed to have fallen to one of the best. Hart Crane's vision of his country starts on Brooklyn Bridge, and looks seaward, invoking the memories of **Melville** and Christopher Columbus. His work in shipyards sated his love of water for a while, as well as his passion for machinery and this adds the modernist edge to his work.

But what is most extraordinary about Crane is his language. His diction is extremely ornate and rather arcane. Words run away with him, and he apostrophises irrepressibly. He will often begin a poem with a clear stanza form, and then transform it as the subject matter takes over. The discipline of his approach seems to come from a reading of **Donne** and **Herbert**; but his rapturous tone shows, perhaps, the most forceful impact **Rimbaud** has had on literature in English.

And indeed, Crane has much in common with the French Symbolist: the alarming precocity, the restless experimentation and the sudden end of a writing career. This has led to his reputation becoming mythical and makes his poetry sound prophetic. It is true that his descriptions never shrink from the sublime, but his verse is frequently forced enough that we are witnessing something very human. His effort and pyrotechnics – his failure even – show the mechanics of rendering the ineffable. In Crane's hands, it is as high an achievement as bringing it off.

MAJOR WORKS

White Buildings (1926)

The Bridge (1930)

Collected Poems (ed. Waldo Frank, 1933)

Complete Poems and Selected Letters and Prose (ed. Brom Weber, 1966)

cummings

e.e.   **born Boston, Massachusetts 1894; died New Hampshire 1962**

and may myself do nothing usefully

and love yourself so more than truly

there's never been quite such a fool who

  could fail

pulling all the sky over him with one

  smile

SPRING

THOSE LITTLE LETTERS MIGHT have done for cummings' reputation. They are the first thing his readers notice, and even quite sensible critics cite typographical innovation as his principal achievement. **Apollinaire** used it, but it never proved quite the same distraction.

Still, it is integral to cummings' work. He was a painter, but his visual daring helps the hearer of poetry as much as the reader. A poem like *ygUDuh* only hits you when you've cracked it. Elsewhere, the poet's emphasis on seemingly random syllables lifts a verse to the pitch of singing. Often, his words hardly need the help. For cummings, capital letters and spaces are obstacles, as are distinctions between parts of speech. This is not to say his poems avoid syntax, rather that his supreme control over it allows him to explore it more acutely. He uses verbs as nouns, finding more life in them ("Scorning the pomp of must and shall/ my father moved through dooms of feel"); and sets advertising slogans beside national songs and natural speech – something which make his satirical poems so catchy. In this, his vocabulary may be conventional, but his words breathe.

This is why it is so hard to find rivals to his love poetry. His theme is traditional enough. The more unpredictable his combination of images, the more we imagine we've seen it before. One can attribute this to a mixture of his Cubist instincts in painting (he exhibited in Paris) and his New England Transcendentalist background (his father was a preacher, and made his son read **Emerson**). But there is a romantic singularity in cummings' achievement. He found a distinct mode of self-expression and, unlike the Cubists, never exhausted it.

Dante

ALIGHIERI

born Florence 1265; died Ravenna 1321

How I became so frozen and so faint,

reader, don't ask: I cannot write it down,

because no utterance comes near to it.

I didn't die, and didn't stay alive.

INFERNO

IN *THE DIVINE COMEDY*, Dante gives a complete and self-contained view of the universe. It is a spiritual vision, founded on the cosmography and philosophy of his day. The poet is taken by the poet **Virgil** on a tour of Hell. His path is strewn with obstacles and prevaricators – Satan's kingdom is full of political rivals, abusers of papal power, usurers and people born too early to have received the Gospel.

In keeping with the contemporary theology, the ascent to Heaven is via Purgatory, a vast spiralling mountain. Dante's guide here describes the structure of the cosmos and the workings of love. The presentation of these derives from Aristotle, whom, we learn, only Christians have interpreted correctly. The principle of Divine Love as Aristotle's Prime Mover of all things is developed further in the heavenly journey around the planets to the realm of the angels. Here the poet's difficulties in facing the Inferno are mirrored by his senses' inability to comprehend, save by degrees, the blinding light of God's glory.

Dante's extraordinary achievement is to make this vision utterly possible. He does this by working even chaos into a coherent system. Moreover, he does it in the execution: he is a master poet, whose very psychology fits in as well with modern views of appetitive love as with Aristotle's; and whose imagery carries this by making the most surprising, and yet the most exact, mental connections since **Homer**. While the rhetorical patterns owe much to his epic antecedents, his own verse-style is a three-line rhyming stanza whose order is a microcosm of the tripartite universe.

Here Dante is the self-aware poet, especially in knowing where words become powerless and truths too fantastic to unfold. His other works discuss the pioneering work he did in making poetry Italian. The finest, *The New Life*, is a treatise incorporating lyric verse on the love he first felt for that same Beatrice who guided him through Paradise. Only **Proust** since has really rivalled the Florentine for approaching love with an academic rigour that never robs it of its mystery.

Davies

ROBERTSON   **born Thamesville, Ontario 1913; died Ontario 1995**

Drug addiction is horrible, addiction to drink is pitiable, but to be a slave of the salted-nut habit is to be lost indeed.

THE DIARY OF SAMUEL MARCHBANKS

ROBERTSON DAVIES' BOOKS exude refinement. From small-town Canada to unchanging Oxbridge, his characters are restrained in speech, usually cultured, putting on *The Tempest* or *St. Matthew's Passion* and often willing to tell you what they're reading at the time.

It is an alluring world and one which leads critics to consider Davies a natural conservative. But he is not without a sense of perspective. Early on in his career, he produced a newspaper column using the persona of Samuel Marchbanks, a Dr. Johnson for the 20th Century, with blusterous opinions on just about everything. In giving him to the world, Davies seems capable of self-parody and so keeps even his innate control under control. In this, his writings show a constant awareness of the literary world's machinations: his disdain for them led him to comment once that "critics are like eunuchs who complain about other people's children."

His writings were the first to have brought Canadian literature to international attention. His stories often begin in his native Ontario, where his home town of Kingston became fictionalised as Salterton in the eponymous trilogy – and his characters can fetch up in the England he knew as a student and actor. In a large body of work, to which he was still adding to in spry old age, he explores guilt, memory and "the isolation of the human spirit". He brings it off with a delicacy of touch which has earned him respect as a humourist. In his hands, seemingly small events can have epic, even tragic consequences, such as a mix-up over a wedding announcement, or a fatefully misdirected snowball. In the latter, when the intended target realises what has happened, his 10-year-old thoughts are already on **Dante**.

Defoe

DANIEL

Wherever God erects a house of prayer,

The devil always builds a chapel there;

And 'twill be found, upon examination,

The latter has the largest congregation.

THE TRUE-BORN ENGLISHMAN

IF DEFOE'S MOST FAMOUS works cannot properly be called novels, it is because he wrote all of them as factual accounts and with an apparent purpose beyond the desire to divert his readers. To do this, he had to invest his prose with absolute accuracy where possible and minutely-imagined detail where not. Moreover, he had to immerse himself in the personality of his narrators, using all the psychological research of his day. As if for further authenticity, he eschewed the well-made plot. Finally, he always concealed his identity.

Although this was common practice in his day, Defoe had special reason to worry. He had worked as a spy and a spin-doctor both for Tories and Whigs. He had been pilloried (literally) and imprisoned for a pro-Dissenter pamphlet and for libel. As a journalist and confidant of William III, he had been active in the making of policy and, as a former merchant who had travelled Europe extensively, he had gone bankrupt.

Given such a life, Defoe's works had much to teach. *Robinson Crusoe* and *Moll Flanders* both tell the stories of tenacious survivors. The former is a fictionalised account of the sailor Alexander Selkirk's real experiences; the latter tells of a girl's life as a whore and robber in London until her repentance, as recounted to our anonymous author in Newgate

Prison. As so often in Defoe's writing, the protagonists here need to be saved, either physically or spiritually. Elsewhere in his massive *oeuvre*, we find heroes with sensational lives turning penitent: only for *Roxana, The Fortunate Mistress,* was it too late.

These books sit beside his real histories, but even then Defoe embellishes and pretends to be a witness. In his *Journal of the Plague Year,* he invites speculation that the writer might have been his uncle (Defoe would have been five during the plague). All his works are full of information, which in themselves would justify their appearance; but in prefaces he would insist, even as he titillated, that it was for the reader to find a moral for him or herself.

MAJOR WORKS

The True-born Englishman (1701)

A True Relation of the Apparition of One Mrs. Veal (1706)

A General History of the Union of Great Britain (1709)

Robinson Crusoe (1719)

Memoirs of a Cavalier (1720)

Captain Singleton (1720)

Colonel Jacque (1722)

Journal of the Plague Year (1722)

Religious Courtship (1722)

Moll Flanders (1722)

A General History of the Most Notorious Pirates (1724, 1728)

A Narrative of All the Robberies, Escapes, etc. of John Sheppard (1724)

Roxana (1724)

A Political History of the Devil (1726)

Dickens

CHARLES

born Portsmouth 1812; died London 1870

Such was the pleasant little family circle now assembled in Mr Pecksniff's best parlour, agreeably prepared to fall foul of Mr Pecksniff or anybody else who might venture to say anything whatever upon any subject.

MARTIN CHUZZLEWIT

DICKENS' NOVELS ARE many things to many readers. They can be read for their rhetorical flourish or for their extraordinary caricatures; as page-turners, or as rich historical documents; savoured for their unpredictable dialogue, or revered for their social concern.

Their author left school when he was 15, taught himself short-hand and became a court reporter. In the meantime, he became well-acquainted with the streets of London and the terrifying plight of the capital's poor. As his newspaper columns grew ever larger, he campaigned against the Corn Laws and child-labour. When his journalism evolved into fiction he was still fighting for legal reform.

Most of Dickens' work was initially published in serial-form in the popular newspapers of the day. A great populist writer, Dickens knew how to please his audience as well as escalate sales with devices such as the now well-established cliff-hanger.

In his depiction of children, Dickens found, perhaps, his most effective register for engineering change. Today, his treatment of childhood may strikes us as mawkish, but his dark fascination with the criminal underworld, captured so brilliantly in his work, often provides a perfect counterbalance and his work is shot through with brutal murders. If Dickens had a weakness for crime, however, he was tough on its causes, which he identified strongly with institutionalised poverty.

His characters, some enchanting, many more disgusting, enact these themes through ad-libbed plots. Their wild range of idiolects draws on the author's marvellous ear, and his passion for amateur dramatics. The scenic form of the novels betrays their sketch-like origins. Often stories within a novel appear as self-contained episodes. The first book, *The Pickwick Papers*, grew out of individual observations by the Pickwick Club. In later works, narrators and their juxtaposition would give the stories a more controlled shape. Phiz's illustrations enhance the whole throughout, brimming with caricatures and set pieces; speedily drawn, they cap the entertainments and enhance with detail… as if the story-teller needed help.

Dickinson

EMILY   **born Amherst, Massachusetts 1830; died Amherst 1886**

I'm Nobody! Who are you?
Are you – Nobody – too?
Then there's a pair of us!
Don't tell! they'd advertise – you know!

How dreary – to be – Somebody!
How public – like a Frog –
To tell one's name – the livelong June –
To an admiring Bog!

NO. 288

"PHOSPHORESCENCE...   that's the genius behind poetry." These words are attributed to Dickinson in a play, and indeed her poems are full of light: the poet craves for summer, and admires bees, "the Buccaneers of buzz" as she calls them; while her language wanders into hot places, "This January Day/ Jamaicas of Remembrance stir". These visions stream into the wintery world of a reclusive writer, who never visited such spots but whose imagination reaches for them, selects them for their random connotations and their euphony, and makes them real for a reader.

Dickinson's poems seem uncontrollable. Some readers hear popular tunes jingling along with the words, and the rhymes feel hymn-like, but within these ad-hoc metres, words can pause, and dashes supply much of the punctuation, as though language breaks off. And Dickinson takes it as far as it can go. She jumbles the senses – "Inebriate of Air – am I/ And Debauchee of Dew –" and reaches a satiety of synaesthesia – "I could not see to see", compressing near-ungraspable states of mind into tiny stanzas and short lines. Often one feels as though one has stumbled on a moment of revelation half-way through.

Much has been made of Dickinson's unhappy life – she harboured literary ambitions, but published only seven out of some 1,800 poems in her lifetime; and many have speculated on the identity of the beloved who caused the pain in her verse. But "Death is the supple suitor/ That wins at last" and her work is all the more extraordinary for lacking any thought that it might itself be immortal. The poetry's fullness of life and absorption with death seems all the truer for having such little self-regard, as much as for the unforgettable rightness of its phrases.

MAJOR WORKS

The Complete Poems of
Emily Dickinson, ed.
Thomas H. Johnson
(1960)

Dostoyevsky

FYODOR

born Moscow 1821; died St. Petersburg 1881

If, when you tell a lie, you skilfully put in something not quite ordinary – something eccentric, I mean, something, you know, that very rarely or even never happens – it sounds much more plausible.

THE IDIOT, TR. DAVID MAGARSHACK

DOSTOYEVSKY'S TALENT was barely controllable. It remains barely surpassable.

He abandoned a career as a military engineer to write. His first novel, *Poor Folk*, was well-received, especially in progressive quarters, but his next, *The Double*, failed to match such success. In 1849, he drifted into radical politics, was rounded up with the Petrashevsky circle, sentenced to a mock execution and then sent to Siberia where he served as prisoner and then soldier for eight years. The experience left him epileptic and prone to compulsive gambling.

The House of the Dead is an account of his prison years, while *Crime and Punishment* is filled with his insights into criminal psychology. Dostoyevsky's feel for the extremities of personality, and his ability to write through them without wasting a word, make this novel an extraordinary experience. Here the author's preoccupations appear in their simplest form – the vanity of violent action and redemption through Christ.

Later, these ideas appear within the context of Dostoyevsky's virulent pan-Slavic religiosity, which dominates his public diaries and often gives way to anti-semitism. But it never disfigures his novels.

The Idiot sets a Christ-like, epileptic prince into a world of rogues, radicals and frustrated aristocrats, to leave us nearly as bewildered as the hero. *The Brothers Karamazov*, meanwhile, gives Dostoyevsky's beliefs their most compelling expression: but the narrative's energy seems torn between Father Zossima's preachings and their atheistic counter.

The artist's hectic soul is bound up in this. Dostoyevsky complained that he could never write a perfect novel like those of **Tolstoy** or **Turgenev**, given the circumstances under which he worked. Still, each of his novels went through several drafts, however rapid they were, and were full of babbling lovers, repentant sinners, and people in whom mercy and brutality contend with each other. Though they often come from newspaper stories and speak with voices that we think we hear every day, they go to the limits of what is human and take us with them in the process.

Doyle

SIR ARTHUR CONAN

born Edinburgh 1859; died Sussex 1930

As Cuvier could correctly describe a whole animal by the contemplation of a single bone, so the observer who has thoroughly understood one link in a series of incidents, should be able accurately to state all the other ones, both before and after.

THE FIVE ORANGE PIPS

SIR ARTHUR CONAN DOYLE was internationally renowned, even in his own time, as the creator of Sherlock Holmes.

Holmes' methods derived from Doyle's teacher of medicine at Edinburgh University, Dr Joseph Bell. They involve a rigorous use of deduction. A Sherlock Holmes story is always told by the detective's companion, Dr Watson. He is the perfect foil: a medic, like the author, he is drawn into the mystery so deeply he can't regard the facts of the story with his friend's dispassion but he can recount it with real verve. His own attempts to emulate his live-in hero may lead the reader down false trails, but always succeed in communicating real atmosphere as he takes special pains to illuminate a very murky London.

Early on in the tales, Doyle was careful to introduce the possibility that Holmes might be fallible. While his arch-rival was always the nefarious Moriarty, his most impressive adversary must remain 'the woman,' Irene Adler.

Despite their enormous popularity, Doyle grew bored of writing Sherlock Holmes stories by 1893,

and plunged Holmes and Moriarty to their deaths in the Reichenbach Falls in what was supposed to be the last story about the Baker Street sleuth, *The Final Problem*. His readership, however, clamoured for more and, after an eight-year gap *The Hound of the Baskervilles* finally appeared, with the hero miraculously saved. Still, Doyle was happy to divert his considerable energies to causes about which he was more passionate, including his defence of Britain's conduct up to and during the Boer War, in which he served as a physician. He also worked as a missionary and his interest in the spiritual grew after the First World War in which he lost his son. Besides the Sherlock Holmes stories, he left behind the adventures of the scientist Professor Challenger, who would have been well at home in Jurassic Park, and a six-volume history of the Western Front from 1916–1919.

Dryden

JOHN   **born Aldwinkle All Saints, Northamptonshire 1631; died London 1700**

Death in itself is nothing; but we fear
To be we know not what, we know not
where.

AURUNG-ZEBE

DRYDEN WAS THE MOST versatile and influential man of letters in 17th-century England. His output covers an immense range – some 30 dramatic works, including operas and a masque (he and Purcell had the luck to be collaborators and on the latter's death,

Dryden wrote a lament of singular grace); sustained satirical poems; translations from Latin and **Chaucer**; as well as literary criticism.

His fortunes were bound up with the times. He was born a Puritan and along with **Milton** and **Marvell**, was a civil servant in the Protectorate. He continued as an administrator during the Restoration, writing an elegy on the death of Cromwell and verses welcoming Charles II. His poetry was always topical; *Annus Mirabilis* commemorates the events of 1666, dwelling on naval victory over the Dutch of that year, while *Absalom and Achitophel* puts the leading figures of the Court at the time of the Popish plot into a Biblical setting. So it is appropriate that before becoming Poet Laureate, he was appointed Historiographer Royal, in 1669.

His forthright lampoons, particularly of Shadwell and Rochester, left him prone to literary and even physical attack (he was mugged at Covent Garden by Rochester's hired heavies). Although he was a fashionable figure, even when being mocked, he did not join in the public rejoicing with the accession of William and Mary, choosing to retain his new Catholic faith. It cost him his court position and he was banned from commenting on public affairs

This left him translating **Virgil**, **Ovid**, **Juvenal** and **Lucretius**, with no obvious allegorical intent. For a man who had frequently adapted other works (producing an operatic version of *Paradise Lost* and basing his play *All for Love* on *Antony and Cleopatra*), it is fitting that he should have spent his final years in bringing his own pellucid verse as close as English has yet come to the elegance of his originals. In this, as in all else, he enriched the language amply and made the way plain for **Pope**.

Dumas

ALEXANDRE THE ELDER   **born Villers-Cotteràts 1802; died Dieppe 1870**

ALEXANDRE THE YOUNGER   **born Paris 1824; died 1895**

The resemblance between heroes and the earthly is too great, the analogy too close; the spectator who follows the development of a passion in the actor will want to check it just at the point where it would be checked in himself.

DUMAS THE ELDER, ANTONY

Theatre is as unpitying as arithmetic.

DUMAS THE YOUNGER,
PREFACE TO A PRODIGAL FATHER

DUMAS THE ELDER ONLY admitted to being the father of Dumas the Younger when the was seven years old – and the latter struggled with his illegitimacy throughout his life. They were both compulsive womanisers, however, and both found it possible to examine the consequences of private indiscretion in their public work.

The elder Dumas' play *Antony* not only contains discussion of what theatre goers expect from tales of heroism: it also portrays a man who kills his mistress to avoid scandal. The audience recognises this as abnormal behaviour and yet, 42 years later, the younger Dumas presents an equally shocking story in a much more realistic setting: *Claude's Wife* has Claude killing his spouse as moral retribution for her infidelity. (The author had himself fathered a child with a married Russian countess.)

Both managed to titillate the Paris of their day with their treatment of scandal, from the orgies and bloodbaths of the Elder's *La Tour de Nesle* – with its glimpses of a former aristocracy that were sure to offend the new Royalist régime – to the Younger's *Camille*, which mobilised the censor for having a courtisan as its heroine (the play is the basis of Verdi's *La Traviata*).

The Elder's more enduring popularity rests on his novels, especially *The Three Musketeers* and *The Count of Monte-Cristo*. In these he continued with his brand of historical romance à la **Victor Hugo**, but with a lightness of touch which charmed his public enough to save him from financial ruin. His son kept the crowds coming to his increasingly moralising plays by guaranteeing quality of structure and an excellent ear for how dialogue works on stage. Together the two Alexandres Dumas dominated French letters for most of the 19th Century.

du Maurier

DAPHNE   **born London 1907; died Cornwall 1989**

We are all ghosts of yesterday, and the phantom of tomorrow awaits us alike in the sunshine or in shadow, dimly perceived at times, never entirely lost.

GROWING PAINS (PUBLISHED IN THE USA
AS MYSELF WHEN YOUNG)

DAPHNE DU MAURIER wrote numerous short stories, memoirs, histories and a notable biography of Branwell Brontë (see under **Anne Brontë**). Two of her short stories have been famously filmed: Alfred Hitchcock's *The Birds* and Nicholas Roeg's *Don't Look Now*. Both stand as chilling realisations of her power as a suspense writer.

Her best-loved accomplishments in this field are her six historical romances, on widely varying themes. The first four of them hark back to the Cornwall she first saw when was 20. She was born into an artistic family: her father was George Du Maurier, the theatrical manager and creator of the rôle Bulldog Drummond, She received a cosmopolitan education, growing up in Hampstead and going to school in Paris. But she stayed in Cornwall and her writing would constantly return to the West Country. Eventually she lived in Menabilly, the 70-room mansion which became the Manderley of *Rebecca*, which remains her most popular work.

It is as Gothic as the novel, which owes some of its plot to *Jane Eyre*, as a young wife wonders what happened to her predecessor, the first Mrs de Winter (who dies in the beginning). The heroine of *Rebecca* is typical of the central character in a du Maurier story: she has an innocence and trust, together with a natural curiosity, which echoes the plight of Mary Yellan arriving among smugglers on the Cornish coast in *Jamaica Inn*, and anticipates the abandon of Dora St. Columb, as she finds liberation in the piracy of *Frenchman's Creek*.

Much of the suspense draws on the uncovering of evil, and the over-bearing sense of guilt which haunts even the most benign characters as if forever. The three mentioned above have all been filmed, as was her next work, *My Cousin Rachel*. On the page, the rhythm of du Maurier's prose can attain great elegance: The opening paragraph of *Rebecca* is the most famous example.

Duras

MARGUERITE

born Indochina 1914

If the very fact of being alive means that we can do harm, however much we don't want to, just by choosing or making mistakes … why then, I too will go through with it.

THE SQUARE,
TR. SONIA PITT-RIVERS AND IRINA
MORDUCH

MARGUERITE DURAS' WORK explores the problem of love and the world that impedes it. Over her long career, she used widely different novelistic techniques to discuss this, as well as producing a large number of screenplays.

She began to write shortly after the outbreak of the Second World War. A memoir of those times appeared in 1985. Called *Pain*, it tells how her husband, Robert Antelme, was deported to Germany for being a Communist and contains her reflections on the genocide as it became revealed. She concludes that the guilt of these crimes is so enormous that it must be shared by us all. Her most famous writing, the screenplay *Hiroshima, Mon Amour*, focuses on two parallel relationships as a way to confront the horror.

After the war, she divorced Antelme. She had already published two realist novels, and a third would follow in 1951, *The Sea Wall*. Here women struggle with their environment and wonder to what extent their lives might be different. Her next two books took a more ironic look at the search for love, represented in *The Sailor of Gibraltar* by the heroine Anna scouring the Mediterranean for her lover, and

in *The Little Horses of Tarquinia* by a situation that results in perpetual bickering.

Later, her treatment of such love becomes more stylised, notably in *The Square*, which is almost exclusively dialogue between a young maid and a travelling salesman, who meet one another by chance. Their immediate ease with one another allows them not only to discuss the unvarying quality of their lives in a probing, theoretical way, but also to find in each other some hope.

In her latest novels, she began to rework earlier plots, and twice portrayed men paying women to help establish their ideal of love.

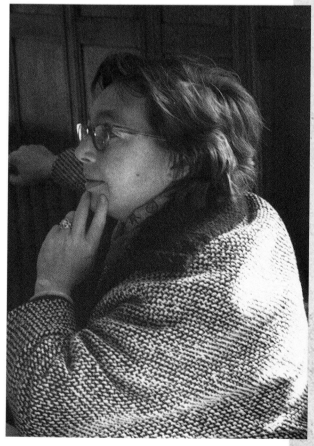

MAJOR WORKS

The Quiet Life (1944)

The Sea Wall (1951)

The Sailor of Gibraltar (1952)

The Little Horses of Tarquinia (1953)

The Square (1955)

Moderato Cantabile (1958)

Hiroshima, My Love (1960)

10.30 on a Summer Night (1960)

The Ravishing of Lol V. Stein (1964)

The Vice-Consul (1966)

The English Lover (1967)

Destroy, She Said (1969)

The Lover (1984)

Pain (1985)

Blue Eyes, Black Hair (1986)

Durrell

LAWRENCE   **born Julundur, India 1912; died Avignon 1990**

Journeys, like artists, are born and not made. A thousand differing circumstances contribute to them, few of them willed or determined by the will - whatever we may think.

BITTER LEMONS

LAWRENCE DURRELL'S WRITING stands self-consciously outside the British literary tradition. The author found England uncongenial – he was born in India and persuaded his parents to move from Kent to Corfu – and lived around the Mediterranean for most of his life. It is here that his series of novels are set.

These show a sympathy for the thinking of Freud and Einstein, and the influence of **Joyce**'s technique in fictionalising their ideas of identity and time. Durrell takes the former's account of sexuality as something that defines the personality and uses eroticism as a means of exploring his characters. He was encouraged in his sensual expression of this theme by his correspondence with **Henry Miller**. Einstein's theory that time is relative is echoed in the books' structures with the author hardly ever telling a story in chronological order – although this very much depends on which author is telling the story.

The first novel of The Alexandria Quartet, *Justine,* for example, is the product of a novelist within the whole opus, while *Balthazar*, the subsequent volume, throws it into a completely different perspective. Throughout the tetralogy, Durrell plays with different points of view on the same episodes and builds up ironies as characters act in ignorance of what the reader understands has already happened.

He writes with a travel writer's sense of place and his locations shape the characters as much as events do, even declaring at one point in his work that "We are the children of our landscape". His settings show all the signs of decay from their mythical past. The Alexandria he describes is the city of **Cavafy**, whose poetry and presence hovers over his books. The same sensual and complex prose characterises the later Avignon Quincunx. Durrell also made a name for himself as a poet and his verse reads as a luxuriant response to the work of **T.S. Eliot.**

Eco

UMBERTO   **born Alessandria, Italy 1932**

Scratch the heresy and you will find the leper. Every battle against heresy wants only this: to keep the leper as he is. As for the lepers, what can you ask of them? That they distinguish in the Trinitarian dogma or in the definition of the Eucharist how much is correct and how much is wrong?

THE NAME OF THE ROSE

UMBERTO ECO IS AN academic with a staggering range of interests and reference. His professional field is semiotics – the interpretation of signs – and he finds them everywhere. He produces linguistic

texts of unsurpassed rigour and newspaper columns scrutinising current trends with a jolly scholar's eye. But his finest, most durable offering so far must be the novel, *The Name of the Rose*.

It is a murder mystery set in a medieval monastery. Brother William of Baskerville's Holmes-like hunt for clues leads the narrator, a young monk, to ponder signs and their meanings. In an intellectual climate founded on faith and reason, the things signified point, however logically, towards an irrational core: although the killer is unmasked, the quest for knowledge appears to lead nowhere.

Still, Eco's own knowledge makes the journey to chaos sublime. From his research into Aquinas' aesthetics and his inexhaustible supply of information on 14th-century heresy, botany, illumination and witchcraft, he has constructed a tale for our own times. While some think of it as a whodunit with some literary theory on top, the whole – however ironic its intention, and however parodic its execution – unites form and meaning to pose the most fundamental questions about human existence.

The scepticism of empirical systems to understand the world is akin to that of **Borges**, who is represented by the manic master of a labyrinthian library in the novel. This stance is similar in Eco's next novel, *Foucault's Pendulum*, where three dodgy publishers start investigating a document which describes a secret energy source known only to a league of Medieval knights. Their findings lead to a complete re-interpretation of history, with much satire on the way. The scientific erudition explored here here takes over in his latest offering, *The Island of the Day Before Tomorrow*, which explores our arbitrary ways of measuring and defining time.

Eliot

GEORGE   **born Warwickshire 1819; died London 1880**

We see no white-winged angels now. But yet men are led away from threatening destructions; a hand is put into theirs, which leads them forth gently towards a calm and bright land, so that they look no more backward; and the hand may be a little child's.

SILAS MARNER

GEORGE ELIOT WROTE NOVELS of great stature. Queen Victoria devoured them, and while Eliot captured her age, she never pandered to its strictures.

She keenly observed the effects of the Industrial Revolution and the sudden transferences of wealth in her novels become, not so much the plot motivations that we find in **Jane Austen**, as an element that colours human relations more subtly. For Eliot, psychology and motivation take precedence. *Adam Bede* contains the line, "Our deeds determine us, as much as we determine our deeds," and much of her books' interest comes from the response of her characters to crises.

In *Silas Marner*, this idea is played out in comparative miniature: a miser loses his horde and it is replaced, as if by a miracle, by a golden-haired foundling. The moral is obvious; subtler is the way his affection is transferred, almost as if his want of an object precipitated the child's arrival.

Here, as elsewhere, Eliot's skill relies on her telling stories in a recognisable form, but allowing readers to form their own conclusions about the structure of life. In *Middlemarch*, widely held as her finest work, the process is likened to the scratches on a table which only seem to form a pattern when a candle is held over them. This illuminates *Middlemarch* itself, which sets two men off in their contrasting bids to make complete sense of the world as they see it. Here the work relies on both writer and reader to construe its meaning. Eliot performed her part by drawing on her sensitivity, especially in the equitable treatment of men and women in her fiction. Ultimately, her work was a plea for progress, that set out to expose hypocrisy, champion the poor over the rich and the individual over gossiping communities – urgencies she very much felt in her own life, living in sin on the Strand.

Eliot

T.S.

born St. Louis, Missouri 1888; died London 1965

The progress of an artist is a continual self-sacrifice, a continual extinction of the personality.

TRADITION AND THE INDIVIDUAL TALENT

AT HARVARD, Eliot aspired to be a philosopher. But his vast reading of religion and anthropology as well as Elizabethan poets and the latest French imagists, left him writing a completely new kind of English verse.

Although technically 'free verse,' it never sounds liberated. Although crammed with allusions and tongues, it never feels fussy. Eliot handled *personae*: his most famous poem, *The Waste Land*, was originally titled *He Do the Police in Different Voices*, and while still a young man, he found the voice of a timid, middle-aged, middle-class American called J. Alfred Prufrock.

The technique gains its effect from the verse's immense musicality. Although he was helped in this by **Pound**'s fine ear (and new research is discovering just how much), Eliot's own instincts were to hear a rhythm and only then supply the words. Indeed, he explained that his *Four Quartets* were an attempt to capture the melancholy of Beethoven's last string quartets.

All this enabled him to keep his poetry objective, rather than let words topple out. For Eliot, it was a key to disengaging his own personality, so great a step after the Romantic obsession with that aspect of the poet. It made him a dazzling critic too, more willing to argue about empirical criteria for good writing than good or bad taste. This meant that, though his conclusions could be as arbitrary as anyone's, he could argue them forcibly – qualities which helped him as a playwright (nominally as a verse one) and allowed him to steer his characters away from Shavian ranting.

Much of this, however, articulated a particular world-view – that of the English establishment, albeit an Anglo-Catholic one. Subsequently, his noblest theme is atonement; although he makes this a clearer goal for Celia in *The Cocktail Party* at the end of his career than for any of the lost voices that speak his words throughout it, it is nevertheless a hope in all his writing. He was awarded the Nobel Prize for Literature in 1948.

MAJOR WORKS

Prufrock and Other Observations (1917)

The Waste Land (1922)

The Hollow Men (1925)

Ash Wednesday (1930)

Four Quartets (1944)

Murder in the Cathedral (1935)

The Cocktail Party (1949)

Ellison

RALPH WALDO   **born Oklahoma 1914; died Oklahoma City 1994**

The question of how the sociology of his existence presses upon a Negro writer's work depends on how much of his life the individual writer is able to transform into art. What moves a writer to eloquence is less meaningful than what he makes of it.

THE WORLD AND THE JUG

APART FROM A COLLECTION of essays, Ralph Ellison published little except the novel that made him famous: *The Invisible Man*. It is narrated by an unnamed black man in 1952, from a room underground in Harlem. He talks of his own search for identity – one which takes him all over the United States, and through the diverse strands of opinion represented by the Civil Rights movement. His "invisibility" lies in his being treated as a number only, not just by white society, but also by black political extremists.

It was the latter which brought the book so much controversy. He was fiercely opposed to segregation between the races: this led him to the conclusion that black separatism was also wrong. But if he seemed overly eager to compromise and co-operate with white society, it was because he had a multi-cultural vision of America.

It was as a student of history and literature that he found ways to express himself. **Joyce** was a key influence; and his project has much in common with Stephen Dedalus's mission (in *Ulysses*) to forge a national identity. But perhaps his musical training provided the real impetus to write *The Invisible Man*. For Ellison, jazz was a uniquely American art form that black people had given to America, and even famously declared that one Fats Waller lyric posed the central problem of race for the entire continent: "What did I do/ To be so black and blue?"

His own childhood was spent in Oklahoma, in a house where white and black people mixed freely. His writing would plead for such tolerance everywhere. He developed this stance in subsequent essays. The bulk of a second novel was destroyed in a fire: he never really recovered from the loss.

Emerson

RALPH WALDO   born Boston, Mass. 1803; died Concord, Mass. 1882

'Tis the good reader that makes the good book; in every book he finds passages which seem confidences or asides hidden from all else and unmistakably meant for his ear.

SUCCESS

RALPH WALDO EMERSON'S spiritualism and his effusive expressions of it, are key to an understanding of American Romantic writing.

His faith in the soul was formal at first. He was born into a long line of preachers and was himself ordained as a Unitarian pastor in 1829. However, his wide reading and questioning mind led him to doubt the sacraments, a scepticism he shared with his congregation before leaving it. A fusion of Swedenborg's philosophy, the poetry of **Coleridge** and **Wordsworth**, and a fair smattering of German and Hindu thought poured into Emerson's own Pantheistic view of the universe.

Although he is chiefly considered to be a philosopher and essayist, his response to this all-pervading soul is profoundly that of an artist. He wrote some poems, but considered all his writing to be poetry. He found a poetic language in Creation's coherence, and a metaphysical counterpart to every physical law. In response to this, the poet must become one transparent eye.

He was disappointed by his travels to Europe, however, where these notions of beauty seemed to him repressed. On meeting Wordsworth, he found him reactionary and rambling. While his reflections on England provide excellent satire, his visit to Paris' Jardin des Plantes proved epiphanic.

In these stances he was ever the American — Oliver Wendell Holmes called his lecture, *The American Scholar*, an intellectual Declaration of Independence — and he was the mentor to a whole school of American poets. His home in Concord, Massachusetts, was the centre of Transcendentalist philosophy, from where he'd correspond with other writers or else set out from to lecture all around the country. While his own work became less coherent as he approached old age, the help and encouragement he gave to the likes of **Walt Whitman** rendered literature an inestimable service.

Erasmus

DESIDERIUS

born Gouda 1466; died Basle 1536

If anyone is shocked at this being more frivolous than theology should be, or more trenchant than befits a Christian, then I didn't say it – Democritus did.

IN PRAISE OF FOLLY

ERASMUS OF ROTTERDAM was a Renaissance scholar and theologian, who was probably born in Gouda. As a philosopher and literary giant, his chief attributes were his intimate grasp of Greek thought,

at a time when Western Europeans were only just re-learning how to read it in the original, his independence of mind and a wit that was as merry as it was subtle. The first two inform all his voluminous writings, while the last is especially evident in his satire, *In Praise of Folly*, which is still widely read today.

He wrote it while he was staying with Thomas More. Together they had studied Greek and translated Lucian, the satirist who began his account of lunar exploration saying, 'Everything here is a lie.' *In Praise of Folly* employs the same technique. Folly speaks throughout, reminding us that we shouldn't take her too seriously. Her gender is significant; while the voice the author gives her is dizzy, the choice of speaker becomes more interesting as she concludes that fools can often make sense, too. She ends by explaining **Platonic** theories of love, which Socrates acquires from a woman in *The Symposium*. It is one of many moments when the author wrong-foots the reader, and allows us to be convinced by the literal interpretation of a discourse we had taken for pure irony. Even what looks like manifest chauvinism might admit an alternative slant.

In this way, Erasmus finds the perfect medium for his views on love (at once scholarly and mystical), and on society, particularly ecclesiastical. These were humanist: he was unashamed about bringing all classical literature to the service of theology, not just **Plato** and Aristotle. He had a liberal view of salvation, which extended to those who had not heard the gospel but were still redeemable. His satire is at the church's expense, and particularly Pope Julius II's, and his books were later burnt. He anticipated the Reformation but was innately ecumenical, and opposed a split.

Euripides

born Phyla? c. 485 BC; died Macedonia c. 406 BC

I want to be under high hiding-places

so that God might make me fly upon a

  bird's wing

with the fluttering flocks elsewhere

HIPPOLYTUS

GREEK TRAGEDY was an art form which played to all sections of the (male) Athenian community, however drunk the audience was. Of the three great tragedians, Euripides understood this best, and delivered plays of the highest quality.

He won the tragedy prize six times only (on 23 known attempts); but public familiarity with his work is evident in the laughs **Aristophanes** expected from mocking it.

Euripides would write for ordinary characters: the deferential nurse, or the farmer living as Electra's husband, who boasts that he never laid a hand on her. He uses simpler language than his predecessors used. Most of his audience would have sat as jurors, so his use of legal oratory, with characters "contesting" a point, made his drama still more accessible. In this way, he could explore motivation more fully, and try to explain the most extreme actions.

These included matricide, infanticide, and incest: in testing the limits of morality, he bent the rules of theatre too. His chorus became increasingly engaged in the action; in *Hippolytus* he used two choruses and possibly a fourth actor. His musical settings stretched words: even without singing, we can hear that the energy and pulse of his lyric episodes are stunning.

Although he could present scarily sexist

characters, his championing of women set him at the opposite extreme to **Aeschylus** and unlike **Sophocles**, he preferred the thorough exploration of psychological crises to architectural plots. So he explored passion fully, especially female; and in the *Bacchae*, gives us a temptation scene held out over a lengthy, metrically-controlled exchange. When the curious party breaks down, so does the metre. Although his verbal tricks make him difficult to render into theatrically-viable English (for in spite of his comic skill, we risk finding him unintentionally funny or pedantic) moments like this abound, when we can appreciate Euripides' amazing facility, both as dramatist and poet, for finding the right stroke at the right moment.

Hippolytus (428 BC)

Andromache (426 BC)

Hecuba (424 BC)

Alcestis (438 BC)

Medea (431 BC)

Electra (417 BC)

Heracles (417 BC)

Trojan Women (415 BC)

Helen (412 BC)

Orestes (408 BC)

Bacchae (405? BC)

Fielding

HENRY born nr. Glastonbury, Somerset 1707; died Lisbon 1754

The first care I always take is of a boy's morals; I had rather he should be a blockhead than an atheist or a Presbyterian.

JOSEPH ANDREWS

FIELDING'S WRITINGS were often about literature itself. But if his work only seemed to exist as glosses in the margins of other books, his own sprawled out of them to be some of the greatest in English.

His youthful plays dealt with the theatre and scholars and he enjoyed great success. **Swift** recalls that he laughed for only the second time in his life during *Tom Thumb*, a spoof of revenge tragedies, which ran for 40 nights. Fielding's last play, *The Historical Register*, was about drama critics, and caused Walpole to introduce severe censorship into the London stage.

He continued his campaign against Walpole, as a journalist in *The Champion*. Then he took an approach similar to Gay's *Beggar's Opera*, and in *Jonathan Wild* likened Walpole to the man who had monopolised London's organised crime by turning informer: in later life Fielding, as a magistrate and early advocate of a police force, was to play a great part in the breaking up of criminal gangs.

But Fielding's greatest target was **Richardson**, whose epistolary tale *Pamela* captivated the reading public in 1740. *Shamela* appeared soon after, treating the earlier book's moral tone as hypocritical. Fielding never denied authorship and Richardson never forgave him. *Joseph Andrews* followed, again using Richardson's characters, but along a wandering story line conceived more in homage to **Cervantes**. The author, however, styled the book in a new genre, which he called the 'comic epic in prose.' It was a form he would make his own.

When Richardson's *Clarissa* appeared, Fielding hailed it as a masterpiece and just had time to pay tribute to it in his own greatest triumph, *Tom Jones*, which was published soon after. It is a huge work, chronicling its foundling hero's seemingly random amorous progress in spite of his remaining in love with the heroine Sophia. Fielding never quite found the same form, although his last book, *Amelia*, sold out instantly. He died in Lisbon three years later, trying to relieve his chronic gout.

Fitzgerald

F. SCOTT

born St. Paul, Minnesota 1896; died Hollywood 1940

*'Fixed the World's Series?' I repeated.
It never occurred to me that one man
could start to play with the faith of fifty
million people – with the single-
mindedness of a burglar blowing a safe.*

THE GREAT GATSBY

F. SCOTT FITZGERALD'S elegiac novels chronicled the hedonism of booming America. He continued to do so when the boom had disappeared and this accounted for a decline in his popularity; but the causes of the era's passing are clear in *The Great Gatsby*, a book published at the height of the Jazz Age.

For many, Fitzgerald embodied the glamour of those times, just as his great fictitious creation, Jay Gatsby, represented its tragic flaws. He shared his extravagant lifestyle with his wife Zelda, gave lavish parties and paid large bills by writing for glossy magazines. His friend **Ernest Hemingway** strongly disapproved of this, considering him a fine and serious writer, and certainly Fitzgerald had the turn of mind to see the superficiality of much around him.

The perfect form and symbolism of *The Great Gatsby* makes it a timeless tale, but it has singular importance in the history of literature on "The American Dream". Like **Henry James**'s novels on the 'international situation', it portrayed a national temperament ill-fitted to gratuitous sophistication and, like subsequent writers, Fitzgerald showed how impossible it would be to realise that dream and maintain the sense of innocence on which it depended.

This kind of disillusionment marks all his work, from *The Beautiful and the Damned* through to *The Last Tycoon*. This latter was left unfinished on his death. It tells the story of a movie executive who has moved from rags in New York to riches in Los Angeles; the megalomania that has driven him there leads him to contemplate murder. On the posthumous publication of what Fitzgerald wrote (drafts and an entire plot summary), critics felt that at last the author was finding the form of his greatest work, and through the reworked drafts could witness the level of perfectionism that he demanded before he could consider a book finished. He was mourned as the writer of one of America's greatest novels.

MAJOR WORKS

This Side of Paradise (1920)

Flappers and Philosophers (1920)

The Beautiful and the Damned (1922)

The Great Gatsby (1925)

Tender is the Night (1934)

The Last Tycoon (1941)

Forster

E.M.   **born London 1879; died Cambridge 1970**

I hate the idea of causes, and if I had to choose between betraying my friend and betraying my country, I hope I should have the guts to betray my country.

TWO CHEERS FOR DEMOCRACY

Ronny had repressed his mother when she enquired after his viola; a viola was almost a demerit, and certainly not the sort of instrument one mentioned in public.

A PASSAGE TO INDIA

E.M. FORSTER WROTE short stories, essays and biographies, as well as five novels – the last in 1924. All these are touched with an instinctive compassion.

Forster spent his school days in misery and this left him timid. He was always modest about his literary achievement, and shy in company: though he was intimate with members of the Bloomsbury set, he was closer to the edge than the centre of that circle.

He wrote especially well of outsiders, many of them victims of a peculiarly English way of life. *The Longest Journey* tells the apparently personal tale of a would-be writer still traumatised by bullying at school. Forster's own first published tale, *The Story of a Panic*, places English picnickers in Italy under the spell of Pan and explores English discomfort with other cultures – a theme which resurfaces throughout Forster's work: the spontaneity of the Italians

unsettles travellers in *Where Angels Fear to Tread* and again in *A Room With a View* in which a girl's awakening to aesthetic forces seem almost indecent to those around her.

A Passage to India is Forster's most complex investigation of these themes. It sets English people against the oppressive background of the Raj, whose strict racial taboos they flout in a quest either for 'the real India' or uncomplicated friendship. They go in too deep: unlike Italy, the subcontinent remains beyond their grasp, not least because of the country's own rigorous social stratifications. The author's frequent plea, that we should connect more with our true feelings and with nature, finds its frustration here, where the very land seems hostile. But even when anticipating the problems of Indian Independence and partition, for many inconceivable at the time of publication, still nowhere does Forster relinquish his faith in people over principles.

Fowles

JOHN

born Leigh-on-Sea 1926

When they were nearer land he said, 'I wish you hadn't told me the sordid facts. That's the trouble with provincial life. Everyone knows everyone and there is no mystery. No romance.'

She teased him then: the scientist, the despiser of novels.

THE FRENCH LIEUTENANT'S WOMAN

JOHN FOWLES' NOVELS and stories have consistently evoked a rich aesthetic world to explore the themes of personal freedom and self-knowledge.

As a result, he produces very aware texts: aware of their own status as art, and aware of their authorial source. There is the writerly self-analysis of *Daniel Martin*; but *The French Lieutenant's Woman* is perhaps the best example of this process, and certainly his most famous work. The novel is set in Victorian Dorset, and nods towards conventional 19th-century plotting and narrative; but it is full of authorial comment, and manipulates the unnatural constraints of the past by forcing events to a conclusion more likely in the present. Or rather, two conclusions. The book belongs more to the writer than the reader. Fowles admitted that he had to let the lovers part, but couldn't, and so gave the work two endings, giving the reader the choice – although even this recalls the previous century and **Charlotte Brontë's** *Villette*.

The book's hero and heroine are echoed elsewhere in the Fowles corpus. Sarah is an idealised, elusive woman – the author has said as much – and for her, Charles suffers almost sadistic trials, while the *ingénu* schoolmaster in *The Magus* is plagued still further by his own "master" in a struggle for control of what Fowles calls "the godgame." Control, over people and art simultaneously, was his earliest theme. *The Collector* kidnaps an art student, kills her and analyses her as an object, beginning a soulless aesthetic project. The story involves class differences, as does the next: *The Aristos* argue over élite and popular views of culture. In *A Maggot*, Fowles finds support for the latter, arguing that we learn more about the 18th century from its mediocre writers than we do from **Pope** or **Dr Johnson.**

Frost

ROBERT

born San Francisco 1874; died Amherst 1963

That day she put our heads together,

Fate had her imagination about her,

Your head so much concerned with outer,

Mine with inner, weather.

TREE AT MY WINDOW

IT HAS BECOME AXIOMATIC to say that Robert Frost was something like America's Poet Laureate. He was an unusually public writer. Although he left Dartmouth College and Harvard without a degree, he had 44 conferred upon him subsequently; he won four Pulitzer prizes; the Senate formally congratulated him on his 75th and 85th birthdays; his visits to Russia and Israel assumed a diplomatic significance; and he read at President Kennedy's inauguration.

But if anything, Frost's reputation has suffered from this prominence. His achievements, and his pride in them, have led critics to attack him for being too popular or low-brow. To the world, Frost presented himself as a simple farmer (he had run a farm in Massachusetts for five years); with his literary peers he could display his erudition.

This has a curious effect on Frost's poetry, such that it is better read when one forgets the hype. It is at once simple and formal: his great trick is to incorporate speech rhythms into blank verse, and to keep each line at once controlled and relaxed. The result is a kind of home-spun wisdom delivered with lyrical grace, as though the poet were less a seer than a good neighbour. His insights often came from nature, and he had a closer affinity with the English poets of the Georgian school than with his American contemporaries (though he was much admired by **Pound**). He observes, and reports; but he has an ear for the one-line dictum. These are characteristically stoical, and lend themselves readily to quotation. His most famous poems, like "Out, Out", are even more celebrated for their grimness. But generally Frost uses his craft to put us in a resigned frame of mind in the way he tells his story, so that his own conclusions don't alarm us.

Gaddis

WILLIAM

born New York 1922

– No but here's a pin. For where your coat's torn. You shouldn't be upset about this appointment, she went on, pulling the tear together, – but I'm glad it's so important to you. There, she straightened the pocket flap and sat away, – but I wish it were a novel.

– Why would you say that, he muttered.

– The way you look, she said not looking.

– Like a novelist? Only problem is a novelist has to understand women.

J R

MAJOR WORKS

The Recognitions (1955)

J R (1975)

Carpenter's Gothic (1985)

WILLIAM GADDIS IS THE author of three novels, each of them highly experimental, each using a highly stylised brand of satire to assess the plight of the soul in post-war America.

At the root of his work is a hope in salvation; but to establish a viable means of achieving it, when contemporary life offers such a babble of temptations and alternative theories, takes the narrative hundreds of pages. Gaddis' technique strives to mimic this kind of chaos, with plot conveyed mostly in dialogue in which only verbal tics can tell us who's talking, and leads some to find his texts unreadable. Still, he uses his own artistry, not only to posit art as a redeeming force, but also to question even that while he is doing it. His first novel, *The Recognitions*, has a hero who,

like Gaddis himself, is the son of a preacher and has artistic ambitions. But he discovers that even artistic endeavour can be flawed, as forgery and commercialism dog his progress around the international art scene.

The book's guiding principle is contained in the palindrome, "trade ye no mere moneyed art", which was to inform the long-awaited second novel, *J R*. Its protagonist is an eleven-year-old masterminding a business empire from payphones around his school. But his mission is set against that of a composer, who suffers as he avoids selling out. This sounds a note of hope, which was to echo in Gaddis' most recent book, *Carpenter's Gothic*, about a misunderstood Vietnam veteran who works for a preacher.

George

STEFAN

born Büdesheim 1868; died Minusio, Switzerland 1933

Now the dream, highest pride, upward springs,

Boldly quells then the god who lent wings...

Till a cry to the depths thrusts us all,

We so bare, face with death, we so small!

DREAM OF DEATH, TR. CAROL NORTH
VALHOPE AND ERNST MORWITZ

STEFAN GEORGE EMBRACED the idea of a higher reality beyond the tangible world. His work seems to aspire for a greater purity still: he thought wine and women were both deleterious to the poet's song, and surrounded himself with male aesthetes whom he could persuade of the same. This circle was called the Georgekreis, within which he was the autocrat.

As a German, he wanted his nation to attain a similar refinement. He was frustrated by what he considered the crudeness of those around him, and by a language too ornate to articulate his ideals. He craved the abstractions of **Nietzsche**, and echoed the philosopher's praise of strength. George expressed this patriotically. His verse would speak of a new Reich, and a Führer, which the incipient Nazi movement found extremely useful. This appalled him. He was too much the poet to care for their politics, and had no sympathy with their anti-semitism. In 1933, he rejected Goebbel's offer of high honours in the new régime and left for Switzerland, where he died later that year.

If his verse had nationalistic leanings, it was in the name of beauty. He combined the two in his view of the youth of Maximilian Kronberger, whom he mythologised as a boy emperor, dead at 16. His earlier work was more decadent and espoused the aestheticism of **Oscar Wilde**; then his model of the young despot was the debauched Heliogabalus. Even then, his verse remained pure. He would execute it under rigorous constraints and avoided repeating any rhyme. His determination to blend form with content meant that he had to express his meaning with whatever vocabulary his rules left him, accounting in part for his distinct style.

Gide

ANDRÉ   **born Paris 1869; died Paris 1951**

"Put as little order into your story as you please," said Jammes. ...

"Then you must allow me to talk a great deal about myself."

"Which of us ever does anything else?" was Jammes' rejoinder.

ISABELLE, TR. DOROTHY BUSSY

ANDRÉ GIDE'S STYLISH and sometimes exotic handling of prose touched on many concerns sure to arouse controversy. He was a forthright critic of French imperialism and, after his visits to Chad and the Congo, became a Communist for a while. **E.M. Forster** considered him the perfect humanist, particularly for the way Gide's love of mankind balanced a natural curiosity. The latter attracted more attention.

In moral matters, he anticipated the work of **Sartre** and **Genet**, and in *The Immoralist*, wondered how far people are constrained by their environments: can they reinvent themselves? But Gide's exploration was more guided by the battle between the sensual and the spiritual than by the needs of the hour. In *Strait is the Gate*, the spirit seems to prevail; but this is partly because of pride militating against freedom, and the sensuality of religion itself.

His fictional treatments complement what appear to be his more atobiographical works. He was a bisexual wanderer married to his devout cousin, and during that time strove to explain his soul's struggle to her in writing. But even his memoirs show the artistry of his story-telling. In his largest, most complex work, *The Counterfeiters*, a novelist is writing the novel *The Counterfeiters*, sharing Gide's own dependence on structure and frame devices to make sense of the vaguely connected plots occurring around him. Here the real author shows his admiration for **Dostoyevsky**, borrowing stories from newspapers, snipping from them at moments of crisis. But, as elsewhere, he retains a love of beauty, and in writing of forgery, asks the question that rises throughout his *oeuvre*: how successfully could the form and elegance of his art render the truths of his life?

Ginsberg

ALLEN   **born Newark, New Jersey 1926; died New York 1997**

Poets be fools of their own desire – O

Anacreon and angelic Shelley!

Guide these new-nippled generations on

space ships to Mars' next universe

WHO BE KIND TO

ALLEN GINSBERG WAS THE POET of the Beat generation. Although his work exists beyond that time, we know it comes from a survivor of that hazardous age who handed it down in all its detail.

His poetry is a rich mix. His method, as he describes it, is a form of meditation, using the mantra "Om": while the altered state of consciousness this produces would seem to generate "automatic writing", Ginsberg juggles a range of sources and allu-

sions. He cites many precedents for *Howl*, the poem which made him famous, including other poems with refrains, such as Christopher Smart's mad *Jubilate Agno*. For all his verse's abundant freedom, however, Ginsberg spent a long time mastering classical metres, translating **Catullus**, or working with Elizabethan models.

A Ginsberg poem, however, could not be mistaken for any of these. His writing is confessional and often vast. It takes on folklore and mysticism, sensuality and religion (especially Buddhist and Jewish: his most harrowing poem is *Kaddish*, a Hebrew-styled lament for his mother). Whatever it takes to combat his enemies – the CIA, sexual repression, the atom bomb, colour TV – he prosecutes his cause with anything from ballads to harangues.

His graphic and unflinching accounts of gay sex, his forthright language, and openly drug-induced streams of consciousness, have led him to be censored and arrested. This alone would give him authority as a leading counter-cultural figure but he is more than just this. He has given the cause a poetry which can reach **Whitman**'s expanses and attain **William Carlos Williams**' delicacy of cadence. He has acknowledged both these as influences and the latter helped his early career considerably.

Nevertheless, he stamps his own name, and those of his friends, all over his volumes, filling them with unpunctuated anecdotes which sometimes make the reader feel he or she just had to be there. All this might seem like vanity, but in being the first to own up to it (Ginsberg frequently complained about his deteriorating looks) his candour seems more generous than self-seeking.

Goethe

JOHANN WOLFGANG VON   born Frankfurt 1749; died Weimar 1832

Now slants the fiery god toward the west,

Hasting away, but seeking in his round

New life afar: I long to join his quest,

On tireless wings uplifted from the

ground.

FAUST, PART ONE, TR. PHILIP WAYNE

GOETHE MIGHT STAND as Germany's finest poet, yet he embraced all Europe. His juvenilia includes work in English and French; he broke off government work to explore Italy, and entered a classical period of writing, translating Latin authors and imitating their metres. At the end of his life, he was a huge fan of **Byron**'s *Don Juan*, and wished his own language capable of such comic rhyme. But he did more than any of his compatriots to extend the range and power of German, stretching its natural capacity for new words, taking on its folk poetry and its song rhythms, as much as its philosophical diction.

His career spanned the end of Classicism, and the beginning of Romanticism. But for all his involvement with the German 'storm and stress' movement, he had more faith in controlled poetics and an ordered world view than in spontaneous outpourings of emotion. Not that he was incapable of these. He could write poetry anywhere and all Europe was caught up in its passion. His prose work, *The Sorrows of Young Werther*, for example, was supposed to have men on the wrong corners of love-triangles reaching for their guns. Goethe's concerns went beyond the individual's emotions, however: as a polymath, with interests including all branches of science as well as the arts of painting, music and theatre, he formulated theories of evolution and light in which he saw a unity in creation, and a kind of Pantheism.

This is especially strong in the mighty *Faust*, his life's work. Taking the 16th-century legend of a man tempted by a pact with the Devil, he portrayed a scholar wracked by his vision of the world's beauties (which Goethe incomparably glossed, even marrying Faust to Helen of Troy), and in doing so reflected his own quest for knowledge and faith in salvation.

Gogol

NIKOLAI

born Sorochintsy 1809; died Moscow 1852

This world is full of the most outrageous nonsense. Sometimes things happen which you would hardly think possible: that very same nose, which had paraded itself as a state councillor and created such an uproar in the city, suddenly turned up, as if nothing had happened, plonk where it had been before, i.e. right between Major Kovalyov's two cheeks.

THE NOSE

GOGOL'S CHARACTERS BEGIN with all-too human delusions, which usually escalate into madness. Readers are tempted to see Gogol's own obsessions and literary ambitions (not to mention sexual hang-ups) as an explanation for this, as well as for his own bizarre end; but his literary and historical sources, together with his own magnificent comic style, are vital.

Literary aspirations took him to St Petersburg, where he worked as a public official and even as Professor of History at the university. The crazed types who people his stories are often frustrated civil servants who lose it completely, or dignitaries undone by embarrassment (like that of losing one's nose at the barber's). These figures waver between fear of humiliation (having too shabby an overcoat) and hope for unattainable social rank (becoming the King of Spain, in *The Diary of a Madman*, for example). These conflicts generally precede lunacy.

They are first-person narratives: Gogol's use of speech, random thought patterns and even typography at once pay homage to his model **Sterne** and go to the roots of personality. This explains why his one play is the constant joy of Russian theatre. *The Government Inspector* blends his old theme of provincial pettiness with an identity mix-up, leading a nobody to believe that he really is the inspector that a corrupt community holds in such dread. While nobody survives this satire, the piece's importance is more than social; where public honesty is at stake, so is honesty to oneself.

Gogol craved a moral element in his work and a holy man talked him into burning much of his largest work, *Dead Souls*, for failing to achieve it. What **Pushkin** read of it had a profound effect on him: the extant text gives us the clearest glimpse of his talent for sheer poetry, with its apostrophes on the progress both of Russia and the human spirit.

Golding

WILLIAM

born St Columb Minor, Cornwall 1911;
died Newquay, Cornwall 1993

I have hung all systems on the wall like a row of useless hats. They do not fit. They have come in from outside, they are suggested patterns, some dull and some of great beauty. But I have lived enough of my life to require a pattern that fits over everything; and where shall I find that?

FREE FALL

WILLIAM GOLDING'S NOVELS characteristically approach the battle good and evil fight over human beings, by setting it in isolation. The first, and the most famous, is *The Lord of the Flies*. It follows a group of boys stranded on an island, whose attempts to establish order descend into anarchy and murder. It presents a view of morality the author could not escape after the Second World War, during which he served in the Navy; but the means of expressing it came from his dislike, both of Ballantyne's insular idyll, *The Coral Island*, and of having taught schoolchildren in Salisbury.

The sea brings the worst out of people in his other novels; in *Pincher Martin*, a naval officer struggles to survive the elements once he is washed up on a rock – but at length we come to realise that it is nothing less than his salvation at stake. In a late trilogy, Golding sends a group off from 19th-century England to settle in Australia. The trip takes the Victorian image of life itself being a journey, while the peculiarly English make-up of the crew, with its attitudes on class and religion, make the vessel in *Rites of Passage* a ship of state.

The sin inherent in Golding's tales is ineluctable. Mankind has fallen already. Rather than go back to Genesis, he returns to the dawn of *homo sapiens*. From *The Inheritors*, we emerge as an innately aggressive, cunning species. A religious reading of the problems we have reconciling morality with our flawed nature occurs in *The Spire*; it tells of a medieval churchman's architectural plea for redemption, in which his human frailties have their counterpart in the building's own structural faults. The very title of *Darkness Visible* recalls **Milton**, and his own poem of the atonement.

Golding was awarded the Nobel Prize for Literature In 1983.

Goldsmith

OLIVER

born Co. Longford, Ireland c. 1730; died London 1774

But me, not destined such

delights to share,

My prime of life in wandering

spent and care;

Impelled, with steps unceasing, to pursue

Some fleeting good, that mocks me

with the view...

My fortune leads to traverse

realms alone,

And find no spot of all the

world my own.

THE TRAVELLER

THROUGHOUT HIS SHORT LIFE, Oliver Goldsmith embraced a wide range of experience, and explained to his brother, "I had learn'd from books to love virtue, before I was taught from experience the necessity of being selfish." His youthful travels rendered him penniless, and must have showed him how to survive – he got by as a busker, an apothecary's assistant and an usher at a school in Peckham – and yet his dealings in practical matters show naivety. When threatened with the debtor's prison, it was **Dr Johnson** who sold Goldsmith's *The Vicar of Wakefield* for the necessary £60.

That book was criticised for its lack of insight into human behaviour, but praised for its morality – the opposite of what his brother might have expected. His characters seemed too romantic, even his vicar too virtuous. The qualities it displayed resembled those his theoretical writings disparaged: he preferred harder, realer truths to the more inflated sentiments of **Richardson**; but Goldsmith's work shows a family prevailing over disasters by the dozen – a contingency real enough to the author.

The events of his best-known play, *She Stoops to Conquer*, appear still more implausible, in which a young suitor mistakes the home of his prospective bride's parents for a pub, and behaves accordingly. Still, we could regard this as portraying each setting more faithfully through comparison with the other, even were it not likely that Goldsmith had made a similar error in his own youth. In the piece, he continued his assault on all that he considered trite in contemporary writing. He sustained it with great distinction as a poet, using an epigrammatic, even bitchy kind of wit to repudiate the fault of taking the world too much at face value.

Goll

YVAN   **born St. Dié, Vosges 1891; died Paris 1950**

And this single dusk

When even the gods are jealous

Of a kiss made of honey and electricity

Is worth more than the centuries of

*   centuries.*

DO NOT CALL DEATH!

YVAN GOLL WAS A Jewish poet born in Alsace-Lorraine, an area which has repeatedly swung from French to German control. His background already gave him a rich cultural mixture – he was fluent in both French and German, and wrote poetry in both languages. He tried writing in English, and produced a German translation of *Ulysses*. His linguistic journeys bespeak the kind of rootlessness that would be his most dominant theme, most notably in the poems of a wondering Everyman, *John Without Land*, whose peregrinations follow Goll's, with no more hope of settling anywhere. This enables the poet to embrace the whole of human experience, as did **Whitman**; but he does it in remarkably controlled, rhyming quatrains, and with epigrammatic elegance: "I buy Manhattan with a single smile/ I sell it back for immortality."

He resembled that other polyglot **Paul Celan** in his range of influences: he spent the First World War in Switzerland writing Expressionist poetry, and in France would champion Surrealism. The two poets were working with such similar subject matter and resources that Goll's wife Claire accused Celan of plagiarism, upsetting the latter deeply.

But it was Claire, a fellow poet, who would inspire Goll most, and give him his best hope of happiness. Many poems show him finding a refuge in his love that saves him from the world's otherwise overwhelming horrors. His work is more approachable than Celan's in this respect, especially when Goll is being lyrical: "When you cry, the sun is eclipsed/ But when you smile, new stars are born."

After the war, he wrote very little in German, until the very end of his life, when he began work on *Traumkraut*. It was published after his death from leukaemia.

Gorky

MAXIM

born Nizhniy-Novgorod 1868; died Moscow 1936

I sought the friendship of those who were foreigners even in their own country.

MY UNIVERSITIES

GORKY'S WRITING is notable for introducing the technique called "socialist realism", which became the prescribed approach for writers working in the Soviet Union. He began his career with the short stories that brought him widespread attention: that of **Chekhov** welcome, that of the authorities less so. The former encouraged him in letters which read like a masterclass; he praised whatever in Gorky was sparing, and advised him against words which swung the narrative too much, and against rhetoric. However, Gorky was to be a political writer and the traits some have regarded negatively, for their want of refinement, were to become Gorky's tools.

Although he is now read chiefly for his memoirs, and his reminiscences of **Tolstoy**, his reputation was sustained by in his novels and plays. His most political play was *The Lower Depths*, which expressed much of Gorky's philosophy and the punishing life he'd led as a labourer even before he was orphaned at the age of 10. His two most famous novels are *Foma Godeiev*, in which a father embodies the insurgent capitalism at the expense of his sensitive son, and *Mother*, about Bolshevik activity in an industrial town. He was indispensable to the Bolsheviks, both before and after the Revolution, trying to collect funds in America in 1905, and controlling the crowds in the excesses of the October Revolution in 1917.

He was a key link between the intellectual and popular movements, but he was regarded with suspicion by both. Although his death invites conspiracy theories from either side, there can be no doubt that Stalin must have been a little comforted by the health concerns that kept the nation's gadfly in Capri for much of his later life. From there, Gorky continued to encourage and advise young writers. His home town of Nizhniy-Novgorod adopted his name as its own. His pen-name at least: for Alexei Mikhailovitch Peshkov changed his name too, to the Russian for "bitter".

Grass

GÜNTHER

born Danzig 1927

And so from this Yorrick came no citizen, but rather a Hamlet, a fool.

THE TIN DRUM

GRASS IS A HIGHLY cultured writer who remains extremely critical of his country. Germany's history has made a profound personal impact on him, and he has been bound up with its public events during the war and beyond.

His most famous and daring response to this has been the Danzig Trilogy, particularly its first book, *The Tin Drum*. Throughout, the narrator,

who has refused to grow physically since the age of three, languishes in an asylum for a murder he didn't commit. He emerges as a brilliant outsider, a *faux naif* and the best hope his delirious nation has of being restored to humanity. His drum beats steadily through the age's hysteria, while his gift for screaming can wreck Nazi rallies. Grass's own book can be read as a similarly alarming shriek aiming to awaken Germany's conscience.

The allure of Hitler reaches deeper into the trilogy's other two books. *Cat and Mouse* depicts a man impelled to join the Nazis by another physical peculiarity (this time a huge Adam's Apple). *Dog Years* follows the rage of a character who embraces and then rejects Nazism, driven to beat his half-Jewish friend, before plaguing his former military colleagues with sexual diseases.

Grass himself joined Hitler Youth, and was drafted into the air force during the war. His experimental and allusive work offers a first-hand, hideously real account of National Socialism's power, using often unreal plots and authorial comment to drive his point further home. He has continued this as a playwright, poet and political thinker. In the last rôle, he has written speeches for Willy Brandt (stung by the personal assaults Chancellor Adenauer launched against his friend), persistently scrutinised public life in open letters, and produced essays arguing against German reunification. His versatility extends to music and the plastic arts, influencing respectively the inner content of his books and their outer design.

Graves

ROBERT

born London 1895; died Majorca 1985

Gone are the drab monosyllabic days

When 'agricultural labour' was still tilth;

And '100% approbation', praise;

And 'pornographic modernism' filth;

Yet still I stand by tilth and filth and

praise.

TILTH

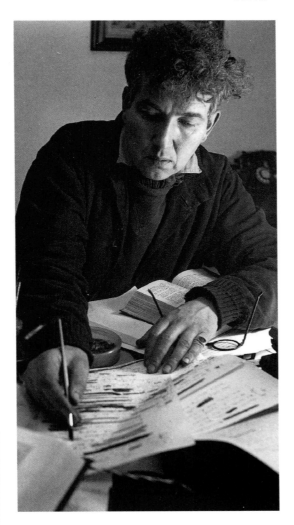

BEFORE ONE OF THE LECTURES Robert Graves delivered as Professor of Poetry at Oxford, an undergraduate was heard to remark that his value lay in the fact that he was "wrong about everything". Indeed Graves tended to avoid agreeing with people.

For sure, he wrote fiction unashamedly for money, in order to sustain his true passion for poetry, and in so doing disciplined himself to write economically and in accordance with public taste, but even his novels were aimed to cause upset. *King Jesus* for example, showed a Christ who had not died on the cross. Other projects and sentiments, meanwhile, showed breath-taking hubris. He modernised **Shakespeare**, and re-translated *The Rubáiyát of 'Omar Khayyám* with his usual freedoms, only to contest that he was using a better manuscript. His poetry, however, is conventional, and while his lyrics are lovely, his premise, "Man Does, Woman Is" has become outmoded and his views on fellow poets such as **Eliot** and **Auden** frankly laughable.

That said, Graves' knowledge was vast. His scholarship did not stop with the classics. His control of mythological sources was enormous, and his ability to communicate it unmatched. Indeed, his novels have popularised Ancient Rome nearly as much as Asterix has. A polyglot and a polymath who gleaned his knowledge as much from life as from books, he was as complex as he was clever. There's no doubt he knew the horror of war – having read his own obituary after mistakenly being reported dead at the age of 21 – and yet he spoke out against poets like Auden and **Virgil** who never saw military action. Through all these contradictions, however, emerges a kind of incomprehensible bravery that make Robert Graves' convictions as bold as his insights.

Greene

GRAHAM   **born Berkhamsted 1904; died Antibes 1991**

If I love or if I hate, let me love or hate as an individual. I will not be 59200/5 in anyone's global war.

OUR MAN IN HAVANA

GRAHAM GREENE'S NOVELS can be read just as he styled many of them – as entertainments – but with his wit and control of tension comes perhaps the most profound examination of morality in 20th-century English fiction.

A constant theme with Greene is betrayal. His work in intelligence, notably under the double agent Kim Philby, informs his treatment of espionage; but for all the 'thriller' content of his books, he is most acute on human motivations rather than political ones.

This shows in his earliest 'romances', and their historical settings; and in the years before the war, his exploration of the international situation focused on individuals acting out of private malaise rather than public feeling. If Greene's characters act politically, it is out of personal anxiety, like their espousal of Communism in *It's a Battlefield* and *The Confidential Agent*.

With Greene's conversion to Catholicism, these themes emerge in a religious context, and with greater vehemence after 1938, when the Church sent him to Mexico to report on state persecution of Christianity. Greene felt that a sense of religion enriched the novel (impoverished, for him, since the death of **Henry James**), and he expressed it in plots handling the most agonising dilemmas. Priests frequently appear either to instil meaning into a moral void, as in *Brighton Rock*, or to articulate their own doubts. This latter alarmed many in the Catholic Church, especially with the frankness of the "whisky priest" in *The Power and the Glory*.

Later work described turbulent landscapes like Cuba and Haiti; the Anglo-Saxon characters caught in these spots try to face pressures while maintaining their integrity. They are in life-or-death situations: in West Africa, as in Brighton, Greene realises the full dramatic potential of the troubled conscience facing impossible decisions.

Hardy

THOMAS   **born Upper Bockhampton, Dorset 1840; died Dorchester 1928**

Yonder a maid and her wight

Come whispering by:

War's annals will cloud into night

Ere their story die.

IN TIME OF "THE BREAKING OF NATIONS"

HARDY'S THIRD NOVEL finds a young, self-taught scholar restoring a Cornish church, and falling in love with Elfrida Swancourt, the daughter of a disapproving priest. *A Pair of Blue Eyes* holds many clues to the author's life and work: he trained as an architect, and his plots stand as structural wholes, each action leading logically to the next, and supported by the rhythm of the seasons. Often, the result is finely-wrought tragedy; this novel features the independent but doomed heroine that would recur in Hardy's books, to be represented most ruthlessly in his penultimate novel, *Tess of the D'Urbervilles*. The end of that novel invokes the pitiless progress of tragedy in its quotation of **Aeschylus**.

He was born in Dorset, where he played the fiddle at weddings and was later engaged to disinter bodies making way for a road. Nearly all his stories take place in Wessex. He gives real locations fictional names; but visitors find that what they read is real enough. Like the poet Richard Jeffries, he portrayed the dignity and suffering of the rural poor, in the face of such obstacles as industry, new wealth, and uncomprehending idealism. But more than that, they contend with the universe's injustice and, from *The Return of the Native* onwards, they never win.

His work was increasingly attacked for its atheism and supposed immorality. He revised his novels right until his death, often toning down his earlier, sensual instincts; but with the outrage that greeted *Jude the Obscure*, he abandoned novel-writing and began publishing his poems. Throughout 900 of them, he never used the same verse form twice. These brought him the fame we now associate with his prose (his most admired verse then was an epic, *The Dynasts*, now largely ignored). They compress the theme of an unsympathetic world into song-like stanzas, whose cadences are as irresistible as the fate they describe.

Hardy died in Dorset, at Max Gate; he designed the house himself.

Harrison

TONY

born Leeds 1937

Hindu/Sikh, soul/body, heart v. mind,
East/West, male/female, and the ground
these fixtures are fought out on Man,
*   resigned*
to hope from his future what his past
*   never found.*

v

MAJOR WORKS

The Loiners (1972)

The Oresteia (1981)

v (1984)

The Trackers of Oxyrhynchus (1990)

IN CONTEMPORARY BRITAIN, Tony Harrison is a poet of rare social importance and technical accomplishment. His poems address a divided nation, and hit home.

He does this in clear language, whose frankness offends some. As well as being an astounding handler of form, he is also a polyglot; he mastered Latin and Greek before his teens and has translated opera libretti from Czech. His verse includes snippets of other languages, including the endangered Cornish.

Harrison himself is from Leeds. His stated poetic goal is to write poetry his father would understand. His sonnet sequence, *The School of Eloquence*, articulates this with unerring pathos. Rather than parade his learning in front of the reader, he draws attention to the difference between his classical education and much of his audience's experience. But his use of the classics is invaluable to today's problems. As well as rendering **Aeschylus** with a rare immediacy, he has written an extraordinary verse play, *The Trackers of Oxyrhynchus*, which follows the Greek scholars Grenfell and Hunt on their trail for lost tragedies. All they turn up are a **Sophocles** satyr play full of the plum lewdness that genre requires, and appeals from the homeless. The analogy between their priorities and ours becomes stark.

Harrison's poetry reaches an unusually large public, through his drama (he has written adaptations of medieval mystery plays) and television. He continues to address urgent social concerns, like Alzheimer's Disease, the Gulf War, and the controversy over Rushdie's *The Satanic Verses*. The earliest remains the best. *v* addresses all the opposing factions of society, in a response which begins with rage at the graffiti on his family graves and works towards an understanding of its deeper causes.

Throughout, he maintains a poet's self-consciousness, leading him to find much guilt in himself: for Harrison, poetry is *The Heartless Art*, and his work strives as much to heal itself as those around him.

Hartley

L.P.

born Peterborough 1895; died London 1972

The life of facts proved no bad substitute for the facts of life.

THE GO-BETWEEN

L.P. HARTLEY'S NOVELS and short stories examine the roots of personality. His characters strive for self-knowledge and the quest often begins in childhood. His world is one of lost innocence and just as children are robbed of their illusions, so is Hartley's age. The Victorian values of the well-to-do figures who people his work disappear in the social change for which he accounts so subtlely.

The lush background of his tales can betray his own origins: action frequently takes place in the countryside of East Anglia, and can wander into the fashionable sets of Oxford and Venice. But Hartley undermines the formality and expectations of such locales with his own prose style. His sentences are finely balanced, and his structure rigorously controlled, all the while depicting an old order of strained elegance in decay.

Hartley can offer some comfort to people who feel they have wasted their lives for ignorance of themselves. Eustace emerges from the *Eustace and Hilda* trilogy, which follows its hero's emotional development from childhood to his death bed, less in the shadow of his sister, and at last capable of love, however long this has taken. The narrator of Hartley's most famous book, *The Go-Between*, has less to console him. He recalls a hot, hot summer holiday spent in Norfolk, and how events showed him, not only what sex was, but also how tragic its consequences could be when transgressing social niceties. Leo Coulston is now a bitter, solitary man, caught in the past until the final page; but his recollections are childhood ones. What he doesn't understand literally is conveyed with an exact symbolism: the thermometer that measures the rising tension; the dreamed-up magic spells that assume lives of their own; the green bicycle that compounds at once the boy's innocence and how he loses it – by taking messages between lovers divided by class. As elsewhere, Hartley's exquisite articulation of his themes owes much to **Henry James**; but the tragic effect he achieves is rare indeed.

Hašek

JAROSLAV

I am very fond of the good soldier Schweik, and in presenting an account of his adventures during the World War, I am convinced that you will sympathise with this modest, unrecognised hero. He did not set fire to the temple of the goddess at Ephesus, like that fool of a Herostratus, merely in order to get his name into the newspapers and the school reading books.

And that, in itself, is enough.

THE GOOD SOLDIER SCHWEIK,
TR. PAUL SELVER

JAROSLAV HAŠEK WAS a prankster and short-story writer who was well-known and liked in Prague, where he lived in the years before the First World War. During the conflict he fought first for the Austro-Hungarian Empire, which ruled Czech-oslovakia, before deserting to join the cause of Czech independence. When the war ended, he joined the Russian Communist party.

In 1921, he began work on his one novel, *The Good Soldier Schweik*. In its meandering, episodic form, it resembles **Cervantes**' *Don Quixote*, and shares that work's use of a character whose incomplete but charming personality sets him at odds with the world around him.

But Schweik is different. He is a little man who has no idea that he is anything else. He is a dog breeder caught up in the Great War. His weakness is that he craves the quiet life in a time of chaos, and yet his docility leads him into the kind of situations where his cheery co-operation with absolutely everyone looks like stoicism. His guilelessness is worthy of a **Shakespearean** fool, and his insights consequently as profound. By sheer accident, he finds himself at the hub of global events, and a part-time national hero.

Hašek's prose collaborates with this notion of the heroic. All the corrupt officials Schweik encounters in his picaresque rise through an army he barely even joined are presented with a kind of nobility of purpose; the writing does nearly as much as Schweik does to expose their shallowness and hypocrisy. The work's own rambling and unfinished character is worthy of its protagonist, and is almost too charming for the mordant satire it conveys.

HD

born Bethlehem, Pennsylvania 1886; died Lake Geneva 1961

I saw it now

as men must see it ever afterwards;

no poet could write again

'the red lily,

a girl's laugh caught in a kiss'

it was his to pour into the vat

from which all poets dip and quaff,

for poets are brothers in this

HELIODORA

THE STYLE OF THE NAME is **Ezra Pound's** fault. He published Hilda Doolittle's work under the sobriquet "HD, Imagiste", and the name stuck. She considered herself at once "discovered" and "dubbed" by this man who – according to **William Carlos Williams** – was in love with her, and to whom she was engaged in 1907. In 1913, however, she married Richard Aldington, whom she succeeded as editor of *The Egoist* while he was way during the war, and who defended her Modernist poetry.

In many respects, however, she was an unlikely Modernist. Her poetry was taken up by Pound in his gathering of poetry tending away from Romantic lyrics towards sparing, *haiku*-like 'images', and these remain her most anthologised pieces. Her work was certainly experimental, however, and her husband declared her to be one of the first writing *vers libre* in English, while her prose work drew on **Joyce**'s techniques of interior monologues and contrasting styles. But throughout she maintained a refinement and tone that is markedly personal and confessional. Her novels are heavily biographical, with *Bid Me to Live*, her most accomplished novel, following the poet to London and Cornwall.

Her prose drew on her poetic ear and reveals her reliance on the classics to reflect her own experiences. She wrote the verse drama *Hippolytus Temporizes*, and the great poem *Helen in Egypt* published posthumously. She knew her Latin and Greek much better than Pound did, but displayed it more modestly, having narrators seeming to forget their Classics even when it would prove most handy to them. Her poem *Heliodora* provides a superb gloss on a fragment to raise questions about originality and possession of literature. Here, she recognises problems that were hers: her work has taken a long time to be assessed fully and in its own right.

Heaney

SEAMUS

born Castledawson, County Derry, Northern Ireland 1939

And we lifted our eyes to the nouns.

Altar-stone was dawn and monstrance
*   noon,*

the word rubric itself a bloodshot sunset.

IN ILLO TEMPORE

HEANEY HAS AN ACUTE consciousness of what writing is, and what it must do. It is rare that a reader can be given so strong a sense that words are things in themselves, and that language is a tool for putting them together.

The poem *Digging* came at the beginning of his career. He describes his forefathers' farm-work, and concludes, "Between my finger and my thumb/ the squat pen rests./ I'll dig with it." Later, *The Haw Lantern* has a poem, *Alphabets*, in which the very letters become objects. Heaney often begins a poem with a sequence of nouns, broken up by full stops. Things become whole sentences; a recent collection is called *Seeing Things*.

What he makes us see most is rural Ireland. Violence drove him to leave Ulster for the Republic in 1972. His verse has little room for causes and, if politics enters his work, it is drawn from more tangible phenomena. It is hard to ignore a feeling of group brutality in his description of a bog woman unearthed and found garrotted; while the sexual imagery in *Act of Union* tells us more about sex than the Irish situation. *Casualty*, though clearly from a Catholic, is more a human response to the Troubles than an ideological one.

But his poems have work to do for society as well. *The Haw Lantern* contains more poems on the writer's rôle as a conscience, guarding justice. He addresses public concerns, like human rights, in work set in imaginary states (more states of mind than nation states) owing much to **Czeslaw Milosz**. He has recently spoken of Ireland's need to recognise its dual nationality as the only way to approach peace. People in his verse always strive for contact and understanding, nowhere more movingly than in *Clearances*, the sonnet sequence in memory of his mother. Peeling potatoes, they are, "never closer the whole rest of [their] lives". What brings a community together in another poem is a *Mud Vision*. The Swedish Academy spoke of his "ethical depth" when awarding him the Nobel Prize in 1996 (he was rambling around Greece when it was announced); and he got deep by digging up things.

Heine

HEINRICH

born Düsseldorf 1797; died Paris 1856

The story is an old one,

but stays forever new;

and when it falls to someone,

it breaks his heart in two.

BOOK OF SONGS

SCHUMANN'S SETTINGS of poems in Heine's first collection, *The Book of Songs*, provide an alluring introduction to this lyricist's strange world. They mix tenderness with the macabre, and the natural with the supernatural (when a lover's paranoia leads him to think the flowers are talking about him); in doing so, the work is always harmonious *per se*, but marked by violent swings of mood. Schumann's piano postludes fill the silence which must confound a reader who has just put down one of Heine's terse epigrammatic poems. For in the verse, so much makes musical sense, but fails to cohere. Why should requited love occasion weeping?

Heine's bitter irony – sometimes even sarcasm – is meant to leave us restless. He was that way himself. He was born to Jewish parents in Düsseldorf, converted to Christianity out of what seems like pragmatism, and moved to Paris in 1831. In this last, he continued to embrace foreignness, writing about the French for German readers, and essaying introductions to German thought to the French. His poetry represents his cultural range, as he hymns Greek gods, Jewish food, Cologne Cathedral, and further, more imagined locations.

In these, as elsewhere, Heine expresses himself with a beguiling simplicity. He takes a straightforward story-telling style into a fairy-tale atmosphere, and keeps the consequences inexplicable. Joyous examples open what some consider his finest book, *Romanzero* – Rhampsenit shows us a kingdom full of laughter, whose monarch stops a thief by offering his daughter's hand and, ultimately, the throne. Heine extends these fantasies in his longer poetry, especially the mock-epic *Atta Troll*, in which a dancing bear on the loose in the mountains lectures on themes related to contemporary German life. Here he combines the satire and symbolism which collude to bewitch readers throughout his corpus.

Heller

JOSEPH   **born Brooklyn 1923**

But that girl who wants to play the accordion for you today is old enough to be a mother. How would you feel if your own mother travelled over three thousand miles to play the accordion for some troops that didn't want to watch her? How is the kid, whose mother that accordion player is old enough to be, going to feel when he grows up and learns about it? We all know the answer to that one.

CATCH-22

JOSEPH HELLER IS GLOBALLY famous for his first novel, *Catch-22*. It is a vast satire which draws on all the tiniest aspects of military life, as seen during the campaign in Italy during the Second World War. Almost every episode is structured as a self-sustaining feedback loop, whose inevitability helps to carry the work's main thesis: there's no way out. The hero, Yossarian, has flown the requisite number of bombing missions, but must prove his insanity to avoid further duty. Such action would prove his sanity.

The work's virtuosity lies in sustaining this for nearly 600 pages (even though Norman Mailer has claimed that 100 could go without the author noticing). The author's eye for absurd details gives the book its energy: he depicts vain military potentates preening with their cigarette holders, agonising about their prose styles, or desperate to win marching competitions. It is as much a satire on bureaucracy and big business as it is on war, although the figure of Milo Minderbinder combines all three, and the currency of the book's title in English shows that the approach is applicable to any situation.

This triumph was hard to follow. Many years later, *Something Happened* appeared, and disappointed critics. *Good as Gold* places an academic in a current Presidential administration, and *God Knows* has King David tell his story as a Yiddisher wise-guy. *Picture This* is a strange attempt to link ancient and modern ideas of Imperialism starting from Rembrandt's painting of aristotle contemplating a bust of **Homer.** Here as elsewhere, Heller is a wry enough commentator on contemporary America to rival **Gore Vidal**; his success comes from the timelessness of his insights, and a logic worthy of the Talmud.

Hemingway

ERNEST · born Oak Park, Chicago 1899; died Ketchum, Idaho 1961

"Love is a dunghill," said Harry. "And I'm the cock that gets on it to crow."

THE SNOWS OF KILIMANJARO

FEW WRITERS HAVE MADE more use of their individuality than Ernest Hemingway. For not only did he consistently portray a singular kind of heroism and solitude in his characters, but he did so in a style that was inventive, and remains unique. It is now hard to say whether Hemingway provides the very type of manhood, or the model of rivetting yet economical prose.

From an early age he was obsessed with athletic prowess. He received his first fishing rod at the age of three and excelled at sports. His first literary rôle-model was Ring Lardner, the sports journalist, and his non-fiction work deals with bull-fighting (*Death in the Afternoon*) and big game-hunting (*Green Hills of Africa*). The allure of the toreador leads to the crisis point in *The Sun Also Rises*, which many consider his finest novel.

A need to test his heroism to its limits led him to join the Red Cross in 1918. He was badly wounded in Italy, and fell in love with a nurse while in hospital recovering. *A Farewell to Arms* draws on these experiences to depict all-destroying war; but Hemingway did not stop fighting for causes he believed in them. He donated $40,000 to the Republicans during the Spanish civil war, and was with the French Resistance in 1944 when the Allied forces liberated Paris. The political convictions that impelled such stands pervade *For Whom the Bell Tolls* and *Across the River and into the Trees*, with a slight loss of the objectivity Hemingway had acquired as a journalist, and which distinguished his earlier work.

In fact, he told a story very much as a reporter would, succinctly and eschewing emotion. Instead, feeling emerges as a natural consequence of the action, and becomes an action in itself – but the narrator never indulges in it. From this kind of understatement comes the remarkable power of Hemingway's prose. While the style is apparently simple, the variation in rhythm and the development of echoes within paragraphs control the tale's pace and pathos with a true poet's ear.

He was awarded the Nobel Prize for Literature in 1954, but thereafter found his powers failing. He shot himself in a fit of depression seven years later.

Henry

O.

born Greenboro, North Carolina 1862; died New York 1910

Life is made up of sobs, sniffles, and smiles, with sniffles predominating.

THE GIFT OF THE MAGI

O. HENRY'S FIRST BIOGRAPHER described him as the writer who "humanised the short story." Henry's pieces attained a huge readership during his lifetime, and their author could command enormous fees for them. After a spell of disfavour with critics, his work is enjoying reassessments from all angles, and over the years has been cherished as much by Soviet commentators and formalists as by his fellow Americans.

He owes this to his accessible style, his chatty dialogue, his warm, jokey humour, his romantic world and his careful plotting. This last keeps a tale progressing as if naturally, with an ending that is anything but improvised. He is most famous for his concluding twists. As for his world-view, it derives from meticulous observation of people around him, particularly in their urban environments. He would give much of his sudden fortune to people on the street, or leave it in lavish tips: anything for a story. He reckoned this an investment, but soon it became an indulgence, and he died of alcohol abuse.

His stories seem to present a world for which he hankered in his life. His characters are often poor; their curiosity about how richer people live regularly leads them to save and mix with swells. This brief fulfilment of fantasies is enough for them. It was not so simple for Henry himself. He was born into a poor Texan family, and worked at his uncle's pharmacy before becoming a bank clerk. His dreams of literary fortune and helping his wife culminated in embezzle-ment, and he evaded justice briefly by fleeing to Honduras. He returned when his wife became terminally ill, and he served three years in prison. He had been published before, and began a humorous paper he called *The Rolling Stone* and wrote almost single-handed; but it was in prison that he began producing the three hundred or so stories that brought him fame under a number of pseudonyms. His recurring theme of disguise and assumed identity served him well in his own life.

Herbert

GEORGE born Montgomery, Wales 1593; died Bemerton, Wiltshire 1633

Wit fancies beautie, beautie raiseth wit:

The world is theirs; they two play out the

   game,

Thou standing by: and though thy

   glorious name

Wrought out deliverance from

   th'infernall pit,

Who sings thy praise? onely a skarf or

   glove

Doth warm our hands, and make them

   write of love.

LOVE

GEORGE HERBERT'S POETRY sounds a genuine note of contrition and humility. When he knew that he would die of consumption, he charged his friend Nicholas Ferrar of Little Gidding with the fate of his poems, collected in *The Temple*, saying that he might burn them unless they might "turn to the advantage of any dejected soul". If this request seems modest, and all the more genuine for the poet seeking an expressly posthumous fame, then it represents a triumph of Herbert's spirituality over his earlier, worldly achievements.

For he was a Fellow at Cambridge, and University Public Orator there. The former post obliged him to take holy orders within seven years, while the latter introduced him to court circles. He did not become a priest when statutes dictated, but rather when he was ready. Throughout his poetry, there is rage, and resistance to the religious life, always yielding to a quiet submission to the will of God; while we recognise the struggle, we know we are reading the work of an Anglican priest.

This shows in his use of the *Book of Common Prayer*, and in his poems on the sacraments (*The H. Communion*), on the church calendar (*Whitsunday*) or specific services (*Mattens*); but more immediately, it shows in his verbal music. He uses anthem forms, with antiphons and hymns, and was a keen musician. This gives his thought a beguiling kind of simplicity, as opposed to **Donne**'s "meaning's press and screw"; Herbert tends to invoke things as well as arguments to convey his message, describing a state of mind, such as in *Sinne* or *Prayer*, in verbless clauses.

Although he draws on rhetoric to convince, as a preacher might, the conviction and repentance remains a personal one, born of self-examination.

Herodotus

born Halicarnassus, c. 484 BC; died Thurii, Southern Italy c. 420 BC

Within a long period of time, anything might happen.

THE HISTORIES

God tends to curb all arrogance.

IBID

HERODOTUS HAS BEEN CALLED the father of History and of Greek prose. The Greek word 'Historia' means enquiry, and like the early philosophers, Herodotus was investigating causes – in this case, of the great war between Greece and Persia. He traced its origins beyond history as we consider it, through reminiscences transmitted orally over generations to myth of the pre-Homeric age, with a sequence of women snatched back and forth across the Bosphorus. Some, from Thucydides onwards,

have criticised him for being too credulous of his sources; but generally Herodotus keeps his sense of perspective.

He does so rigorously in his discussion of other cultures. For all the panegyrics on his adopted Athens, he was called a barbarian-lover: the Greeks gave barbarians that name because they were supposed to communicate by saying "bar-bar", although this is not Herodotus' view at all. He starts from the position that "Custom is king of all", and strives to understand other peoples within the context of their traditions. Most of these ethnic groups he discusses in lengthy digressions, notably on Egypt and Scythia. He had travelled as a merchant, but may have undertaken journeys simply for research. His improbable description of Scythian burial customs have recently been validated by archaeological evidence, but when his narrative takes him to what he imagines to be the ends of the earth, we can accuse him of making it up: the race of people with feet so big that they can lie down and use them as a parasol has yet to be discovered.

Herodotus is a born story-teller and his prose has a smoothness unexpected in so early a story-teller. He is as concerned as his contemporaries, the tragedians, with the roots of character, and the problem of motivation. This outweighs his interest in political, economic and military affairs, making him no worse a historian, and a better read.

Herodotus' popularity rose again in 1997 when, for a few brief weeks *The Histories* (in a harshly abridged format) were in the bestsellers listings in the UK following the enormous success of the film of Michael Ondaatje's book *The English Patient,* in which they had a starring rôle.

Hesse

HERMANN **born Calw, Germany 1877; died Montagnola, Switzerland 1962**

Virgil had many lines not half so beautiful, so clearly and yet cunningly wrought, so full of meaning and delight, as this spiral of leaves upon a stalk.

NARZISS AND GOLDMUND

NARZISS AND GOLDMUND tells the story of an unworldly monk charged with the education of a boy who is a beautiful but inattentive student. They commend themselves equally to the reader's attention; but the situation of reading might incline us towards the bookish scholar. That the roving pupil should prove to be (not just physically) more attractive helps to show that Hesse's writings acquired a new type of reader altogether.

He had devoured 18th- and 19th-century novels and his prose was in the fine German tradition; **Thomas Mann** adored his work. But Hesse reached a younger audience. Even before *Narziss and Goldmund*, his autobiographical *Under the Wheel* had spoken for rebellious students everywhere. But his novels of "awakening" became touched by the horror of the First World War.

By then he had left Germany, become a Swiss national and volunteered for the Red Cross. But it was his need for analysis, after the spiritual death he felt he'd suffered as a result of the war, that started him on "the journey within". *Demian* was the first result of this quest, telling a war story similar to Hesse's own. His journey continued to the East, as he sought enlightenment in India. He never arrived, but in *Siddartha* tells the story of a Brahmin seeking salvation. He cannot accept Buddha's example of suffering, nor does he find any comfort in sensualism. Bliss only befalls him as he ferries people back and forth across the river.

Here enlightenment arrives from balance. In *Steppenwolf*, a vision of Mozart prescribes laughter to tame the animal within us. Music is vital to the author, and prevails throughout *The Glass Bead Game*, a world in which a musician is the acknowledged legislator. The choice Hesse's characters face elsewhere challenges the inhabitants of this artistic Utopia: is purity or recklessness better for the soul? If the last book finds for the latter, the message remains that it is a discovery we must make for ourselves.

Hesse was awarded the Nobel Prize for Literature in 1946.

Highsmith

PATRICIA

born Fort Worth, Texas 1921

She knew that the burning had been an action on her part to get rid of a feeling within her, a primitive action, if she thought about. Because, though the basket had been tangible, her thoughts were not tangible. And they proved damned hard to destroy.

THE TERRORS OF BASKET WEAVING

PATRICIA HIGHSMITH IS NOTED for her distinctive handling of the suspense novel. Her treatment of murder plots is rooted less in the tradition of thrillers and action stories than in a more acute approach to the problems of criminal motivation and psychology. She has made clarity her main aesthetic goal, rather than the generation of mystery. For some readers this comes across as a scientific exercise; for others it is more imaginative than that. The actions of her characters can be brutally sadistic, but often shock more for being founded in seemingly rational responses to desperate situations. A natural sympathy for a murderer's suffering, even at the expense of pity for the victim, compounds this horror. She is especially interested in the deeper causes of crime, as if exploring **Auden**'s lines, "Those to whom evil is done/ Do evil in return."

Her first novel remains the most famous: *Strangers on a Train* introduces Highsmith's recurring gambit of presenting two apparently opposite characters who find a sudden kinship in guilt and intrigue. She takes this kind of relationship to a more intense pitch in *The Boy Who Followed Ripley*, the concluding novel in her series about a charming killer whose need to dissemble and make money leads him into farce-like situations which easily turn murderous. But Ripley's strengths as a character come as much from his smoothness as his ability to kill: he aspires to a kind of suavity that he is uniquely able to emulate, while the reader can never forget the roughness beneath.

Later Highsmith books blend grimness with satire to comment on contemporary America (although she has moved to France). She attacks sexism in *Edith's Diary*, and in the short stories contained in *Little Tales of Misogyny* of the same year. Born-again Christians and the effects their strictures on abortion have on a family prompt the violence of *The People Who Knock on the Door*. When Highsmith turns on the law itself, she mocks its dithering with a teasing example: a detective fails to capture a man who kidnaps a woman's poodle and demands $1,000 as ransom.

MAJOR WORKS

Strangers on a Train (1950)

The Blunderer (1954)

The Talented Mr. Ripley (1955)

Ripley under Ground (1970)

A Dog's Ransom (1972)

Ripley's Game (1974)

Edith's Diary (1977)

Little Tales of Misogyny (1977)

The Boy Who Followed Ripley (1980)

The People Who Knock on the Door (1983)

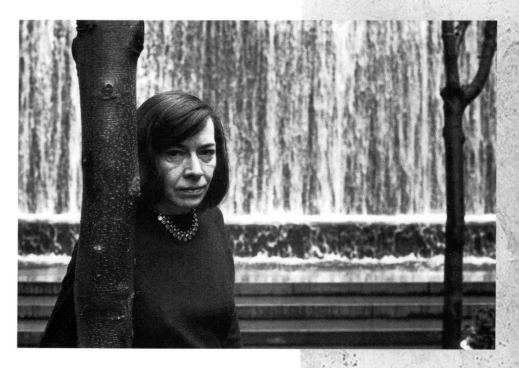

Hoffman

E.T.A.

born Königsberg 1776; died Berlin 1822

*Can anything else but poesy reveal itself
as the sacred harmony of all beings, as
the deepest secret of nature?*

THE GOLDEN POT

THE 'A' STANDS FOR Amadeus: Hoffman gave himself the same middle name as Mozart. He would have agreed with Pater that all arts should aspire to the condition of music – and few writers have written on music so well, with such a grasp of form. In his stories, he would apply the instincts of a composer to create effects beyond reason, leaving readers reeling.

In music, he preferred bold combinations of different harmonies to delicate counterpoint. His fictions are similar. He introduces science into the world of the imagination. His stories are full of automata that take on human form, and scare children who can never be believed; of clock-makers, indifferent to the powers their creations unleash. In *The Golden Pot*, Hoffman takes us into a dreamscape where eligible snakes haunt an apple-thief. His most daring juxtaposition is his funniest: he gives us his largely autobiographical reflections on a frustrated but promising musical career through the fictionalised figure of Kreisler, whose memoirs are interrupted page after page by the musings of the tomcat Murr. The tone is marvellously captured in Schumann's manic piano pieces in response to it, *Kreisleriana*.

As a critic, he headed straight for the darker side of Mozart, in an essay on *Don Giovanni*, and was Beethoven's earliest apologist. In this, he was Romanticism's champion. He embraced an age when the subjective apprehension of artistic forms was more vital than dry analysis. For Freud, he understood the word 'aesthetics' in its original sense, of feeling. Hoffman's own ability to feel, and to make his readers feel for themselves, make him key to any history of the imagination; **Heine**, **Poe**, **Dostoyevsky** and **Baudelaire** all owe him a great deal.

Hölderlin

FRIEDRICH

born Lauffen, Germany 1770; died Tübingen 1843

I want to celebrate; but what? want to

sing with the others,

But I'm alone, and I feel there's nothing

godly in me.

MENON'S LAMENT FOR DIOTIMA

ONLY LONG AFTER HIS DEATH was Hölderlin considered to be in the first rank of German poets; indeed, in the writings of Heidigger, his importance as a thinker is counted as inestimable. And Heidigger was analysing the work Hölderlin produced in his long, last period of schizophrenia.

If Hölderlin could make a sublime kind of sense even in madness, it was due to his **Coleridge**-like

gift for feeling ideas, and giving them poetic expression. He was often afraid that his thinking would disfigure his verse, and so welded his subject matter to the medium in which he was expressing it. His medium was the Greek metrical patterns adopted by the mystic poet Klopstock: Hölderlin would write in the rhythms of Alcaeus and even Pindar, and elegiac couplets flowed from him. He translated **Sophocles** with a rigid adherence to the quantities of the original.

He was as absorbed by the cultural supremacy of the Greeks as he was by their Pantheism. He studied for the priesthood, but found his beliefs incompatible with orthodox creeds; he chose instead to work as a tutor and his verse spoke of the human yearning for God. It blended classical forms with a hymn-like vocabulary to form a rapturous, love-craving poetry, focusing on the divine figures of Christ and Dionysus (whom Hölderlin saw as one), or Diotima, the woman who taught Socrates how to define love. This last was a manifestation of an employer's wife Hölderlin had adored.

Hölderlin was much troubled by the emergent philosophy (expounded by his classmate Schelling, and derived from Kant) which dwelt on the individual nature of our response to natural phenomena. He was depressed by the loneliness this doctrine entailed, and believed that the only refuge from such solipsism was a love which transcended the senses and which was waiting beyond this world: it is the thesis of his poem *Menon's Lament for Diotima*. It is characteristic of his range — at once ecstatic and despairing — which shows forth in language of singular purity, directness and elegance.

MAJOR WORKS

Best work written between 1798 and 1801, uncollected in his lifetime:

Odes (1797–1798)

Hyperion (epistolary novel, 1797–1799)

Empedokles (unfinished verse drama)

Holtby

WINIFRED

born Rudston, Yorkshire 1898; died London 1935

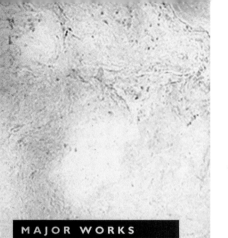

Councillor Saxon, after 52 years of childless married life, had suddenly lost his heart and virtue to a blonde in a tobacconist's kiosk on Kingsport Station and found himself at 74 the proud but embarrassed father of a son. The whole of South Riding, apart from Mrs Saxon, appeared aware of this achievement. Most of the South Riding, whatever its outward disapproval, was delighted. It enjoyed all feats of procreation.

SOUTH RIDING

WINIFRED HOLTBY IS DUE for a revival. Posterity has treated her with scant regard. During her short life, she was among London's best-known literary journalists and wrote the first critical study of **Virginia Woolf**. Her death from kidney failure came four weeks after she had finished *South Riding*, her most ambitious work, which caused a sensation when it appeared in print the next year. It was filmed, but today only this and her first novel remain in print.

She wrote six novels in all – a remarkable output, even more so given the hectic work-rate which hastened her death. She was director of the journal *Time and Tide*, and wrote frequently for *The Manchester Guardian*. She fought tirelessly for women's rights, and campaigned against racism: indeed, her novel *Mandoa!*

Mandoa! satirises the attempts of a travel agency to market a fictionalised principality in Central Africa. She was a pacifist too, but interrupting her studies at Oxford to work with the Women's Auxiliary Army Corps during the First World War. Here she met Vera Brittain. They became inseparable and lived together even after the latter married: Brittain's *Testament of Friendship* commemorates Holtby.

South Riding shows the understanding Holtby had of local politics: her mother was the first female Alderman in the East Riding of Yorkshire (South Riding is a fictional name). The author was fascinated by the motivations and potentially huge effects at play in administrative decisions. The love-triangles, the feel for local community, and the enormous range of characters presented in most stages between triumph and despair, suggest to the modern reader a mini-series – which would at least have the effect of getting her four remaining books back on the shelves.

Holub

MIROSLAW

born Plezn 1923

You only love

when you love in vain...

Like caryatids

our lifted arms

hold up time's granite load

and defeated

we shall always win.

ODE TO JOY,
TR. IAN MILNER, GEORGE THEINER

MIROSLAV HOLUB IS KEEN that people read his "poems as naturally as they read the papers, or go to a football match". This may seem an ambitious goal for a Czech writer as influenced by the French Surrealists as he is by his work as a Professor of Immunology, but his verse remains remarkably accessible. He avoids using arcane words for their own sake and when he chooses a scientific term, it's as much for its resonance in ordinary language as for its exact interpretation. He has done much to popularise science, both in newspaper columns and in his own magazine *Vesmir*, and sees a poem as something organic, with a life of its own and a capacity for growth. His verse frequently examines microscopic things and finds in them analogies for vaster entities.

The most appealing thing about Holub's poetry is the sense of hope. Although he shares his bleaker visions, such as *Five Minutes After the Air Raid*, there is still, a sense that life — as it evolves — offers the promise that things might improve. He has made an art form out of **Beckett**'s dictum, "Fail again, fail better" – a belief Holub takes from laboratory experiments into the world of emotions.

He has always been modest about his literary achievement. He began writing during his postgraduate research, at the age of 30, and is deferential towards younger Czech poets. His uncomplicated syntax and ear for a conclusive aphorism have maintained his popularity: his books have regularly sold out and, in 1982, his first book to be published in his homeland for 10 years was bought up on the first day of publication. The official reason for issuing no reprint was a paper shortage. Prior to that Holub had been silenced by the Soviet regime since 1968.

MAJOR WORKS

Day Duty (1958)

Achilles and the Tortoise (1960)

Go and Open the Door (1962)

Although (1971)

Sagittal Section (1980)

On the Contrary (1982)

The Dimension of the Present Moment (essays, 1990)

Homer

Great Priam slipped by, took
*   Achilles' hands,*
beseeched him, then he kissed those
*   slaughtering hands,*
awful, which had cut down a city's sons

ILIAD

He recognised the smooth coat
*   on his shoulders,*
so like the skin upon an onion dried.

ODYSSEY

WE HAVE TWO TEXTS that are attributed to someone called Homer, the *Iliad* and the *Odyssey*. Seven towns claim to be his birthplace and the writings are in the Ionic dialect: their source was Greek-speaking Asia Minor. They are the finest poems ever written.

Written: it was perhaps as late as the eighth century BC that these perfect compactions of myths and sailor's tales appeared to readers. Research into repeated phrases, rhythmic patterns and recurring structures within structures starts to explain how a bard could have recited line after line, elaborating with each performance. How this way of telling it evolved, we can never know; scholars still argue over which passages might have been appended gradually.

Still, we have two finished works of art. The *Iliad* tells of a brief spell during the war which resulted in the Greeks sacking Troy. The stated theme is the wrath of Achilles. His bitterness and lust for revenge seem to obscure his human sense of compassion; but in conceding the mutilated body of his enemy to the family for burial, he shows the qualities of heroism and dignity the narrative explores. The *Odyssey*, meanwhile, follows Odysseus home from the Trojan War. His 10-year passage, the lies by which he survives, his nakedness and guises, show a search for self-definition. The layers of his personality are like an onion, to be peeled off one by one. The goddess Athene gets to the core – as, finally, does his wife.

These processes have dominated most literature ever since. Imagery describes war and crisis with reference to bees or falling leaves; the subject matter can move to distant places too, as digressions lead to stories within stories. In so controlled a form, each speaker retains a voice of his or her own, from Nestor's rambling to Helen's quiet lament. The poems are composed of many narrative levels, and the *Odyssey* in particular invites us to question which is closest to truth; still, so extraordinary is the work that when "Homer" asks, "Daughter of God, tell us, and start whenever", we believe.

Hopkins

GERARD MANLEY

born Stratford, London 1844; died Dublin 1889

Whatever is fickle, freckled

(who knows how?)

With swift, slow; sweet, sour;

adazzle, dim;

He fathers-forth whose beauty

is past change:

Praise him.

PIED BEAUTY

GERARD MANLEY HOPKINS wrote the most innovative Christian poetry in English since **Milton.** Like Milton, his experiments had a theoretical basis, that was firmly grounded in the classics. He believed that a poet's genius was in originality: just as Milton discarded the tyranny of rhyme, so Hopkins strove to transform rhythms. He wrote a number of sonnets, but in metres of his own devising, with regulated stresses but ample supporting syllables thrown in.

This was an expression of his aesthetic beliefs which, like his religious ones, were formed while at Oxford. Two influences there were the great Walter Pater, and Cardinal John Henry Newman. The former was his tutor, and believed that the artist should take pains to render natural phenomena in purest form; the latter admitted him into the Catholic Church.

Hopkins certainly took pains to express his own spirituality – a fusion of these two creeds. He coined the terms "inscape" and "instress", the former being the perceptible manifestation of the latter, the energy that generates it. This was to dictate his thoughts on poetry, but so was a sense of guilt. He burnt most of his early work and only resumed once he had become a Jesuit priest, encouraged by his colleagues. In this he was much comforted by reading the theologian Duns Scotus, who seemed to have anticipated this kind of thinking.

The result is a poetry in which language becomes that pure form. Internal rhymes, compound words and puns bounce into metres which focus all that neighbouring words have in common, to convey an often ecstatic vision of the world. This comes from the religious symbolism he found in nature (*The Windhover* is a bird representing Christ), or from theological issues (such as how a compassionate God could work His purpose through the nuns who died in *The Wreck of the Deutschland*). In his later years, his loneliness as Professor of Classics at University College, Dublin, drew more despairing verse from him, but he died at peace with the world. His fame as a poet was to be posthumous, when his friend Robert Bridges published the surviving work in 1918.

MAJOR WORKS

Poems (1918)

Horace

born Venusia 65 BC; died Tibur 8 BC

... now the betraying giggle of a girl

hidden in a snug corner happily,

the keep-sake snatched from arms, or

held by a mere finger, pretty limply.

ODES I, 9.

HORACE WAS THE FINEST lyric poet in Latin; and if versatility in tone and metre, absolute grace in form and the knack of surprise in cadence be considered criteria above the spontaneous overflow of powerful feelings, perhaps he is the finest ever. Given so towering a precedent, subsequent practitioners can scarce help but be judged by the standard of what **Petronius** called "Horace's curious felicity".

He had some fine models, too. In an ode, his claim to have "built a monument more lasting than bronze" rests on the introduction of Greek verse techniques to Italy. His chief models were Archilocus of Paros and Alcaeus of Lesbos, both noted for their drinking songs. Horace was from southern Italy, whose Greek colonial past was still evident, and he studied in Athens. In his odes, he eases Greek names into the sturdier Latin, and subverts that language's toughness with his anti-epic stance, referring to Achilles' "stomach" rather than wrath. Even when writing in the standard epic meter, he writes satires and rambling discourses, with conversational rhythms which sound clumsy when compared with **Virgil**. (He called his friend "half his soul", and the two parts complement each other wonderfully.)

This is all part of Horace's celebrated mock modesty. In some poems, he is as unexcited about his ambitions as he is elsewhere about his appearance. For all the sophistication of his poetry, the persona most often favours the simple life. If this attitude seems Epicurean, then it is accompanied by Epicurus' belief in restraint and control. This leads some to view Horace as a moral writer. For sure, he was an establishment poet, writing an increasing number of odes to the Emperor Augustus; but even when his patron was Maecenas, effectively Minister of the Interior, his work was allowed its mild naughtiness. He prefigured **Propertius** and **Ovid**, poets who distanced themselves from the Roman rat-race, as a bard in an Imperial culture who preferred love to war – as, perhaps, in private, did his Roman readers.

Housman

A.E.   **born Fockbury, Worcestershire 1859; died Cambridge 1936**

They say my verse is sad: no wonder;

Its narrow measure spans

Tears of eternity, and sorrow,

Not mine, but man's.

FOREWORD TO MORE POEMS

IT IS UNLIKELY THAT someone's reputation as a poet should be rivalled by fame as a classical scholar; but A.E. Housman came close. This has a little to do with the quality of his scholarship. Many of his amendments of corrupt **Propertius** texts have been adopted; in his day he was the only scholar who could translate (or admit to being able to translate, albeit in private memos) the ruder parts of **Juvenal**; and he published a collection of such passages (although only in Germany).

Still, the least characteristic of his poetic works is a skit on **Euripides**, in which he bundles together the most extreme examples of the playwright's pedantry, and translates them as literally as possible. For the rest, his verse is not at all classical. Indeed, in his lecture, *The Name and Nature of Poetry*, his activity as a poet seems to be completely separate from his academic life. It is something that occupies him when relaxing on walks. His approach to the art is physical rather than intellectual: he confessed that he had to be careful when shaving, "because, if a line of poetry strays into my memory, my skin bristles and the razor ceases to act".

A Shropshire Lad is full of this immediacy. The poems are written in an easy, ballad style, focusing on the vulnerability of the rural idyll. There is the shadow of war, and the deaths of fit youths, which became more urgently popular during the First World War than on their publication in 1896. At that time, the work was already nostalgic and its wistfulness and melancholy have earned it affection and mockery in equal measure. **Ezra Pound**'s parody, *Mr. Housman's Message*, lampoons the tone succinctly; but **W.H. Auden**'s poem *A.E. Housman* comes closer to the man's more private misery.

MAJOR WORKS

A Shropshire Lad (1896)

Last Poems (1922)

The Name and Nature of Poetry (1933)

More Poems (1936)

Jacobson

DAN

born Johannesburg 1929

It seemed that in England even the calendar had visible external meanings that I had not fully understood before. And the chief of these meanings was movement; the passage of time made manifest.

TIME AND TIME AGAIN

DAN JACOBSON IS A SOUTH African-born novelist, now resident in the United Kingdom, of Jewish descent. He has often been praised for bringing his own race consciousness to bear on an exploration of the differences between white and black. In his work, it is more than superficial colour that divides people. Jacobson uses a novelist's empathy with his characters to bring about a greater understanding between apparently irreconcilable groups, such as in *Evidence of Love*, which tells the story of an interracial romance.

Such compassion is not forced, for his novels frequently reflect his own experiences, which he discusses directly in *Time of Arrival* and later in *The Electronic Elephant*. Again, the perspective is a Jewish one, which he fictionalises most ambitiously in *The Beginners*. The story follows four generations of settlers, to South Africa in the last century and over to London in the 1960s.

Jacobson's own arrival in England seems to lie behind the narrative of *The Trap*, the first novel to bring him acclaim. A book set in California, *No Further West*, sprang from his subsequent experience teaching at Stanford University. For most critics, such personally-felt work has resulted in completely convincing prose with less even structures.

He is Professor of English at University College, London. If anything, he is writing more imaginatively now: his latest work, *The God-Fearer*, presents the history of Europe as though the Jewish faith had prevailed, and not the Christian. As elsewhere, his natural sensitivities demonstrate that the capacity for acting on prejudices can exist in anyone: this inversion of events continues to excoriate it where he finds it.

James

HENRY

born New York 1843; died Rye, Sussex 1916

Her cherished desire had long been to come to Europe and write a series of letters to the Interview from the radical point of view – an enterprise made the less difficult as she knew perfectly in advance what her opinions would be.

THE PORTRAIT OF A LADY

HENRY JAMES WROTE forgotten plays and vivid travel sketches; but his fame rests on some 20 novels and 100 short stories. These are distinguished by their great elegance and delicacy, often dealing with what the author called "the international situation."

He was born an American citizen, but caught the "Europe virus" during his youthful travels, when he had an influential meeting with **Turgenev**. He settled in Europe in 1875, the year of his first novel, *Roderick Hudson*. Its appearance was a triumph, and the plight of its hero presaged the theme that would dominate James's writing: the contrast between the New World and the continent. The former produces characters with an unaffected naïvety of the more sophisticated old world. Like the author himself, they are lured into this atmosphere, often with less happy consequences.

Daisy Miller struggles with this, as does Isabel Archer in *The Portrait of a Lady*. Elsewhere, the dilemmas are personal – between love and political conviction in *The Princess Casamassima*, or feminism and the *status quo* in *The Bostonians*. But James avoided being simply a novelist of ideas, thanks to the subtlety of his technique. As brother of the philosopher William James, who coined the phrase "stream of consciousness," he could describe acutely what was "beneath the surface of things," without taking sides. In *What Maisie Knew*, he portrays a young girl's view of her parents' divorce, while balancing her knowledge with her innocence.

In 1898, James moved to Rye House, Sussex, where he wrote his last three novels. For all his stunning descriptions of the continent (such as the Paris of *The Ambassadors*) he became ever more an Anglophile, adopting British citizenship in 1915. The next year, his last, he received the Order of Merit.

MAJOR WORKS

Roderick Hudson (1875)

Daisy Miller (1879)

The Portrait of a Lady (1881)

The Bostonians (1886)

What Maisie Knew (1897)

The Turn of the Screw (1898)

The Awkward Age (1899)

The Ambassadors (1903)

Jean Paul

born Wunsiedel 1763; died Bayreuth 1825

Creation hangs a veil, woven out of suns and spirits, over the Infinite, and the eternities pass by before the veil, and draw it not away from the splendour which it hides.

HESPERUS

JEAN PAUL'S COLLECTED WRITINGS fill 65 volumes of memoirs, essays, letters, sketches, philosophy, and extraordinary novels. It is hard to know where these last begin, and the rest leave off, for his fictions take in such extensive digressions, with cross-references, personal reflections and arcane citations, that they can appear like rambling tracts of their own. Jean Paul took **Sterne** as his model in this, and he styled his first two names in French in homage to **Rousseau.**

His literary skittishness serves the turn of his thought. The humour throughout belies a disaffection with the surrounding world. This is not to speak of pessimism, although his early sketches born of childhood poverty, and his visionary pieces – arising from deaths around him, including his brother's suicide in 1790 – would seem more than enough to occasion it. Rather, it is a Platonic belief in the purity of things beyond the earth. Albano, the hero of *Titan*, his most read work, can see beyond the clouds, and like Socrates, can look forward to death.

Although Jean Paul's plots are wild and complex, being sometimes delivered by dogs or making random demands of characters (one must become a piano tuner, and then a lawyer), it is the turn of thought and rapturous response to emotion and landscape that most defines his work. Random characters peopling his extraordinary forms can pour forth joyous critiques of the subjective philosophies the author abjured. Unlike **Hölderlin**, he is unswayed by Fichte's and Schelling's arguments that our impression of things is unique, and he recoiled from solipsism. If he introduces dream sequences into his work, it is not to provide insights into the workings of a single mind, but to represent thoughts in their most abstract form. Still, in structure and mood, he is as manic as he is Manichaean, which helps to explain why he was the composer Robert Schumann's favourite writer.

Jhabvala

RUTH PRAWER

born Cologne 1927

There are many ways of loving India, many things to love her for – the scenery, the history, the poetry, the music, and indeed the physical beauty of its men and women – but all, said the Major, are dangerous for the European who allows himself to love too much.

HEAT AND DUST

WHEN WRITING OF INDIA, Ruth Prawer Jhabvala is well placed to bring the international perspective to her subject. Born to Polish Jews, she fled from the Nazis in 1939, settling in England, where she was educated and met her Indian husband, with whom she moved to Delhi in 1951. She now lives in New York. She creates characters with an Indian perspective, but during her time in India felt herself to be neither an insider nor an outsider.

She explores this ambiguity in her novels and short stories. She introduces foreigners to a land she portrays as a harsh one and shows how incompatible the two worlds are. The approach is similar to **Forster**'s; but Jhabvala's concern is the way Westerners entertain sentimental and unobtainable hopes for the country. In *Esmond in India*, a philandering civil servant arrives from England, imagining that he is in love with an Indian woman and all that is mysterious about the subcontinent. Elsewhere in her work, travellers arrive in search of enlightenment, only to encounter crime or *swamis* with a craving for power.

For her delicate handling of the social dilemmas facing the better-off, she has been compared to **Jane Austen**; some critics have thought that this aspect of her work precludes a fuller discussion of India's grinding poverty. But in her first novel, *Amrita*, a listless rich family is contrasted with a poorer one in the Punjab. Their stories cross in Jhabvala's examination of arranged marriages and the caste system and while neither house is free of them, the narrative favours the less privileged and their zestful wedding preparations.

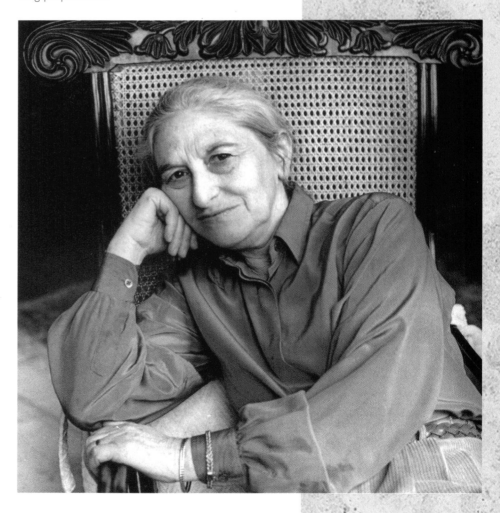

Joyce

JAMES

Tell me, where is fancy bread? At Rourke's the baker's, it is said

ULYSSES

JAMES JOYCE HAS PROVED to be the most influential novelist of the 20th century. Born in Dublin, he was educated by Jesuits and at the Catholic University College, Dublin. Throughout his work, Joyce struggles with this religious legacy and, like Stephen Dedalus, the hero of two novels, he adopted art as a faith. He was made for it: at eighteen, he had an extraordinary gift for languages (he wrote a letter of admiration to **Ibsen** in Dano-Norwegian) and a fine tenor voice. His musicianship and profound understanding of words' possibilities are evident in all his writing.

Although he was an instinctive nationalist, wanting to send the English tongue "off the face of the Erse," he left Ireland for good in 1912. His last visit was to his dying mother. Earlier publications include **Yeats**-influenced poetry and a play, *Exiles*: but it was in novels that he found his unique voice. The auto-biographical *A Portrait of the Artist as a Young Man* brought him attention and patronage in 1915, when he was already at work on *Ulysses*. This was published in 1922, on his fortieth birthday, and is considered his masterpiece.

The book was banned in Britain and America for obscenity. The text follows the most intimate thoughts and actions of many characters, in as many styles. Each chapter takes a different episode from **Homer**'s *Odyssey*, and documents an nour of 16 June 1904, when Joyce first met Nora Barnacle, his future wife. For all the novel's complexity, it offers the simple message of the power of love.

Joyce took language and structure further still in *Finnegans Wake*. This is a vast dream novel, following the nocturnal thoughts of Humphrey Chimpden Earwicker. It is full of vast sentences, lists and multilingual puns, and occupied his last 17 years, a period made more painful by glaucoma and his daughter's schizophrenia. He died in 1941, the acclaimed giant of Modernist literature.

Juvenal

born Aquinum c. 60 AD; died Egypt? c. 136 AD

So give yourself a break. When did you last
stop for a whole day?
No talk of that debtor,
none of your wife giving you silent rage
if she goes out at dawn and comes home late
with dresses drenched and those
suspicious cheeks
and tousled hair and golden face aglow ...

SATIRE 11

JUVENAL'S SATIRES give such a clear and consistent an idea of the poet's personality that we almost think we know him: a middle-aged, bitter man who is no longer ashamed to give his spleen free reign, or to let his more wretched thoughts run away with him. So full of gossip and conviction does he seem that commentators feel tempted to fit him into the picture he paints with such detail — to speak of his hard climb to social rank, his rage at having lost it, exiled for a jibe at his hated emperor Domitian's boyfriend, and his eventual death commanding a military campaign in Egypt at the age of 80.

What of this is not unlikely is uncertain; but Juvenal's genre and technique are so much his own that we can't conclude easily that he was writing to formula. For he blends rhetorical commonplaces with parody to present a world which is completely upside-down, such that "it is hard *not* to write satire". His targets include the moral frailty of the aristocracy, the spitefulness of women, the duplicity of patrons, the habits of homosexuals, and anything else that annoys him at the time. He constantly takes a stern, Stoic attitude — frugality is best, we should learn by example, there's such a thing as decency — while rehearsing often outrageous subject matter.

The result is hilarious. Juvenal has a gift for drawing very economical conclusions from lavish subject matter, many of which remain proverbial: all they want is bread and circuses; pray for a sound mind in a sound body; who guards the guards themselves? In this he displays the knack of timing that enables him to shock as well as titillate and scorn; such that he has left a lurid, unflinching account of his own age and a model for those who have striven to correct with laughter ever since.

MAJOR WORKS

The Satires (110–130 AD)

JUVENALLS SATYRS. By Sᵗ Robert Stapylton Kᵗ Gent: of the Penry Chamber to the Prince.

Kafka

FRANZ   **born Prague 1883; died Kierling Sanatorium, nr. Vienna 1924**

In the battle between you and the world, back the world.

REFLECTIONS ON SIN, SORROW, HOPE AND THE TRUE WAY

GEORGES PEREC WOULD OFTEN try to convince people that he looked like Kafka. It is as though someone lonely, labouring under an intolerable burden of guilt, can find a comfort in sharing anything

with the gaunt figure of the Czech novelist, with his wide eyes staring back at terror. As though someone else had imagined himself in a universe whose powers to crush are exercised uniquely on him. For Franz Kafka, though, there was no such comfort.

For such is Kafka's world. In *The Castle*, it is a village he visits to take up a clerical job which appears not to exist, and where personal destinies are determined by forces always just outside your reach. It is a land organised by a laborious communications system, as in *The Great Wall of China*, where no-one can know who is sending the messages.

Worse still, it is a world whose victims cannot understand why they cannot be understood. Gregor Samsa turns into a giant insect for no good reason in *Metamorphosis*, to be mocked and then ignored. In *The Trial*, Joseph K. is the object of judicial proceedings he cannot witness, when no charge has been made. The more he tries to defend himself, the more hopeless his plight becomes.

It is a world which might seem trivialised by comparison to the Austro-Hungarian bureaucracy which employed Kafka in labyrinthian Prague; but it takes such arbitrary systems to their extreme. Because it is incomprehensible, the storyteller makes no effort to complicate it. All is simple, and events happen apparently in sequence, as if in the tradition of Jewish folk tales. Given such plain, horrifying writing, readers have tried to explain away their own fears from within the sparse material: the totalitarian state, sexual anxiety, the dysfunctional family, social collapse... By doing so it is as though we are avoiding Kafka's own process – looking into ourselves. When we turn instead to find some cause in Kafka, we find a man who felt "accused of life" and died young.

Kästner

ERICH

Born Dresden 1899; died Dresden 1974

Poets have their function again. Their occupation is once more a profession. They are probably not as indispensable as bakers and dentists; but only because rumbling stomachs and toothache more obviously call for relief than non-physical ailments.

NOISE IN THE MIRROR

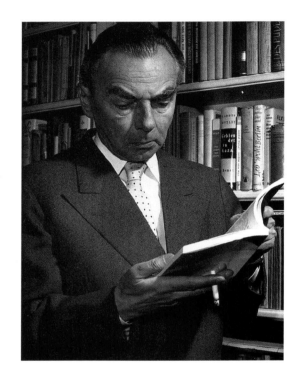

MAJOR WORKS

Heart on Waistline (1927)

Noise in the Mirror (1928)

Emil and the Detectives (1929)

Fabian, the Story of a Moralist (1931)

The Flying Classroom (1933)

Three Men in the Snow (1935)

The Missing Miniature (1936)

When I was a Little Boy (1957)

DRESDEN-BORN NOVELIST and children's writer Erich Kästner found ways of raising his wry, ironic voice in protest at his native Germany's conduct even in its darkest days. Unlike so many other writers and artists, he chose to remain in the country throughout the Second World War. At a public burning of works by 24 authors, he was the only one of those writers who witnessed it. Although the Nazis banned his books, he was still able to publish abroad until 1942, when he sold the script of *Baron Munchhausen* to MGM. He had been placed under surveillance previously, and twice arrested; now he found himself silenced completely.

He had been conscripted into the army during the First World War, and hated militarism of any kind thereafter. His studies might have been hampered by hyperinflation and his parents' poverty, which ren-dered a valuable scholarship virtually worthless at a stroke; but he lived extremely frugally and distinguished himself as a scholar. Shortly afterwards he wrote his best-known work, *Emil and the Detectives*, about a boy who enjoins the children he meets on a visit to the city to help him apprehend a thief. Kästner would continue to write stories with a profound understanding of children, and of the way they speak and think, in books like *Three Men in the Snow* and *The Flying Classroom*.

Throughout his writing life he accumulated a body of poetry, about which he would be unduly modest, and a range of subtly autobiographical work, including the satirical novel *Fabian*. A statue stands to him in Dresden, close to the house where he was born, in tribute to this reserved, often solitary, and always peace-loving writer.

Kawabata

YASUMARI

born Osaka 1899; died Zushi 1972

There were Siberian irises on the girl's obi. Perhaps it was a coincidence. But irises were most ordinary flowers for the season, and perhaps she had planned the combination.

The Japanese irises sent their blossoms and leaves high into the air. One knew that Chikako had arranged them a short time before.

THE GROVE IN THE EVENING SUN, TR.
EDWARD G. SEIDENSTICKER.

In 1968, THE NOVELIST AND short story writer Kawabata became the first Japanese author to win the Nobel Prize for Literature. The event drew attention to a vein of writing of which he was the purest exponent. Unlike **Mishima**, a younger writer whose work he did much to encourage, his style showed barely any Western influences. Still, the two authors shared a fanatical devotion to their country, to the point of right-wing extremism, and both killed themselves – Kawabata died by gas.

Particularly new to Western readers is the emphasis Kawabata's kind of writing places on images rather than the ideas they embody. While this might have much to do with the physical nature of words as he uses them on the page, it is in keeping with his notions of beauty that our eyes remain on the surface of his texts. He had a great love of Noh theatre, and in *The Sound of the Mountain* writes of an actor's mask, which is more real than what it covers. The dream-like properties the narrator attaches to it are comparable to those so desired by an old man in Kawabata's most famous story, *The House of the Sleeping Beauties*, included in the collection *The Snow Country*. The protagonist frequents a house of geishas in which the girls have been drugged or enchanted into a sleep that must leave the patrons' desires insatiable.

It is in the world of the imagination that these hankerings for the beautiful must find fulfilment. Kawabata's sparing mode of story-telling leaves the reader with a series of images which the reader must connect just as the characters do – as if by random associations – towards some kind of knowledge, if anything can be certain at all.

Kazantzakis

NIKOS   **born Heraklion, Crete 1883; died Freisburt im Breisgau 1957**

My inspiration and the guiding force throughout my life has been the continuing, merciless battle between the spirit and the flesh; and the soul is the arena where they meet and clash.

THE LAST TEMPTATION OF CHRIST,
INTRODUCTION

THE THEOLOGIAN PELAGIUS was called "the reluctant heretic"; this is even truer of Kazantzakis, who remains modern Greece's most controversial writer. His work was constantly at odds with Orthodox thought, and he died without the full rites of the Church and, in 1997, Greece's chief school inspector sought to have the author taken off the syllabus. However, Kazantzakis was possessed of a profound spirituality which is imbued with the mysticism of the far East (evident in the late play *Buddha*), but finds echoes in the Orthodox liturgy itself. Its view of the Holy Spirit as a giver of life, filling all things, is very much his own: for him, life is not a dynamic cycle of birth and death, but an independent spirit which vivifies existence.

And his most abidingly popular work abounds with life. The exuberant *Zorba the Greek* loves it completely: he is a man "made of rubber". His story is told by a shrinking academic opening a lignite mine in Crete who finds in the hero an earthly corrective to his own remoter stance. The narrative illuminates the dual nature of Greek rural life with its piety, hospitality and extraordinary violence. Even in mourning, Zorba is irrepressible: on his son's death the only way he can ease his pain is by dancing.

The Last Temptation of Christ caused widespread scandal, but is profoundly Orthodox. Christ is still God; but Kazantzakis embraces the human, doubting part of the Messiah as he too chooses life, in a dream sequence. That this life should involve sex was the grounds for shock; but in exploring the alternatives to a hideous martyrdom – one to which Judas is a reluctant party – the author succeeds in rendering the ultimate sacrifice, in fulfilment of the scriptures, as all the more selfless and saving.

MAJOR WORKS

The Odyssey, a Modern Sequel (1938)

Zorba the Greek (1946)

Christ Recrucified (1954)

The Last Temptation of Christ (1955)

Keats

MAJOR WORKS

Endymion (1818)

Lamia and Other Poems (1820)

Forgive me if I wander a little this evening, for I have been all day employ'd in a very abstract Poem and I am in deep love with you – two things which must excuse me.

LETTER TO FANNY BRAWNE, JULY 25, 1819

THERE IS NO WAY of getting over Keats. His legend presents the very archetype of a poor, dreaming poet who died tragically early; but we must balance the man whose epitaph is, "Here lies one whose name is writ in water" with the writer who could declare, "I will be among the English poets when I die".

From **Byron** and **Shelley** onwards, there has been the romantic belief that hostile reviews of *Endymion* hastened Keats' death. But he always felt that his days were numbered, and his medical training led him to confront the first symptoms of his consumption immediately. Thus he could face the poor notices with pragmatism, recognising his work's need to develop, as well as the snobbery which animated such savage criticism: it was felt outrageous that a Cockney should attempt classical themes when all his Greek came from the British Museum, or translations.

But he was aware of that too and it is the subject of one of the greatest sonnets in English, *On First Looking Into Chapman's Homer*. His mastery of that form's rigours gave him the control to sustain his argument through the exquisite stanzas of his more luxuriant odes. Even when he seems to be apostrophising, it rolls through the Hellenic odes of *To Psyche* and *On a Grecian Urn*, to the incomparable *Ode to a Nightingale*.

Keats has had many imitators, but most fall for a palpable lushness instead of the rich language so apt for his material. For all his sensual verse, he was less concerned with a subject's outer aspects than with its inner life – which he felt could be more sumptuous still: "Into her dream he melted, as the rose/ Blendeth its odour with the violet." Any notions of the poet's vulnerable fragility might not stand up well to a reading of *On Seeing the Elgin Marbles*, however, which presents a world of the imagination sturdier than our own.

Keneally

THOMAS

born Sydney 1935

'Don't kill yourself on the fence, Clara,'
the woman urged her. 'If you do that,
you'll never know what happened to
you.'
It has always been the most powerful of
answers to give the intending suicide.
Kill yourself and you'll never know
how the plot ends.

SCHINDLER'S ARK

THOMAS KENEALLY IS a prolific Australian novelist. He trained for the Catholic priesthood, without becoming a priest; but his books are often concerned with moral dilemmas, and life-or-death decisions. A few of these he has based on fact: *Gossip from the Forest* is about the men chosen to negotiate the Armistice that ended the First World War. Even when not dramatising the actual past, his books are concerned with events real enough to involve Keneally in painstaking research. *Flying Hero Class* intimately observes the psychology of hostage crises in which he depicts the efforts of Palestinian hijackers to win the support of six Aboriginals against their better-off fellow passengers.

Throughout Keneally's writings there is a similar compassion for the poor or dispossessed. The early convicts who arrived in Australia, in a state of exile, are a natural focus for his sympathies, and enable him to invoke the national theme. *The Playmaker* shows illiterate prisoners working on a play in 1787, and restores to them their dignity. This sensitivity is at the core of his best-known work, *Schindler's Ark*, the story of Oskar Schindler's work saving Jewish prisoners from the death camps. The telling involves Keneally's accomplished handling of fact, his eye for the moments when life assumes an art-like quality (the situation is reversed when Schindler himself becomes a prisoner), and his thorough study of heroism. Schindler is a saviour, but no saint; and the author examines moral ambiguities in the face of the ultimate horror. The novel won the Booker Prize in 1982, was filmed in 1994 and has become a vital text in a world that must never forget the Holocaust.

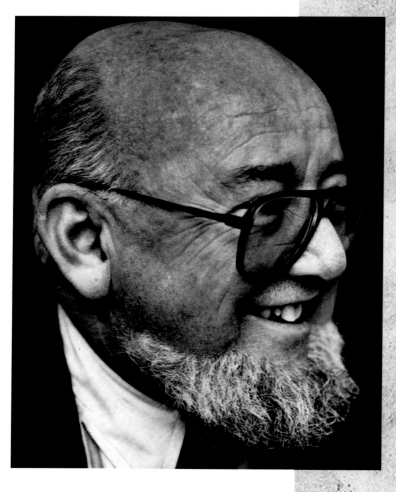

Kerouac

JACK **born Lowell, Massachusetts 1922; died St. Petersburg, Florida 1969**

> *"Darling, you know and I know that everything is straight between us at least beyond the furthest abstract definition in metaphysical terms or any terms you want to specify or sweetly impose or harken back ..."* and so on, and zoom went the car and we were off again for California.

ON THE ROAD

JACK KEROUAC DUBBED HIS circle of writers and adventurers the "beat generation". He meant it to be short for beatific; throughout his writings, he embarks on a quest for all that is holy in his alternative lifestyle, finding benediction in sex, drugs and jazz, as experienced in the light of Neal Cassady's angelic nimbus. Cassady is fictionalised as Dean Moriarty in Kerouac's most cult book, *On the Road*, and as Cody Pomeray in *Big Sur*. **Allen Ginsberg** appears in the former as Carlo Marx; **William Burroughs** as Old Bull Lee.

As in most of Kerouac's work, the journey towards enlightenment in *On the Road* follows tracks truly trodden. It follows his own path, hitching across the States, taking odd jobs and embracing the unpredictable. The prose is faithful to its subject, at times recounting events with **Hemingway's** lack of ornament before losing itself in its own epiphanies. The lengths of paragraphs and the freedom of their direction imitate the course of the narrator's road.

Kerouac's enquiry into the spiritual turned on his upbringing in *Satori in Paris*; he was born into a deeply Catholic family of Breton origins, who were later to repudiate his work publicly. While in France he rhapsodises over candles in empty churches, and elsewhere he explores Buddhism, especially in *The Dharma Bums*.

This last introduces the poet Gary Snyder as Japhy Ryder. Only *Doctor Sax* emerges from Kerouac's writings as pure fiction, but still stands with other works as part of the "Duluoz legend", Kerouac's emulation of **Balzac's** *Comédie Humaine*. He died before he could attempt a further imaginative project, of an abdominal haemorrhage.

Kesey

KEN

born La Junta, Colorado 1935

*What the Chronics are – or most of us –
are machines with flaws inside that can't
be repaired, flaws born in, or flaws beat
in over so many years of the guy running
head-on into solid things, that by the
time the hospital found him he was
bleeding rust in some vacant lot.*

ONE FLEW OVER THE CUCKOO'S NEST

KEN KESEY IS A LIVING legend: he has been the subject of **Tom Wolfe**'s book *The Electric Kool-Aid Acid Test*, **Allen Ginsberg**'s poem *First Party at Ken Kesey's with Hell's Angels* and numerous police investigations.

It is hard to know how much of this attention would have been focused on the founder-member of a proselytising pro-drugs group called The Merry Pranksters, had he not created that at once warming and chilling fable of conformity American-style, *One Flew Over the Cuckoo's Nest*. Set in a mental institution, it shows a sane person's bid to awaken the individual spirits within his fellow inmates, and the efforts of the authorities to repress them. For all its allegorical qualities (with the characters embodying human attributes found throughout the supposedly saner world outside) the novel comes with a realism born of its author's own time spent working on a psychiatric ward.

The narrative technique that achieves this is magnificent. Chief Bromden tells the story. A half-native American schizophrenic, he owes his all-seeing, all-knowing position to others' belief that he can hear and say nothing. In spite of the novel's gloom, this device gives its whole execution a faith in patient listening: it is as though we have a story we weren't meant to read.

Kesey was to experiment further with narrative in *Sometimes a Great Notion*, set in a logging town with a peculiarly high suicide rate in his native Oregon. It was a larger project than the first, and he took further pains to make his characters real, conducting extensive interviews with lumberjacks. What writings have appeared since have indicated a kind of disillusion with the aspirations of the '60s, particularly in his piece, *The Day after Superman Died*, written as a memorial for the 'Beat' hero Neal Cassady.

MAJOR WORKS

*One Flew Over the
    Cuckoo's Nest* (1962)

Sometimes a Great Notion
    (1964)

Ken Kesey's Garage Sale
    (1973)

Demon Box (1986)

Kundera

MILAN   **born Brno 1929**

But all the student could see was the butcher's wife slipping out of his hands that whole month, and hard as it was to do, he shook his head. Kristyna meant as much to him at that moment as all his country's poetry.

THE BOOK OF LAUGHTER
AND FORGETTING

MILAN KUNDERA'S WRITING has the intrinsically Czech quality of being immediately readable, while unsettling the reader as he refrains from offering any empirical truths or entrenched attitudes. Like **Kafka** or **Hašek**, he presents an alternative view of how the world works; and although he guides the reader with a seemingly-tangential commentary, often based on his own experience, the sparing nature of his prose, and the self-conflicting nature of his aphorisms, provide their own refusal to comment.

Still, his analyses are rich in allusions to philosophy, music, poetry and history, which he explains patiently. These take the post-war Czech situation to explore the human condition, and vice versa. He avoids the idealism of his earlier poetry, a forthright defence of Communism, especially for its having prevailed over Fascism; increasingly his work depicted a universal disaffection with the Marxist régime. Until the Prague Spring, he was able to express this quite freely, but in 1967 his first novel *The Joke* worried publishers and was banned on publication in 1969. Kundera was silenced and escaped to France in 1975. He now lives in Paris, in the Montparnasse area.

His work from around the time of his exile onwards has dealt with the effects change has had upon human relations. The totalitarian conditions he describes are dehumanising, and take their toll on people's ability to laugh and love. Seldom in Kundera is even sex free of political significance, and throughout laughter emerges as the only response to a world robbed of meaning – a lightness when things no longer have weight. Even the joke at the expense of Communism becomes a kind of self-mocking on a national scale for ever having espoused it. The recent *Immortality* deals with this more internationally, and makes the point that human beings are more memorable when they are ridiculous; as ever, the quest for meaning finds nothing, and we laugh without knowing why.

Laclos

born Amiens 1741; died Taranto 1803

PIERRE-AMBROISE-FRANÇOIS CHODERLOS DE

MAJOR WORKS

Les Liaisons Dangereuses
(1782)

I am not surprised that, with a licentiousness that one would be wrong to deny you, you did for once deliberately what you have done a thousand times merely as the occasion offered. Everyone knows that this is simply the way of the world: the way of all you whoever you are, Neros or nobodies. The man who behaves otherwise nowadays is taken for a romantic and that is not, I think, the fault I find in you.

LES LIAISONS DANGEREUSES
TRANSLATED BY P.W.K STONE

LES LIAISONS DANGEREUSES is Laclos' one imaginative work. It spins a web of intrigue around the indolent and rotten circles of aristocratic France on the eve of the Revolution. Two characters turned completely sour have nothing to do, and so create situations over which they can wield their power fully.

The novel is executed entirely in letters. Each is vital dramatically, both as a source of plot and a piece of the plot in itself; letters become challenges, highly-charged objects, and even items of evidence. Their tone varies with violence: exchanges of civil enquiry or maternal advice break up the unrestrained cross-fires of two estranged lovers striving to better each other by any means available to them. They destroy everyone in the process, and mean to, but in doing so they ultimately destroy themselves.

The story reaches us thanks to a diffident editor who annotates the letters, sometimes with trivia, sometimes with crucial information. Laclos' artistry consists in appearing to offer this story for moral reasons, but giving something richer. If we are to learn anything, it is that society demands hypocrisy; that young girls are expected at once to be both innocent and compliant. By the self-revelation of the anti-heroine, the Marquise de Merteuil shows us something beyond such values. Her response to that society transcends revenge. It is a brutality born of lust and boredom: she is a greater study than the lesson.

The book was publicly burned after court action. In presenting a world in which discretion is the only virtue and silence the only sanctity, Laclos told all. The novel sets up boundaries for itself and then blasts through them.

Lermontov

MIKHAIL   **born Moscow 1814; died Pyatigorsk 1841**

And I sat alone

for hours, a king upon a fairy throne –
and while

I live I remember, in spite of storms
and doubt; I keep a tiny island green
in an ocean desert.

JANUARY 1ST, TR. RAFFEL

LERMONTOV WROTE at a time when Europe had started mythologising **Byron**, and when Russia had started to prize its own language. In a country which had always seen the source of culture as France, he followed **Pushkin** in exploring the poetic potential of his native tongue, displaying a love of his country but profound distrust of its rulers. He gave his country its first great novel, *A Hero of Our Times*.

This hero is Pechorin. Lermontov considered him to be typical of a generation, but portrayed him as a solitary figure with no apparent concern for others. Most of this small book is taken from Pechorin's journal, as introduced by his friend Maxim Maximich. The confessions seem sincere from their ability to shock, but the story allows us to doubt even this aspect of the narrator's morality. He dislikes posturing, however, and must fight a duel with the self-absorbed Grushnitsky, who wears his epaulettes too high. Throughout stories within stories, the reader questions whether Pechorin can love, or feel anything, even a fear of death: he even reads **Walter Scott** on the eve of his duel. The concluding tale of these loosely-linked episodes depicts a man never beaten in

Russian roulette, who knows exactly when he will die.

The romantic loneliness that Lermontov conveys here finds less dispassionate expression in his verse. The first poem to bring him fame was *The Death of Pushkin*, which pointed to government collusion in Pushkin's death in a duel. For this he was exiled; he too was to die in a duel, which caused others to make similar allegations. His verse is considered more spontaneous than Pushkin's, and is highly rhetorical, especially in his outburst on Napoleon's remains being transferred to France in *The Last House-warming*. His fascination with the misunderstood visionary despot echoes that of Byron's *Childe Harold*, and *personae* of other poems match Byronic mood-swings between rapture and disaffection with love.

Lessing

DORIS   **born Kermanshah, Persia (now Iran) 1919**

*The point is that the function of the
novel seems to be changing; it has been
an outpost of journalism; we read
information about areas of life we don't
know – Nigeria, South Africa, the
American Army, a coal-mining village,
coteries in Chelsea etc. We read to find
out what is going on...*

THE GOLDEN NOTEBOOK

DORIS LESSING'S FICTION provides a personal account of self-realisation; but it is one which reaches beyond the self, from political to increasingly spiritual concerns. She was born in Persia, but spent most of her childhood in Rhodesia, where she encountered apartheid. Her anger at this injustice animates her first novel, *The Grass is Singing*, in which she shows the tensions inherent in the system erupting into violent murder.

Lessing's own journey through radical politics and the relationships that steered it, is chronicled in the *Children of Violence* sequence, describing Martha Quest's coming of age. Among these books comes her most successful, the apparently unrelated *Golden Notebook*, in which a novelist works on a political novel, *Free Women*, which we receive with excerpts from her notebooks, each a different colour, each bringing a different kind of self-awareness to bear on the process of fiction. The novel has been praised for its experimental structure, and its contribution to feminism (although not universally); it sold nearly a million copies in hardback.

The fourth book of her work in progress, *Landlocked*, is more supernatural than its realist antecedents, involving telepathy and the mystical power of Sufism. A final text, *The Four-Gated City*, takes the story into the year 2000.

This began her career as a visionary. Her subsequent stories of Earth, which she calls "the broken planet" or Shikasta, as reported by emissaries trying to correct its course, are attempts at science fiction whose spiritual and utopian leanings bring the project closer to metaphysics.

In 1983, she submitted a novel to publishers under a different name, aware that her own was big enough to prevent readers from approaching her work objectively. The reviews were mixed, but in itself, her ploy showed a sense of responsibility balanced with a sense of the self which has consistently defined her work.

Levi

PRIMO

born Kermanshah, Persia (now Iran)

born Turin 1919; died Turin 1987

Hurbinek, who was three years old and had perhaps been born in Auschwitz and had never seen a tree, died in the first days of March 1945, free but not redeemed. Nothing is left of him: he bears witness through these words of mine.

THE TRUCE

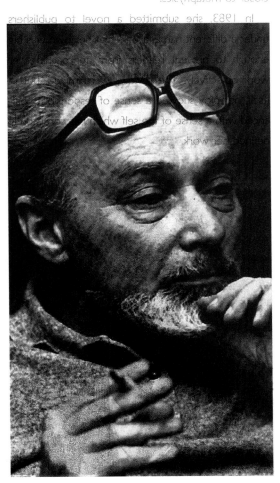

PRIMO LEVI BEGAN WRITING after his experience of Auschwitz. His life's work was to bear witness to the hell he had seen, and the guilt he felt in surviving it. He compared himself to **Coleridge**'s Ancient Mariner, and had a constant need to tell his story. He was a chemist, and found writing science fiction liberating; but his science was to inform his autobiographical books in a way that denied him any escape. He once collaborated on a paper detailing Nazi methods of extermination as a scientific phenomenon rather than a moral outrage.

His knowledge of chemistry and insight into humanity account for *The Periodic Table*, a series of stories and character studies based on the elements. Each element gains its defining quality from being distinct, and finds a corollary in the way people interact. Each carries an immediate association which reflects life, until the last, carbon, which becomes it. The work draws on his experience of growing up with Fascism, and its clinical notions of purity, as well as his time with the anti-Fascist resistance. *If This is a Man* and *The Truce* explore the horror of what followed his capture, from the tattooing of the number 174517 on his arm to the Red Army soldiers discovering him among the handful of survivors. The narrative's increasing awareness of the evil and its fulfilment echoes **Dante**'s descent into hell.

Levi's testimony became more urgent still when historians began to write articles denying Hitler's crimes, and questioning whether so vast and so rigorously documented a mass slaughter could have taken place at all. This, he said, was to "kill the dead twice". Ultimately, Levi did not survive. The nightmare of guilt and terror would never leave him. He killed himself in April 1987.

Lewis

born Belfast 1898; died Oxford 1963

> *People now all seem to want "a slice of life" (the flaccid, tepid, grey-to-brown shapeless object is a better image than they know) or the "comment on life." To me those who merely comment on experience seem to be far less valuable than those who add to it, who make me experience what I never experienced before.*
>
> **LETTER TO MERVYN PEAKE**

C. S. LEWIS APPLIED HIS immense intellect first to the history of English poetry, and then to a defence of Christianity. He drifted from the faith in his youth, only to return to it after rational enquiry, during which he espoused Pantheism before concluding that, for him, Christianity outshone all other religions. Still, he described himself as "the most dejected and reluctant convert in the whole of England". His struggle with the faith gave him acute insights into the psychology of believing, and the nature of temptation. *The Screwtape Letters*, in which a senior devil shows a bungling junior how to sway his "patient" from the path of salvation, applies Christian language rather than Freudian to a study of the mind.

The work emerged from suffering: he had made a pact with a fellow soldier in the First World War that, should one of them die, the other would care for the deceased's mother. Lewis fulfilled his pledge for 20 years of what his brother described as "self-

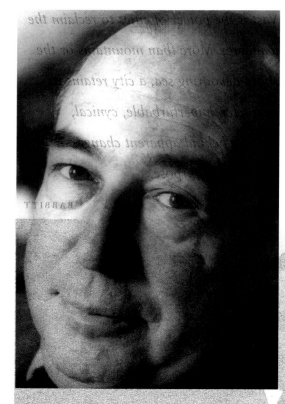

imposed slavery". Similarly, *A Grief Observed* confronts the pain of losing the one person he allowed himself to love since the early death of his mother, as he responds to losing his wife to cancer.

His most famous writing can be read as a Christian apology, although it started as a response to what Lewis perceived as the absence of decent children's literature at the time. But the figures that populate the sequence of seven books, starting with *The Lion, the Witch and the Wardrobe*, become increasingly Christianised. Aslan the lion turns Messianic, after being "crucified" and rising from the dead, and by *The Voyage of the Dawn Treader*, Lewis' allegory is made all but explicit as Aslan declares, "In your world you must know me by another name".

Lochhead

LIZ   **born Motherwell, Lanarkshire 1947**

I only have to pause for breath and in he falls, 'yes, dear I'll have the Steak Tartar medium rare, please!' The girl and I just look at each other ... from then on he can't open his mouth without putting his foot in it. Orders a 'cravat of your house white, please!' Then it's 'As you were, as you were, give me a bottle of Chateaubriand'.

GLASGOW'S NO DIFFERENT

LIZ LOCHHEAD IS ONE of a generation of contemporary poets whose work lends itself best to performance. To see her work on the page is already to be hearing it rapped out in a Glaswegian accent with an authority that leaves you unable to answer back. Many of her poems are really sketches or monologues that form part of her revues. She has written extensively for the stage, including musicals and a rhyming version of **Moliére**'s *Tartuffe.* Here she says, "I have been faithful to the original, in my fashion"; the fashion is emphatically Scots. She is also great news for the cause of poetry on TV.

Television can be seen as a theme of her work as well as a medium for it, whether she is attacking the elitism of the arts coverage, or simply leaving it on in the background of her retelling of fairy stories in *The Grimm Sisters*. These versions of **The Brothers Grimm** leave little room for romance: Rumplestiltskin works through every imaginable way to impress a girl before he can get around to saying "I love you", by which time it's too late.

Lochhead can maintain this level of cynicism about a lot of things. The "Glasgow's Miles Better" campaign comes in for special scorn, as does her home town's recent stint as European City of Culture. But while she makes short work of any urban attempts to sound idyllic, she is herself a vital part of that culture, keeping it strong and defiant.

Lodge

DAVID

born London 1935

'So Puss in Boots is equivalent to the Grail?' Persse said facetiously. Miss Maiden was not discomposed. 'Certainly. Boots are phallic, and you are no doubt familiar with the vulgar expression "pussy"?'

SMALL WORLD

DAVID LODGE IS A NOVELIST and a Structuralist literary critic. His work in the former does much to popularise the latter. Although his fiction addresses serious concerns, such as religion and the state of scholarship, it is consistently hilarious.

His first two books were realistic looks at post-war England: *The Picturegoers* tells of a run-down cinema. He wrote it while doing his National Service, which in turn provided material for the next work, *Ginger, You're Barmy*. It was with *The British Museum is Falling Down* that he introduced the themes of Catholicism and academic research. The book's hero must choose the novels on which to base his thesis on the same day that his wife becomes pregnant again. Throughout the text, the post-graduate encounters novels all around him from the butchers who speak like **Hemingway** to the **Kafka**esque encounter at the British Library Reading Room. Finally the two stories are merged as his wife discusses gynaecology in the style of *Ulysses*, ending with a "perhaps" rather than **James Joyce's** resounding yes.

Literature takes over the plots of his two novels on the international lecture circuit, *Changing Places* and *Small World*. The latter exemplifies Barthes' theory that a text can never quite attain closure, and its constant twists and hiccoughs defer any kind of resolution. The academics involved are happy to explain these ideas as they go, but never at the expense of character and belly-laughs.

These novels are set at Rummidge University, which the author is at pains to dissociate from Birmingham, where he teaches. The more recent *Nice Work* again takes place on a campus, but tackles social issues beyond it, as an industrialist and a lecturer explore one another's realms. Lately Lodge has renewed his investigation of how faith manifests itself in the modern world in *Paradise News*, in which a theologian's idea of heaven clashes with that of the travel agents.

London

JACK   **born San Fancisco 1876; died Glen Ellen, California 1916**

"Never travel alone" is a precept of the north.

HOW TO BUILD A FIRE

JACK LONDON'S RAPIDLY — produced *oeuvre* presents all aspects of America as he saw it — and he really saw it. His childhood was spent in poverty in San Francisco, and he left home early to work in a cannery before becoming an adventurer. He was also an oyster-poacher-turned-fish-patroller and in the former capacity had his first encounter with alcohol (which was to plague him for years), in an incident that nearly drowned him. Even his immense reading was an adventure, and he enrolled at Berkeley in 1896, studying by day, shovelling coal by night, such that he could barely hold a pen. Later, he would suffer similar blisters from his typewriter, which he said was "informed of an evil spirit".

His experiences and education made him at once a Socialist and a Darwinian. He wrote political tracts and memoirs: of the latter, one volume, *John Barleycorn*, tells of his alcoholism, another, *Martin Eden*, of his rise from rags to riches, and the accompanying guilt. He did not finish his degree at Berkeley, instead joining the Klondike gold rush.

This provides the setting for his most famous story, *Call of the Wild*. It incorporates London's beliefs and insights, and is sustained by a strong survival instinct. Its hero is the dog Buck, once a pet, now hauling cargo across the tundra. His rise through the team of dogs reflects at once a sense of collective responsibility and the ruthlessness staying alive requires. The allegory may be read in many ways, but the story derives most of its strength simply from its telling: the author's admiration for the animals' stamina and loyalty points towards qualities which humans can envy, but never possess.

Longfellow

HENRY WADSWORTH   **born Portland, Maine 1807; died Cambridge, Mass. 1882**

Read from some humbler poet

Whose songs gushed from his heart,

As showers from the clouds of summer

Or tears from eyelids start

Who, through long days of labour,

And nights of ease,

Still heard in the soul the music

Of wonderful melodies.

THE DAY IS DONE

LONGFELLOW WROTE SIMPLE unaffected poetry, often of great lyrical charm. He was a New Englander, and went to Bowdoin College with **Nathaniel Hawthorne**. Something of that area's Transcendentalism seems to have touched him, especially in the spirit of **Emerson**, whose view of nature having its own grammar finds fine expression in Longfellow's poem *Snow Flakes*. "This is the poem of the air/ Slowly in silent syllables recorded…"

Like Emerson, too, he campaigned for the abolition of slavery and his humanity is evident in much of his verse. His compassion for the exiled Jew marks his poem *The Jewish Cemetery at Newport*. But most significant is that his attempt at the national epic should be devoted to the native American legend of Hiawatha.

It is in marked contrast to an earlier effort, Joel Barlow's *Columbiad*, preaching simplicity in **Pope**-like rhyming couplets. Longfellow's poem is unrhymed, in short regular lines, that keep the syntax plain. The arguments emerge little by little with lilting echoes mimicking the "rushing of great rivers/ With their frequent repetitions/ And their wild reverberations." The hero's leave-taking has the limpid poignancy of *A Pilgrim's Progress* as it concludes.

But there is still a certain sadness in Longfellow's poetry. He writes as one acquainted with the night, dwelling on scenes of dusk and empty seascapes. He was a man lauded in public life, but one who nursed private unhappiness. His melancholy finds its match in the regretful tone of **Housman**. Both were hugely learned poets who kept their scholarship and verse separate – Longfellow was a Professor of Languages at Harvard. He suffered from outliving two wives, one of whom burned to death with their child in a fire. He won the admiration of Queen Victoria, was awarded honorary degrees from Oxford and Cambridge and is the only American poet to be commemorated in Westminster Abbey.

MAJOR WORKS

Hyperion (prose, 1839)

Voices of the Night (1839)

Ballads and Other Poems (1842)

Poems on Slavery (1842)

The Belfry of Bruges and Other Poems (1847)

Evangeline (1849)

The Song of Hiawatha (1855)

The Courtship of Miles Standish (1858)

Tales of a Wayside Inn (1863)

Christus (1872)

Aftermath (1874)

The Masque of Pandora (1875)

Ultima Thule (1880)

In the Harbor (1882)

Lucretius

born Rome? Campania? 99 BC? 94 BC? died c. 55 BC

Sweet, when the sea swells to the turbulent winds,

to stand on earth and watch another's toil;

not through delight in someone else's struggle –

it's sweet to see the problems you don't have.

ON THE NATURE OF THINGS, BOOK II

LUCRETIUS IS NEARLY as important as a philosopher as he is as a poet. In his extraordinary poem, *On the Nature of Things*, he takes the teachings of his hero Epicurus, and renders them in Latin verse. He was writing in hexameter, the standard Latin and Greek metre, at a time before **Virgil** had perfected it; and because Latin has fewer words than Greek, he coined new ones himself. This is unsurprising, given the complicated nature of his arguments, many of them scientific, and the rigour of his form; only half the words of his language fit into it. Like **Callimachus**, he could claim he was attempting a project never yet undertaken, and treading the Muses' untrodden paths. His poetic skills he considered were the drop of honey meant to make medicine less unpleasant. For all the apparent grimness of Lucretius' own dosage – he believed that the soul died with the body, and that the laws of physics preclude love (which he describes sensually

before censuring it) – his purpose was nonetheless to comfort. If the soul will not survive us, we need not worry about it – and worry is the one thing Epicureans want to avoid.

His poem is a verse compression of the arguments about matter taking place in antiquity. He rejects the theories of the Monists, who tried to posit a universe made of some single stuff, and explains instead the activity of atoms, which move around enough to provide a model of mankind's free will. The poem was much admired by Cicero, who was of the opposing, Stoic camp. But Lucretius' own ethical code, which found more comfort in human tolerance than divine compassion, must have appealed to the statesman for its firm rooting in reason.

McCarthy

MARY born Seattle 1912; died New York 1989

Every word she writes is a lie, including 'and' and 'the'

OF LILLIAN HELLMAN
ON NATIONAL TELEVISION.

MARY McCARTHY'S MOST valued quality has been her honesty; or rather, her bluntness. She made her name more as a critic than a writer of fiction, and became famous for championing unfashionable authors at the expense of fashionable ones. She disliked pretension, and the coteries which would surround experimental dramatists. Her interest in theatre came from an early wish to perform: she was the first to admit that she had no acting talent at all. In self-judgments like this she showed every bit as much candour as she could aim at others. She made many notable enemies, not least Lillian Hellman, the wife of **Dashiell Hammett**: the remark I quoted above resulted in a libel action. The injured party died before the case came to court; McCarthy would have preferred vindication to her enemy's demise. She exercises this in stories and novels with a strong autobiographical line, as well as in actual memoirs. Her first collection was *The Company She Keeps*. It concentrates on Meg and her political ambit, whose involvement in the Trotskyite circles of the thirties resembles McCarthy's: the same is true of the character's sexual intrigues, and a willingness to discuss them openly. This anticipates further appearances of McCarthy figures, notably the Vassar-educated rebel in *The Group*. In *The Oasis* she is taking her progressive friends with a greater pinch of salt. She always comes across as the romantic one, and later remembered pointing out that in a room full of

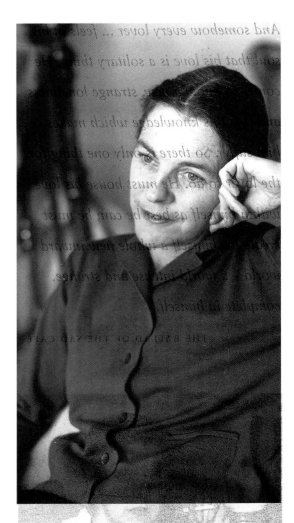

Communist activists, she was the only one who knew it was Valentine's Day.

While she could be humorous at her own expense, she could be earnest too, recalling the miseries of living with a great aunt after losing her affectionate parents (they died in the 'flu epidemic that followed the First World War) at the same time as satirising her Catholic upbringing. Her plain-speaking humanity found its most serious purpose in criticising American involvement in Vietnam.

McCullers

CARSON   **born Columbus, Georgia 1917; died Nyark, New York State 1967**

And somehow every lover ... feels in his soul that his love is a solitary thing. He comes to know a new, strange loneliness and it is this knowledge which makes him suffer. So there is only one thing for the lover to do. He must house his love within himself as best he can; he must create for himself a whole new inward world – a world intense and strange, complete in himself.

THE BALLAD OF THE SAD CAFÉ

CARSON MCCULLERS NEVER fitted into her home town of Columbus, Georgia. Her unconventional behaviour and relationships with those she loved regardless of gender scandalised the community long after she left it, and even after her death. So as a writer, she can immerse herself in a Southern small town, while retaining a prophet's kind of detachment. In that exemplary work, *The Ballad of the Sad Café*, she plumbs the profundity of her theme, love, while observing the action of her tale as might a curious neighbour, describing the landscape, the food and the surrounding characters with a familiarity that charms.

For McCullers, love is an unlikely force. It is animated more by solitude than desire, as in *The Heart is a Lonely Hunter*, where a deaf-mute awakens the solitary souls around her, or in *Reflections in a Golden Eye*, where military men confront their deepest needs. If this seems a pessimistic view of love, still, in McCullers' writing, it redeems the outcast, in a way she describes with a lyricism to match **Plato**'s treatment of it in the *Phaedrus*. And if people's passions are unpredictable, her narrative remains unshocked. This makes her prose a faithful recounting of surprising events happening around a mysterious, unaccountable core. *The Ballad of the Sad Café* has the story-teller giving the whole a song-like quality, with the last verse echoing the first. Her style is direct and economical, sometimes pointing the meaning of a scene, sometimes just reporting it. We are left with characters who have formed new, unanticipated attachments, supported by a commentary which manages to portray love as an even more all-embracing phenomenon than we might have contemplated before.

Maeterlinck

MAURICE

born Ghent 1862; died Nice 1949

Oh Lord, my earthly cravings will

At last expire within my heart!

Lord, let your radiance impart

Light to the hothouses of ill...

TEMPTATIONS

MAURICE MAETERLINCK fell under the spell of Symbolism while studying law at Ghent University, and though his earliest works are books of poems betraying the influence of **Mallarmé** and **Verlaine**, his distinct contribution to the movement was on the stage.

This was an extraordinary step to take. For to attempt the representation of abstract ideas by naming real things is one thing in verse, but to place it in a theatre, where all is to be seen and heard, is quite another. This was Maeterlinck's project, and he undertook it with sonorous dialogue and fairy-tale plots which combine to produce an unreal quality very suggestive of music. His best-known play is still more famous for just that: *Pelléas et Mélisande* has drawn musical responses from Debussy, Schönberg, Fauré and Sibelius.

Maeterlinck conceived his plays as musical wholes. In fact, it was his view that *Macbeth* is not so much a play as a poem and that the unexpected diction it includes is deliberately unlike natural speech. In his dramas, every effect contributes to the symbolic world conceived in a single mind, rather than a world which emerges from the actions of the characters. This extends to the exits and entries on the stage, and even the time-scale of a piece. Developed characters are not what we expect from a Symbolist play, and here the author doesn't shrink from a comparison with puppet shows. If anything, the lifeless movement of those on stage represents the playwright's belief that we have no free will whatsoever, and no guiding spirituality either. Although he has little in common with them in terms of style, still Maeterlinck's experimentation did much to prepare the way for the likes of **Ionesco** and **Pinter**.

Mailer

NORMAN

*It had always been the same, love was
love, one could find it with anyone, one
could find it anywhere. It was just that
you could never keep it. Not unless you
were ready to die for it, dear friend.*

AN AMERICAN DREAM

NORMAN MAILER SEEMS to write with his fists, and he can sting like a bee. His long interest in boxing is a reflection of the combative spirit he brings to his work. He is unafraid of critics, even suggesting that some of them should be "punched out". Such toughness has served him well in the solitary stances he has taken on a wide range of issues, most notably war, sex and politics.

Most of his works are either autobiographical or written out of a deeply-felt personal animus: when he is writing about the Vietnam war (in *Why Are We in Vietnam?*, for example, or *The Armies of the Night,* a memoir of the march on the Pentagon in protest at the war), he is not writing for writing's sake alone, however admirable his prose. And although his writing can contain war heroism and violence, he writes against war – despite seeing violence as inevitable in American society. This is something he exposes in *The Executioner's Song,* a Capote-like study of a man on Death Row who welcomes his own death. In *An American Dream,* the violence is domestic, although a public figure is responsible. The book is notable for containing American literature's first known description of heterosexual anal sex.

Mailer's first success was *The Naked and the Dead,* which drew on his own war experience to find, in the army, a model of his nation's problems. So acclaimed a debut seemed hard to follow, but although he remained his own greatest single theme, he was capable of examining that from a number of different angles, too. He is unembarrassed by his attachment to a wide range of subject matter, from a hagiography of Marilyn Monroe (not alone among works that have riled feminist commentators) to his recent psychological identification with Picasso and first-person telling of the life of Christ. This last especially has proved that Mailer has kept his ability to shock into his seventies.

Mallarmé

STÉPHANE

born Paris 1842; died Valvins 1898

I know that distant from this night, the
*   earth*
Casts unaccustomed awe with a great flair
under the hideous times, which blot
it less.
Growing or shrinking, space its own
*   worth*
Spins in this boredom vile fires to profess
The genius of a flaming, festive star.

WINDOWS

MALLARMÉ'S POETRY is a quest for beauty. The poet is aware of the inability of words to express the truly beautiful, which exists beyond things; so what we have in the poems is a yearning for the rose beyond the rose, the light beyond the window, the world beyond worldliness.

This accounts for the extraordinary style of his verse. It strives to go beyond ordinary language, and packs grammatical complexity into only a few syllables. Mallarmé strives to represent the essence of objects; and just as it is impossible to describe a smell without reference to other smells, so he introduces other images to illuminate the things he presents.

This made him, along with **Verlaine**, the founder of the Symbolist style of poetry. Early on he was influenced by **Baudelaire**, to whose strict verse rules he would always conform; but where Baudelaire would evoke disgust to explore the idea of evil, Mallarmé, would use morbid images to throw into relief the poetic qualities that transcend it. For this, he was at once admired by the younger "decadent" poets, while remaining a leading member of the Parnassian school, a group including Verlaine and Gautier, dedicated to classical purity and elegance.

His work is very difficult to interpret, but always gives the impression, in Pater's phrase, of "aspiring to the condition of music". His poem *Saint* speaks of music by describing a painting, so even the music is silent and inexpressible; in his most famous piece, *The Afternoon of a Faun*, a flute solo takes over where words seem to fail. On reading it, one can understand Mallarmé's gratitude for the shimmering Debussy orchestral prelude these lines inspired, even though at first he characteristically doubted that there could be any way to express his insights.

MAJOR WORKS

The Afternoon of a Faun
    (1876)

The Ancient Gods (1880)

Poetries (1887)

Poems in Prose (1891)

Verse and Prose (1893)

Divagations (1897)

The roll of the dice will
    never abolish chance (1897)

Malraux

ANDRÉ

born Paris 1901; died Paris 1976

Art and death are all I hope to rediscover here.

ANTIMEMOIRS

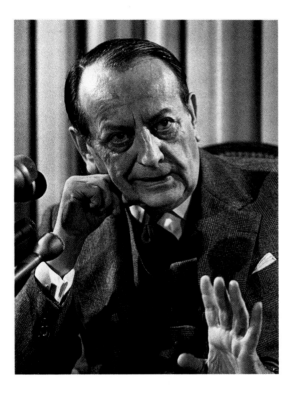

WHEN ANDRÉ MALRAUX WAS WORKING as an archeologist in Cambodia, he was arrested by the colonial service for revolutionary activities. By the end of his career, he would be the Minister for Culture in Charles de Gaulle's cabinet with the specific task of persuading the colonies that they should remain French. Malraux's journey in between, however, was not the normal shift from left to right of the angry young man adopted by the establishment.

Throughout his life he had chronicled uprisings and battles and taken part in many of them: in 1936 he was procuring arms for the Republicans in Spain; in 1939 he joined the French Tank Corps; in 1940 he escaped his German captors and fled to unoccupied France. Throughout, his actions were considered those of a Communist, but despite early Socialist leanings, nothing could have been further from the truth. Malraux was appalled by some of the Left's claims about their activities with the Resistance during the war, by what he considered to be their real ambitions, and most of all by Stalin. For Malraux, one dogma was as bad as another, and to accept unquestioningly was death.

In his books, action takes place in the teeth of such death. The First World War, that marked his adolescence, made him consider God dead. From then on he put his faith in friendships. This is most apparent in *Man's Estate*, Malraux's account of Chiang Kai Shek's battle with the Communists in which feelings preside over politics. Similarly, it is camaraderie which prevails briefly over the Falangists in *Days of Hope*.

This made him seem like an Existentialist, as did his phrase, "A man is what he does". But Malraux went deeper into the brain to confront the trivia that sways people from rational decisions. Ultimately he was concerned with results and permanence. It was this, more than anything, which led him to dig in Cambodia and use his Ministerial brief to preserve buildings in Paris, making him a latter-day Victor Hugo with even more political clout. He found permanence in art, architecture and even in empire; and this makes his art criticism as vital a part of his *oeuvre* as his novels and memoirs. All these works can dart from scene to scene, or subject to subject, as necessity dictates. They sustain life and survive us.

Mandelshtam

OSIP   **born Warsaw, 1891; died Vladivostok 1938**

O indigence at the root of our lives,

how poor is the language of happiness!

Everything's happened before and will

*   happen again,*

but still the moment of each meeting is

*   sweet.*

TRISTIA, TR. BROWN AND MERWIN

FOR MANDELSHTAM, poetry was a matter of life and death. Its pleasure surpasses the praise it accrues; it is as vital as bread. In the end, it would kill him.

For he published a savage denunciation of Stalin in 1934, with the concluding line, "He rolls the executions on his tongue like berries". It led to his arrest. After a second apprehension, he was transported from Moscow to Vladivostok, where he is said to have died, supposedly of heart failure, in a gulag. Only recently have even these details emerged, thanks to his wife Nadia.

For so pure a poet, he was full of a sense of his own times. He had lived through the Revolution, and wrote many poems expressing a change of the ages. If the authorities already had cause to deem him counter-revolutionary, it was because his verse appeared to hark back to an earlier age, and lament its passing. But his work contained this element even before the Revolution, which he had greeted with enthusiasm at the time. His first collection, *Stone*, often talks of twilight, and invokes a lost Classical world. He writes of Caesar's demise, and cites the unfulfilled longings of **Ovid**'s elegies; his reflections on St. Petersburg make it clear that he does not live in a Golden Age.

With **Akhmatova** and Gumilev, he founded the Acmeist school of poetry; its interest in the reality of things, rather than their symbols and ciphers, extends to Mandelshtam's idea of words. In his mouth, they become entities in themselves, and he could ask, "What's meaning but vanity? A word is a sound /one of the handmaidens of the seraphim". This sense of their quiddity, organised in restrained and formal stanzas, makes them so essential.

MAJOR WORKS

Stone (1913)

Tristia (1922)

Poems (1928)

Mann

HEINRICH

born Lübeck 1871; died Los Angeles 1950

Each of us is as nothing, but massed in ranks as neo-Teutons... we taper up like a pyramid to a point at the top where Power itself stands, graven and dazzling...

MAN OF STRAW

HEINRICH MANN'S REPUTATION has long been eclipsed by his brother **Thomas Mann**. It was not always that way, though. Heinrich had once attracted more attention for his fuller treatment of decadence, and Thomas always looked up to him as his big brother figure. They disagreed publicly about Germany's actions during the First World War, and about the use of the novel for political ends. But this was because they shared much of the same subject matter, especially the function of art. Both explore its capacity for good and evil, but Heinrich examined it in more social terms, disdaining bourgeois culture and seeing art as a weapon to combat authoritarianism.

This he did in his two most famous novels, *The Blue Angel* and *The Man of Straw*. The former introduces Professor Unrat, a morbid teacher whose intolerance of class-room disruptions leads him to megalomania, while the latter depicts similar despotism at an imperial level. His hatred of dictators made him one of the first to leave Germany when Hitler became Chancellor in 1933. He headed a group of *émigré* writers in Paris until the city fell to the Nazis in 1940, after which he escaped to California.

Ultimately, apart from the two novels mentioned above, Heinrich Mann is remembered more for his discussion of what a novel should achieve than, say, his characterisation of prose style. His essays on **Flaubert** and **Zola** show him trying to reconcile life with its representation. He practised this most fully in *The Little Town* in which he depicted a theatre company in a small Italian community and showed that while man may be a political animal, he can become more than just that.

Mann

THOMAS   **born Lübeck 1875; died Zürich 1955**

We can only with difficulty imagine such a thing; and yet it will be, and be the natural thing: an art without anguish, psychologically healthy, not solemn, unsadly confiding, an art perdu with humanity.

DOCTOR FAUSTUS

THOMAS MANN'S IMMENSE GIFT to our times has been his unrelenting, peerless enquiry into the rôle and plight of the artist in a sick age.

He achieved this in books charged with ideas, and a Germanic reverence for all that is pure and noble. But although he was an avowedly patriotic, establishment figure during the First World War, he was already the prophet of decline, in *Buddenbrooks*, his astonishingly precocious study of a family in long-term decay, and in *Death in Venice*, where an esteemed German writer falls for a boy in cholera-stricken Italy.

But the war and the persistence of his brother **Heinrich Mann** shook his conservatism, and altered the course of his work then in progress, *The Magic Mountain*. With its new insights into a diseased Europe, the book assumed a modern wisdom, won its author the Nobel Prize, and has been acclaimed as one of the greatest novels ever.

But soon the Nazis would be burning his books, and destroying everything. Mann found his notions of harmony in art unable to face the terror around him. He turned increasingly to allegory, pleading for tolerance in exile with *Joseph and his Brothers*.

In *Doctor Faustus*, he summoned all his powers to confront evil in its purest form. A diffident classical philologist offers us the biography of his late friend, a composer who yields to the Satanic. All notions of form, and all inclinations towards love, are impotent in the face of the ensuing mental and international chaos which engulf so controlled a work.

Mann's last work, *The Confessions of Felix Krull*, tackles artifice with the hilarious recollections of a charming impostor; but even he must conclude, "The most hopeful situation in life is when things are going so badly for us that they can't possibly go worse". If we cannot avoid sharing such pessimism, at least this joyous book shows us how Mann's art can impart delight as well as despair.

Maupassant

GUY DE   **born Miromesnil, Normandy 1850; died Passy 1893**

But yes, she had failed him in her tenderness, failed in pious respect. To him, she had become irreproachable, as all mothers must be to their children. If the fury it had raised almost reached hatred, it was because she had wronged him more criminally even than she had wronged his father.

A LIFE

MAUPASSANT WROTE SIX NOVELS, but is better known for his short stories, of which he wrote some 300. His work in this genre was adopted by **Zola** as representing the aims of the Naturalist movement, and Maupassant contributed one of his earliest, most famous stories, *Boule de Suif,* to the collection Zola edited under the title *Les Soirées de Médan* and and presented to **Flaubert** as a homage to the latter and the influence of Realism.

In fact, Maupassant owed more to Flaubert. They had become related by Maupassant's marriage, which their friendship outlasted. In both their works, they show a strong attachment to their native Normandy. Many of Maupassant's tales depict Norman peasant life, as well as drawing on his own experiences as an administrator during the Franco-Prussian War of 1870-1 and his subsequent work as a civil servant. He avoids sentimentality, and prefers detail. His craft demands that he be economical, and lengthy psychological accounts of a character's motivations do not suit his technique. Instead we see people's actions, and the consequences, which are the more pathetic for being understated. Events lead to tragedy, rather than human attempts to influence them. *A Piece of String* offers a fine example: a peasant dies in disgrace after his neighbours accuse him of finding and keeping someone else's wallet, when he was merely picking up a piece of string. Here the author compresses the passage of time, and the peasant's decline, as effectively as he would record his heroine's boredom in his novel *A Life,* without being boring himself.

His work is considered less finished than Flaubert's. He wrote at a much faster pace throughout an even shorter life – he died insane, capitulating to a form of syphilis which caused him to hallucinate and made him suicidal. He claimed that when he wrote he could sometimes see himself watching himself work. Only when he finished writing did his *alter ego* disappear.

Mauriac

FRANÇOIS

born Bordeaux 1885; died Paris 1950

Maria Cross yielded not so much to drink deep of the branch-encumbered air as to a temptation to lose herself in it, to feel herself dissolved and atomised, till the inner desert of her heart should become one with the emptiness of space, till the silence within her should in no way differ from the silence of the spheres.

THE DESERT OF LOVE

FRANÇOIS MAURIAC'S NOVELS brought him widespread respect and many honours. The conflict in them arises from the clash of spirit with flesh and from the individual with conventional Catholic morality, as played out in the close family units of the rural areas surrounding Bordeaux.

Mauriac empathises with the loneliness of his characters. He places them in a world that God makes miserable by His absence. Instead, nature is present throughout the novels, sometimes oppressively so. Once-benign and desirable features of the landscape can turn menacing when a character's security in the world vanishes. Much of Mauriac's narrative can happen inside someone's head, distorting the timescale with recollected episodes. Thus a story's outer tensions cause inner fury, which his passionate prose captures over lengthy paragraphs. In this way *Thérèse Desqueyroux*, which remains his most widely read and admired work, is made more real to us: we meet a heroine who enjoys an immediate sympathy for nature, but whose instinctive reaction to those around her leads her to feel the universe turn against her, even before she tries to kill her way out of a loveless marriage. The narrative leaves her at the mercy of her vengeful new family.

Love becomes a more potent force in Mauriac's later work. The criticism of colleagues like **André Gide** led him to re-examine his attitudes towards religion and the possibilty of redemption with a degree of humility. As a result, he made his subsequent writing more optimistic, taking Thérèse beyond her spiritual isolation in a sequel and introducing more effective religious figures into other novels. But his realm remained a bleak one, in which sin is still a strong presence and families are ever-ready to turn on individuals to protect their names.

Mauriac was awarded the Nobel Prize for Literature in 1952.

241

Maurois

ANDRÉ

born Elbeuf 1885; died Paris 1967

I think that laughter is produced just when a state of alarm is followed by a state of relief. A young monkey who has the highest regard for the old chief of the tribe sees him slip on a banana skin; he fears an accident and his breast swells with terror, before discovering that it's nothing and all his muscles unclench pleasantly. That was the first joke. And that explains the convulsive movement of laughter.

DR O'GRADY IN
THE SILENCE OF COLONEL BRAMBLE

ANDRÉ MAUROIS WAS a French novelist and belletrist who brought a Gallic refinement to his subject matter. His chief interest was the English-speaking world. During the First World War, he worked as a liaison officer between the British and French armies and launched his literary career with two volumes that shared his insights into the British character. *The Silence of Colonel Bramble* and *The Speeches of Dr O'Grady* remain his most popular works.

Although Maurois can be identified with the novels' French character, Aurelle, the writing is detached from the action, which is realised mostly through speech. The pictures of the phlegmatic Scotsman and the loquacious Irishman take precedence over any account of the fighting: we are firmly in the officers' mess, not the trenches. Here we encounter the British male as he is represented in all classes, and the conflict seems to bring out the best in him – not least the Briton's perceived sense of "fair play". One soldier even goes so far as to propose a toast to the Germans, for providing such excellent sport: he now commands respect on his return home. The images of war are more sentimental than in his later work, such as when the soldier who once toasted the war as a marvellous adventure receives his fatal wound gallantly. Still, the conversations are droll and reveal a French view of the British that remains largely unchanged.

Maurois was drawn to this sporting spirit and lived in England before taking a teaching post at Princeton and settling in the US. He strove to explain both cultures to his compatriots, in his *History of England* and *History of the United States* from Wilson to Kennedy.

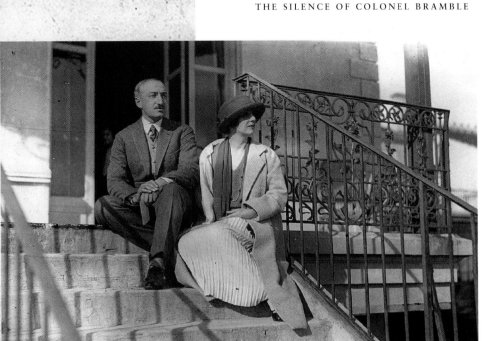

242

Mayakovsky

VLADIMIR **born Mayakovsky, Georgia 1893; died Moscow 1930**

On earth,

my love I could never fulfil.

I was seven foot tall.

To me what's a foot or two?

For such works even a

plant-louse can do.

I scratched with a pen, eyeglasslike

squeezed into

the spectacle case of a little room.

ABOUT THIS, TR. HERBERT MARSHALL

MAJOR WORKS

A Cloud in Trousers (1915)
Mysteriya-Buff (play, 1918)
150 000 000 (1919–1920)
About This (1923)
Vladimir Il'yich Lenin (1924)
Good! (1927)
The Bedbug (play, 1929)
At the Top of My Voice (1930)

VLADIMIR MAYAKOVSKY is the poet of the Russian Revolution, a man who thoroughly embraced the events of 1917. Although only 12 during the 1905 uprising, he busied himself writing propaganda for his classmates. By the time he and the revolutionary movement had matured 12 years later, he was writing such material for the entire nation, as well as producing films and lyrical advertising slogans.

Despite this, his relationship with the new rulers was never easy. Lenin openly disliked his poetry, wrongly linking it to the less social Futurist movement; Stalin publicly praised him, then had him followed by the secret police when he travelled the world to recite his lament for Lenin.

Mayakovsky's artistic problem was reconciling his leanings towards the love lyric with his passionate social concerns. In the former, he is never sentimental, adopting staccato-like lines and modernist images to express the pain of the beloved's failure to "phone" in the most global terms. In the latter he is the prophet of a **Whitman**esque, unselfish and universal love. This balance in his work won him admirers, including **Pasternak** and some in the Soviet establishment, and kept him as deeply in the hearts of his people as any Russian poet.

He shot himself in 1930 – no-one has been able to explain why. His suicide draws attention to his complex private life and the grudges against him, and these are as likely causes as the political climate. A gambler and drinker, he had a morbid turn of mind and had contemplated suicide for many years before he pulled the trigger. The demands he made of himself as a public poet are likely to have led to a sense of failure – Roman Jakobson wrote of Mayakovsky's inability to write epics without making them intimate and episodical. Few people were more alarmed by the author's interest in the human heart and his desire to be loved than he was himself.

Melville

HERMAN

born New York 1819; died New York 1891

Very often do the captains of such ships take those absent-minded young philosophers to task... half-hinting that they are so hopelessly lost to all honourable ambition, as that in their secret souls they would rather not see whales than otherwise. But all in vain; those young Platonists have a notion that their vision is imperfect; they are short-sighted; what use, then, to strain the visual nerve? They have left their opera-glasses at home.

MOBY-DICK

AS WITH OTHER TRULY great American writers, it is deceptively easy to categorise Melville. Although born in New York, his association with **Hawthorne** links him with New England and he lived on Hawthorne's estate for a time. Melville shared his landlord's forebodings of darkness and sin, while having much in common with the transcendentalists living nearby. He embraced the same wildness, if anything more fully; and **Emerson**'s pantheism has its counterpart in Melville's capacity to see the whole of humanity compacted into single things. To Captain Ahab, the great white whale Moby-Dick is such, and it is this vision that rings in our ears as we put down the short story *Bartleby* – "Ah, Bartleby! Ah, humanity!"

Unlike his fellow authors, he died unknown. He wrote incessantly, until it drove him insane. He produced poetry, some in a lyric form, some with **Whitman**'s charge, some endless and rhyming, much of it bleak. This range seems like versatility, but his prose work shows that his method of fitting ideas into language could barely be controlled. In *Moby-Dick*, a description of the slightest thing can become the theme for a discourse on mankind's destiny. Ahab's inner thoughts assume the metre of a **Shakespearean** monologue and characters' interactions can require a staging worthy of **Goethe**'s *Faust*. Melville's utter commitment to his theme dispenses with mere artistry.

Moby-Dick was published in London. It was the culmination of his writings about the sea, which he had known through abandoned adventure, including imprisonment, mutiny and whaling.

Meredith

GEORGE

born Portsmouth 1828; died Box Hill, Surrey 1909

The strangeness of men, young and old, the little things (she regarded a grand wine as a little thing) twisting and changing them, amazed her. And these are they by whom women are abused for variability! Only the most imperious reasons, never mean trifles, move women, thought she. Would women do an injury to one they loved for oceans of that – ah! pah!

THE EGOIST

GEORGE MEREDITH CONSIDERED himself primarily a poet, but he is better known for his novels. Even these have never reached the wide audience he craved, but his ambition did not outweigh his artistic integrity and after a few attempts to address fashionable literary concerns, he decided to write more according to his instincts. Meredith's admirers included **Henry James**, George Gissing and **Thomas Hardy**, whose early works he encouraged when he read them for a publisher.

Like them, Meredith was a progressive. He was a strong advocate of equality for women and is remembered for his particularly sympathetic female characters. In writing, his leanings were towards the poetic. This became exaggerated in later years, when he worried less about attracting new readers; but his earlier work displays a similar richness. His apparently detached narrative technique can suddenly become passionately engaged with a character's thoughts, before leaving them to discuss some idea of his.

His masterpiece is considered to be *The Egoist*. It is the study of an aristocratic figure who cannot understand how his actions can harm other people and so treats them negligently. He displays a callousness towards women and a yen for self-fulfilment, while the narrative concentrates more on those around him. They set off the protagonist, Sir Willoughby Patterne, and reveal aspects of the author's personality – in Vernon's learning and Laetitia's ambition to make a living by writing. Although the love triangles and social dilemmas tend towards a happy conclusion, they oppress the characters throughout, especially the women, who must overcome convention to express themselves.

Metastasio

PIETRO

born Rome 1698; died Vienna 1782

Not only do the things I sing and write

prove to be false, but in

my hopes and fears

I live deliriously, and all's deceit.

My life has been nothing but fantasies.

But Lord, when I have woken

from this night

Then at the heart of truth

may I find peace.

WHILE WRITING THE OLYMPIAD

METASTASIO'S NAME comes from the Greek for change, or passing. He chose it himself, changing it from Pietro Trapassi when he was 20. In fact, he was a poet of the establishment, writing courtly poems for the aristocrats of Naples and serving in Vienna as Caesarean poet under two Holy Roman Emperors (Charles V and VI). His innovations were in dramatic theory rather than in drama – his study of Aristotle's *Poetics* challenged the stage conventions of his time more than his plays did. They were not noted for their characters or plots (enlightened despots become embroiled in affairs of the heart – he was writing tragedy with a strong love interest at 14), but were noted for their poetry.

Even when he was not writing it expressly to be sung, it was always musical. He wrote many melodramas, "lyric scenes" and the libretti for some 27 operas. What his characters lacked in psychological interest, Handel or Mozart provided musically: the latter set Metastasio's *La Clemenza di Tito* sublimely, though only after major structural changes.

Still, Metastasio had extensive practical knowledge of the theatre: he had formed a troupe to perform his plays while working as a lawyer in Naples (financial and amatory problems compelled him to leave his native Rome) and had formative liaisons with actresses. For all his experience of life, he seems to have learned as much from books. He grew up with access to the library of his adoptive father, the poet Gravina: he called it his Arcadia. Henceforth, he immersed himself deeply in the classical temperament of his times and furnished Italian letters with his translations of **Horace** and **Homer**'s *Iliad*. Pope Pius VI is reported to have wept at the news of Metastasio's death.

Miller

ARTHUR

born New York 1915

A man is not a piece of fruit

DEATH OF A SALESMAN

I refuse to believe that man's only way to demonstrate his love for God is to refuse to eat some fruit

LUCIFER IN THE CREATION OF
THE WORLD AND OTHER BUSINESS

ARTHUR MILLER IS a playwright whose works have always been carefully structured, even at their most experimental. In this way he has made palatable the major concerns of post-war America.

He made his name with *All My Sons*. Its representation of a man plagued by guilt at his negligence as an industrialist during the war owes much to **Ibsen**'s *The Master Builder*.

Death of a Salesman tackled more exclusively American dilemmas – Willy Loman's sense of dignity in a modest profession tarnishes with time. He comes to feel disposable, first to society, then his family. Subsequently, Miller's work lost Ibsen's realism, allowing flashbacks and looser time-scales. But he retained his mentor's interest in psychology and the problem of the individual versus society.

He produced his own version of *An Enemy of the People* in 1951. His experience of the play's maxim, "The minority is always right," came during the McCarthy era. *The Crucible* drew on the 17th-century witch-hunts in Salem, which lent their name to McCarthy's hounding of suspected Communists out of public life, often driving them to suicide.

Miller chronicles his refusal to name names in *After the Fall*, which also tackles his marriage to Marilyn Monroe.

Like some of his other plays, it draws on allegory and confronts an issue that recurred, unbidden and unmentionable – the Holocaust. It is a harrowing focus for Miller's abiding preoccupation with guilt and *After the Fall* must face it rather than exorcise it. Miller's plays do not offer us the catharsis we have come to expect from tragedy, but show us a world in which we must remember the past before we can redeem it.

MAJOR WORKS

All My Sons (1947)

Death of a Salesman (1949)

The Crucible (1953)

A View from the Bridge (1955)

The Misfits (screenplay, 1960)

Incident at Vichy (1965)

The Archbishop's Ceiling (1977)

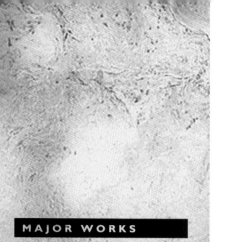

Miller

HENRY   **born New York 1891; died Pacific Palisades 1980**

The books he read – at 18! Not only Homer, Dante, Goethe, not only Aristotle, Plato, Epictetus... but all the small fry in between. Alors, on page 232 he breaks down and confesses. I know nothing, he admits. I know the titles, I have compiled bibliographies... I can talk for five minutes or five days, but then I give out, I am squeezed dry.

TROPIC OF CANCER

HENRY MILLER WAS a wanderer and sexual adventurer who achieved literary fame for his frank books, which would read more like confessions if they were accompanied by a greater sense of guilt. His work has striven to liberate readers from the taboos he found so constraining throughout his upbringing, and which were the reason he left America.

This is what gives his most famous book its joy and freedom. *Tropic of Cancer* celebrates Miller's early years as a writer in France. It broke ground with its expletives and **Lawrence**-influenced rhapsodising of genitalia. But the author's hunger is for food as much as sex and the whole is more interesting for its treatment of Paris than of passion. The latter is urgent, but the former is permanent and Miller finds the city much as **Hemingway** left it in *The Sun Also Rises*.

It is very much a writer's journey – and a solitary one. In an epiphanic passage, he claims to recognise the "absolute". He never tells us what this is, but it gives him an authority that empowers his later books when he rails against American materialism and sexual anxiety, especially in *Tropic of Capricorn*. In the autobiographical trilogy, *Sexus*, *Plexus* and *Nexus*, he describes his odd jobs in prohibition New York, his two marriages, their complications, and ultimately the "Rosy Crucifixion" that gives the books their collective title – it is Miller's "resurrection as a writer".

His generous and seminal output affects readers very differently. **Orwell** welcomed his rendering of real life as that of a proper writer, while for others the apparent sexism is a major obstacle to embracing Miller's profoundly personal vision.

Milne

A.A.   born St. John's Wood, London 1882; died Hartfield, Sussex 1956

If   this   is   shall   really   take   to
                 flying I   never   it.

WINNIE-THE-POOH

'It isn't their necks I mind,' said Piglet earnestly. 'It's their teeth. But if Christopher Robin is coming I don't mind anything.'

WINNIE-THE-POOH

A.A. MILNE'S CAREER as a light poet and sketch-writer led to his assistant editorship of *Punch* magazine. This was interrupted by the First World War, during which he began writing stage comedies, which are barely performed today, although he did dramatise Kenneth Grahame's *The Wind in the Willows*.

He began writing verse for his son Christopher Robin, anthologised in *When We Were Very Young* and *Now We Are Six*. The work displays a neatness and fluency that his great creations Pooh and Eeyore did not share in their lyric efforts. But their bumbling metres and mad lunges for rhymes are truer to the poetic process than the apparent effortlessness that Milne brought to it They consistently defy **Yeats'** dictum that, "a line will take us hours maybe;/ Yet if it does not seem a moment's thought,/ Our stitching and unstitching has been naught".

And yes, it is easy to be smart about Pooh and his friends, who people (or teddy) Christopher Robin's half-imaginary world in the two gems *Winnie-the-Pooh* and *The House at Pooh Corner*. Their utterances have been taken to support any number of philosophies, including Taoism and most schools of literary theory (Frederick Crews' spoof readings are as handy an introduction to F.R. Leavis, Freud and deconstruction as any), and have even been translated into Latin.

But he could be smarter at our expense. "Every age is a Canterbury Pilgrimage", wrote **Blake**, "we all pass on, each sustaining one of these characters..." and it is a lasting comfort to think the same is true of the Milne toy-box. For if we can recognise in ourselves anything of Pooh's driftiness, Piglet's trepidation, Wol's deluded sense of order, Tigger's bounce or Eeyore's resignation to it all, then even in a world that can knock out all our stuffing, there might remain for us something eternally fluffy.

Milosz

CZESLAW

born Wilno, on the Polish/Lithuanian border 1911

At the entrance, my bare
   feet on the dirt floor,
Here, gusts of heat; at my
   back, white clouds.
I stare and stare. It seems
   I was called for this:
To glorify things just because they are.

BLACKSMITH SHOP, IN PROVINCES

THE POET CZESLAW MILOSZ has spent much of his life outside his Polish homeland (he was born in Lithuania); although he had edited a left-wing journal as a student in Warsaw, he left in 1951 to escape the increasingly totalitarian Communist régime. He settled first in France, then in California. His work was banned in Poland until 1981, when he won the Nobel Prize. His presence in the West has done much to promote the work of other Polish poets, and to draw attention to the circumstances under which they have been working. Some of his most read work comes from the Warsaw he knew during the war. With his underground poetry, he supported the Polish Resistance.

War, and the knowledge of its devastation, might have been the source for much poetry, but he takes this further. The constant presence of death can lead his poems to explore the difference between states of being and non-being. A moment may be part of a developing process, or else be frozen in time. His poetry seizes on minute details, which become dis-tinct from a tide of impressions impossible to capture in words: for example, he decides how the eye might fix upon two blades of grass and a stone during an air-raid. It is this kind of memory snatched from moments of historical crisis that have led critics to call him a "witness" – a label he rejects as characterisation of Western triteness. He has become well-known for poems which occupy imaginary territories: here his influence is particularly marked on **Heaney**. The impact seems to be reciprocated in later Milosz poems, which show a delight in actual things. The two poets have shared reading platforms in the States.

Milosz has translated **T.S. Eliot** and **Walt Whitman** into Polish, and his own poetry into English. His English verse-writing is innovative and extremely accomplished; his expression is direct, and he experiments with line-lengths in a way which a different translator, striving for fidelity to the original, might be reluctant to attempt.

Milton

JOHN   **born London 1608; died Chalfont St. Giles, Bucks 1674**

And all amid them stood the tree of life,

High eminent, blooming ambrosial fruit

Of vegetable gold; and next to life

Our death the tree of knowledge grew

   fast by,

Knowledge of good bought dear by

   knowing ill.

PARADISE LOST, BOOK IV

MILTON'S WRITING HAS had so huge an effect on the language of English poetry that it has often seemed hard to respond to it. One contemporary poet has called him "the great closing down sale of English literature", describing his complete mastery of previous poetical forms – the masque (*Comus*), the pastoral (the lament *Lycidas*), the tragedy (*Samson Agonistes*) and the epic (*Paradise Lost*) – and the vision that led him to transform them for his own ends.

These aims are often the same as those of his pamphlets and public campaigning. He was a Puritan and felt the Reformation had not gone far enough in England. He wrote passionately in favour of divorce, then for freedom of speech when these views encountered censorship.

In politics and religion, he fought against oppression. His faith embraced companionship and sex in marriage (the early relationship between Adam and Eve was his ideal) and after the Restoration he was imprisoned for attacking the new regime. **Andrew Marvell** saved his life.

Milton's masterpiece, *Paradise Lost*, threw off "the tyranny of rhyme". Composed in blank verse, it expounds mankind's history from creation to the fall, then forwards to our redemption through Christ. His knowledge of all previous epics and his verse, which is worthy of the best of them, has made any subsequent attempt at the form seem futile. His complete vision of human history and his power to express it make it hard to imagine that he considered any other theme, although King Arthur had been a likely subject. But by going for the more cosmic option, he still enriched his country's poetry to the point of satiety. His Latinate syntax, his ability to make the abstract vivid, his capacity for making "the worse appear/the better reason" in Satanic speech before persuading us of holier truths, and his sheer conviction, have left English poets stammering in admiration.

MAJOR WORKS

Lycidas (1637)

Areopagitica (1644)

Paradise Lost (1667, 1674)

Paradise Regained (1671)

Samson Agonistes (1671)

Mishima

YUKIO

born Tokyo 1925; died Tokyo 1970

Death does not go beyond truth. Suicide might be called death through action. A man cannot be born of his own will, but he can will to die.

FORBIDDEN COLOURS

HOWEVER HARD ONE TRIES to separate art from life, it is almost impossible to consider Mishima's literary career apart from its bloody end. When he had finished the fourth and final book of his masterpiece, he appeared before an assembly of soldiers to harangue them about the Japanese constitution's assaults on the glories of the Emperor and warriordom, before disembowelling himself with unbelievable deftness, assisted by one of his hand-picked troops, who beheaded him.

His work and life over, he had attained *Bunbu-Ryodo* (the union of cultural and warlike excellence) or, in his own phrase, the harmony of pen and sword. Readers asking why often pick through his corpus for clues. His last work, *The Sea of Fertility*, invites the conclusion that Mishima might have anticipated his return to the earth. *The Decay of the Angels* shows a preoccupation with the early, violent death of young men at their most beautiful. This last gesture seems to strive toward the kind of beauty he cherished most.

It was a physical beauty, such as he had desired in other men from youth and which his first novel, *Confessions of a Mask*, explores. And it was a terrible beauty: the novice of *The Temple of the Golden Pavilion* is so drawn yet repelled by the wonder of a building, he must destroy it, then himself.

Mishima's end seems to fulfil aesthetic goals rather than logical ones. He railed against Western materialism, but left a plush flat with Greek statues and foreign novels; he advocated severity, while displaying a merry wit and sociability. In his writing, he can treat what allures him with disgust and his tetralogy shows the appeal of his method of death (called *seppuku*) embraced, only to be dismissed elsewhere. In life, he was a fanatic; in art, an artist.

Mitchell

MARGARET

born Atlanta, Georgia 1900; died Atlanta 1949

He drew a short breath and said lightly but softly: 'My dear, I don't give a damn.'

GONE WITH THE WIND

MARGARET MITCHELL'S ONLY BOOK broke all sales records and, as a historical epic and a sustained romance, it reached wider audiences than any earlier work conceived on the same scale. Readers of *Gone With the Wind* devoured the tale of the American South set around the Civil War, without being daunted by its thousand-odd pages.

Mitchell was born in Georgia and from her youth had absorbed stories passed down through generations of people with long memories of the war. Her novel is written from the Southern point of view, showing sympathy for the Confederates, if not for slavery. The narrative treats black and white characters equally. The scope of the book is immense, beginning with the seeds of the conflict and following the fate of a family plantation, Tara, to the end and beyond into the Reconstruction period. Mitchell introduces the vastness of the battle scenes, but maintains a female perspective on them, tackling the theme of domestic tragedy through her heroine, Scarlett O'Hara.

Scarlett is an intriguing figure, capable of acting without morals in everything, motivated by self-interest and a need to protect her family's fortune. We follow her through three marriages and her progress from loving a childhood sweetheart to her later relationship with the mysterious outcast Rhett Butler. Whether or not she finds true love in the end is left to the reader to decide; he or she will have turned page after page only to be as beguiled by Scarlett as her suitors are. She plays games with everyone.

Margaret Mitchell took 10 years over the work, revising it for years after the first draft before offering it to a publisher. She conceived it while recovering from an injury to her ankle and proposed to call it *Tomorrow is Another Day*. Before that, she had worked on the *Atlanta Journal*. Her achievement with the novel was honoured with a Pulitzer Prize in 1936 – remarkably she was chosen over **Faulkner**, whose literary landscape is very similar, but whose technique could not contrast more strongly with Mitchell's. The classic film version was made in 1939.

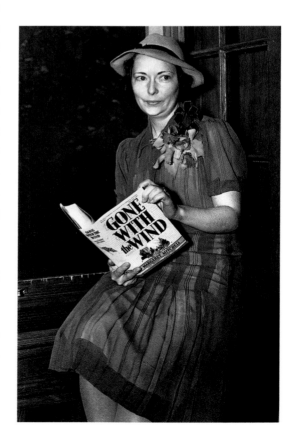

Mitford

NANCY

born London 1904; died Versailles 1973

I have long regarded you as an agitator – agitatrix, agitateuse? of genius. You have only to publish a few cool reflections on 18th-Century furniture to set gangs on the prowl through the Faubourg St Germain splashing the walls with 'Nancy, go home'.

EVELYN WAUGH, AN OPEN LETTER TO THE
HON MRS PETER RODD (NANCY MITFORD)
ON A VERY SERIOUS SUBJECT,
IN NOBLESSE OBLIGE

NANCY MITFORD WAS BORN into an aristocratic family in which eccentricities were not just tolerated, but cultivated. The Mitford sisters' activities were more than just quirks, but were surprising nonetheless. One, Jessica, was a Marxist, as her memoir *Hons and Rebels* recalls; another, Diana, married the Fascist Sir Oswald Mosely and was all but in love with Hitler.

Nancy Mitford's remarkable achievement as a belletriste was to avoid coming down on one side or the other, at least on paper. Her novels present families with intricate histories similar to her own, with youthful English girls at sea in Paris. These comedies of manners look at the English upper class (she would never call it British, nor the Scottish "Scots") with an uncritical eye; her narratives would sooner laugh with her characters than at them.

She comes closer to expressing personal opinions in her most frequently consulted work, *Noblesse Oblige: An Enquiry into the Identifiable Characteristics of the English Aristocracy*, a collection of essays by a number of hands which takes its lead from a lecture on linguistics defining the differences between non-upper-class and upper-class speech. In her work popularising this method of class distinction (which she denies has anything to do with wealth or education), she reveals that her concerns hinge on niceties more than politics. Although she is a keen observer of social change, she perceives it so much in particulars that her tone can become camp. This can turn into self-parody; while she avoided expressing her own feelings, stifling her own cries with a pillow even during a painful death from Hodgkin's Disease, she left as faithful an account of the declining aristocracy as we are likely to have.

Molière

JEAN BAPTISTE POQUELIN

born Paris 1622; died Paris 1673

Madam, it is such a great honour for me to have the fortune to be so glad about being so happy that you might have the goodness to accord me the grace of doing me the honour of honouring me with the pleasure of your presence; and if I have deserved to deserve such deserts as yours, and the sky... envying my well-being... would have accorded... the good luck of rendering me worthy... of...

THE BOURGEOIS GENTLEMAN

FEW PLAYWRIGHTS have been more attuned to the needs of an actor and the requirements of staging than Molière. He was set to follow his father into the textile business, but joined a theatre company when he was 21. He trained in the tradition of the Italian *Commedia dell'Arte* – that is, he learned to improvise set scenes in one of the genre's characters. His role was Sganarelle, the two-faced, embittered steward and this was how he first appeared at Court, following a performance of **Corneille**.

He was soon to become the main attraction of his troupe and he wrote prolifically in his early years. In keeping with this "type"-based theatre, he would build plays around characters who displayed a specific weakness and portray their flawed interactions with the rest of the world. The heroes of Molière's plays are often deluded and accomplish little; rather, they become the butt of everyone else's jokes. The exercise is not merely humorous: in their monomania, people can cause others real pain without realising it, such as the *Misanthrope*; or else they can command our pity, like the *Bourgeois Gentleman*, whose naïve insistence on social rules enables everyone to make him behave according to new ones they've just invented.

His last play presents a character whose weakness was craving that weakness: it is a fitting epitaph that Molière died after a coughing fit that began while he was on stage in the title role of *The Hypochondriac*. Legend has it that as he tried to stifle the cough with mock hilarity he so delighted his audience that he had to beg them to stop laughing at him!

Montaigne

MICHEL DE   born Château Montaigne, Périgord 1533; died there 1592

That day is the master, that day is the judge of all others: it is the day, says an ancient (Seneca), that must judge all my years past. I leave it to death to essay the fruits of my studies. Then we shall see if my discourses come from my mouth, or from my heart.

WE MUST NOT JUDGE OUR TIME EXCEPT
AFTER DEATH

MONTAIGNE INVENTED the essay. It was a form he could adapt to his qualities: he had a mind that was curious, liberal and encyclopedic. This meant he would base his enquiries on his vast range of reading – sometimes endorsing the views he cited to the point of assimilating them – as often as he would his own personal experience. His interest in the latter make his essays read like explorations of his own character, but he never allows his readers to think they are getting to know him too well. He is fond of introducing a passage with the words "I have seen...", or of sounding subjective – "I'm not what you'd call a naturalist but" – before expounding well-rehearsed opinions on human nature.

The joy of Montaigne lies in the way he organises these works. His essays went through four different editions, each acquiring new essays, with none appearing in the order in which he wrote them. This leads commentators to look in vain for the shifts in his thinking. He is capable of contradicting himself from one essay to another, one moment praising the simple life, the next promoting scholarship.

Montaigne shopped around the various schools of classical philosophy, finding **Lucretius** as apt for his own brand of humanism as was Cicero for his more authoritarian stances. In life, he combined both attributes, campaigning in pamphlets and parliament for religious tolerance and serving two terms as Mayor of Bordeaux.

Whether his insights derive from public duties, private friendships (notably his devoted attachment to the younger, less talented writer La Boëtie), or the seclusion of his own vast library in a secluded castle, he expresses them in a French whose elegance owes as much to Latinate grace as to his own measured humanism – for he was a true child of the Renaissance.

Moravia

ALBERTO

born Rome 1907; died Rome 1990

I answer frankly: 'I want you to stop mixing up literature and life. Maybe you're thinking that I go for little girls because I like a poem where a woman has sex with a little girl. But you're wrong, I like the poem, not little girls.'

THE VOYEUR, TR. TIM PARKS

ALBERTO MORAVIA COMBINED a modernist readiness to experiment and surprise with a romantic mission. His books can take on existential angst (especially in his many adolescent characters), can be sexually explicit or just plain ribald and ultimately contemplate nuclear Armageddon. If people are saved from these terrors, it is through the mysteries of a personal relationship rather than simpler creature comforts or fleeting sexual congress. The latter has its consolations, but they are mostly negative ones: someone having sex with a person is seen to have a kind of implicit sympathy with everyone else who has had sex withthe same person.

His early works appeared in Mussolini's Italy. He did everything he could to rile the regime and still get into print. This included the use of pseudonyms: his real name was Alberto Pincherle. His first novel was wilfully out of tune with Fascist aesthetic dictates and those that followed used allegory to lampoon *Il Duce*. Once Mussolini realised that a series of manic authoritarian leaders were thinly disguised versions of himself, he insisted on censoring Moravia's work personally. Until the end of the war, the author had to live in hiding in the Italian hills or America.

In peacetime, his earlier disdain for middle-class apathy and concern for working-class dignity gave his work a specifically Marxist agenda. He continued to champion humanity and spiritual love over materialism and sex, encapsulating both in *The Woman of Rome*, about a prostitute who finds salvation in her suffering.

Sense continues to struggle with spirit in *The Voyeur*, a dialogue between the hero and his penis. It is in a late work that we find the real and the imaginary at their most confused: *1934* offers a nexus of confused identities and faked suicides between Italian and German characters: did the hero fall in love with twins? Their roles are implicitly political: to the end, Moravia's allegory, complex plots and the thirst for love remained as sure as ever.

Musil

ROBERT

born Klagenfurt 1880; died Geneva 1942

For the awakening boy's first passion is not love for the one, but hatred for all. The feeling of not being understood and of not understanding the world is no mere accompaniment of first passion, but its sole non-accidental cause. And the passion itself is a panic-stricken flight in which being together with the other means only a doubled solitude.

YOUNG TÖRLESS, TR. WILKINS AND KAISER

ROBERT MUSIL WROTE *The Man Without Qualities*, the unfinished, multi-volumed novel that has been called the Austrian masterpiece.

It is the culmination of a lifetime's work on the problems of morality and the apparent inconsequence of a person's actions. As he does throughout his work, he raises the question, how do we know things exist? Here the decaying Austro-Hungarian Empire of before the First World War is made real enough for the reader, but not for the hero Ulrich, who seems detached from it. His bid to find a purpose in life within a year cannot be confined by conventional morals: in his search for the perfect balance of erotic and selfless love (the theme of the earlier *Three Women*), he opts for his twin sister, and when he wonders if killing can ever be justified, his working model is a psychopath.

The novel's incomplete state means these issues are never resolved, but as elsewhere in Musil's work, the inner, emotional life takes precedence over the outer world of action. In this he resembles **Proust**: what plots his short stories have are often recurring ones and his analysis of developing feelings maintains a drama of its own. He owes this to expressionism as much as to the philosophical rigours he had pursued in his academic life.

His youthful story *Young Törless* shows this. It is more than a story about brutal retribution at a military school (one attended both by Musil and **Rilke**) and more than an account of a youth's character-building. The work reads as a psychological sketchbook, with a different mental state on each page, often without incident to prompt it. Such clashes always dominated Musil's thinking and twice led to breakdown.

Musset

ALFRED DE

born Paris 1810; died Paris 1857

Thank God that authors now have

different ways,

And we prefer the drama that's the craze

Where intrigue, wrapped up in a pretty

roll,

Turns like a rebus round a rigmarole.

A WASTED EVENING

ALFRED DE MUSSET gave the French the line in which many find an encapsulation of the national temperament: "My glass is little, but I drink from mine." As well as describing the French sense of balance and perspective, it expresses Musset's image as a poet. He uses it to justify his restricted subject matter – mostly the pleasures and pains of love.

It is very much his own glass. What bitterness is in it, he shares with the world. His one gift, he says, is to have cried. His most famous poem, *May Night*, takes the Christian image of what Richard Crashaw calls, "the soft, self-wounding pelican" and reworks it in aesthetic terms: the poet, implicitly Christ-like, lacerates himself for those around him.

Much of this public unhappiness stemmed from his on-off romance with **George Sand**. His fondness for women and wine drove him to despair a situation exacerbated by Sand falling in love with Musset's doctor. Yet for all the sensual and lofty lamentations the poet offers us, he remains as self-contained as his glass. He knew himself too well to keep up such a pitch of pathos. In *Tales of Italy and Spain*, a work that brought him fame at the age of 20, he was already mocking the circle of romantics who

had encouraged him (especially **Hugo**). He was as well-known for his writerly comedies as for his verse, most notably the cautionary *Don't Mess With Love*. He also shared his insights by dramatising well-known proverbs. This unwillingness to be original, together with a certain triteness and reckless versification, earned him the scorn of **Baudelaire** and **Rimbaud**. Had he lived long enough to have heard such criticism, one imagines he would have been ready for it.

Nabokov

VLADIMIR   born St. Petersburg 1899; died Montreux, Switzerland 1977

I am trying to describe these things not to relive them in my present boundless misery, but to sort out the portion of hell and the portion of heaven in that strange, awful, maddening world – nymphet love.

LOLITA

NABOKOV'S WRITING contains unashamed displays of style and sophistication. He was a scholar, of lepidoptery as much as literature, and his knowledge of the latter spanned many languages. His brand of wit enabled him to play with words' meanings in varied tongues, and to mock the fussiness of Europeans as well as the bewildered response they elicit in his adopted America.

His life took him through a range of cultures. He was born into a privileged Russian family and was forced to flee his homeland during the Revolution. He studied at Cambridge, before living in Berlin and Paris, ultimately settling in the United States as an academic. By then he had written a number of novels in Russian, introducing the brilliant but deluded characters who would descend into madness (such as the chess genius in *The Luzhin Defence*, or the schizophrenic murderer, fraudster and would-be writer of *Despair*) and anticipate later creations in the English books, most strikingly Humbert Humbert in Nabokov's *succès de scandale*, *Lolita*.

This account of a European scholar's passion for a 12-year old girl appears as a confessional memoir written in prison – its introduction, signed by a fictional psychiatrist to lend the narrative authenticity, must have surprised those who encountered the book in its first, pulp pornography incarnation. Nabokov's use of frame devices had already adorned *The Real Life of Sebastian Knight*, in which a man writes a biography of someone who turns out not to be his brother. It reached extreme proportions in *Pale Fire*, a novel in a commentary on a poem by an author who proves impossible to trace.

Nabokov's translation of **Pushkin**'s *Eugene Onegin* also ballooned into proportions that dwarf the text under examination. For him, scholarship and flights of creativity were joyously entangled.

Naipaul

V.S.   **born Trinidad 1932**

So step by step, book by book, though seeking each time only to write another book, I eased myself into knowledge. To write was to learn. Beginning a book, I always felt I was in possession of all the facts about myself; at the end I was always surprised.

FINDING THE CENTRE

V.S. NAIPAUL WAS BORN into Trinidad's East Indian community. His novels and travel books use a journalist's instincts to describe the lives and aspirations of people struggling to survive in the world's poorest areas. His enquiries have taken him to India, Africa and through a range of Islamic countries.

But he begins at home, wondering even if he can call it that. His first four books are novels set in Trinidad. *Miguel Street* presents the buoyant characters of his youth, as well as describing the education that distanced him from his homeland: Naipaul left Trinidad for good, to study in London. *A House for Mr Biswas* tells of a man's dream of possessing his own piece of land, with a house. His ambitions are limited and regularly thwarted and his literary goals don't go far beyond scoop reporting.

It was the start of Naipaul's career in showing the developing world as one he wished could develop faster. His view of India shows this. His experiences of the country were not what he expected (he claimed only to know it from the community around him in the West Indies and the works of R.K. Narayan) and he witnessed its least democratic days since Independence – Indira Gandhi's State of Emergency in 1975. He blamed the poverty and chaos on entrenched attitudes and a refusal to break from tradition. He brought the same criticisms to his study of Islam world-wide, *Among the Believers*. This brought further controversy around him: Edward Said accused him of generalisation and of finding only what he expected to find – ultimately of being too pro-West.

These charges were not new to him and his world view has never been optimistic. But his impatience with people's inability to change is balanced by a faith in individuals, treating them with dignity and humanity through the most extreme struggles.

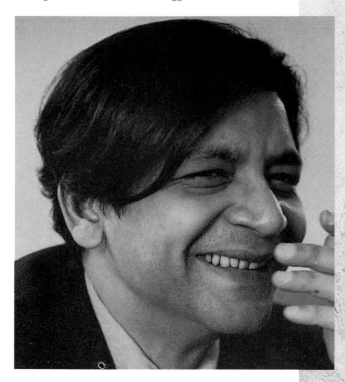

Narayan

R.K.

"What is the meaning of Tim?" asked Gupta irrelevantly.

"Deity in our village temple," replied Nagaraj on an inspiration.

"What God is that?" asked Gupta with curiosity. Nagaraj gave some answer describing the image as possessing four arms and three eyes.

THE WORLD OF NAGARAJ

India will go on

REMARK TO V.S. NAIPAUL, QUOTED IN
INDIA: A WOUNDED CIVILISATION

R.K. NARAYAN'S long storytelling career has charted the vast transformations India has undergone this century. His first novels appeared under the Raj and have covered shifts in thinking and society through to today.

But national trends never dominate. Rather, he portrays them in the more intimate setting of Malgudi, a small town in Mysore (now Karnataka). There, change is a family affair: different attitudes are evident in different generations, with younger characters more willing to embrace the West. Narayan's narrative leaves no-one free from his undermining irony, although he is gentle enough to treat most of his characters with tenderness. In *The Guide*, an amiable con-man attains status as a guru, talking us through all levels of Indian society without taking the holiest of cows too seriously. A more honest protagonist is *The Painter of Signs*, who falls in love with a woman popularising family planning during the 70s. Although this meeting of an accepting man and a progressive woman seems to encapsulate India in transition, it is a love story and the novelist keeps it personal.

Narayan writes in English and is as at home with **Shakespeare** and the Bible as he is with the Indian myths. Still, he has written re-tellings of the *Mahabharata* and the *Ramayana*. He avoids taking either side too dogmatically and is able to satirise the Anglophile lecturers of *The English Teacher* as well as anti-British fanaticism. In the short story *Lawley Road* a crowd bays for the removal of an Englishman's statue only to discover that he was more benefactor than brute. As one of India's finest writers, Narayan combines a love of his country with a reluctance to mysticise it out of existence.

Nash

OGDEN   **born Rye, New York State 1902; died Baltimore 1971**

Croesus was turned to gold by Minos,

And Thomas À Kempis was Thomas

    Aquinas.

Two Irish Saints were Patti and Micah,

The Light Brigade rode at Balalaika,

If you seek a roué to irk your aunt,

    Kubla-Kahn but Immanuel Kant.

WHO DID WHICH? OR WHO INDEED?

OGDEN NASH'S ASTONISHING vocabulary and pertinent humour was a regular feature of the *New Yorker* magazine, of which he was editor. He gave the world a unique brand of nonsense verse. Like that of **Lewis Carroll** and **Edward Lear**, it owed much to the verse of his time. But where other parodists could be biting, Nash could really gnash. Terrible puns were key to his technique, redeemed chiefly by the amazing words he invented expressly to play on them. His lengthy, often deliberately non-metrical lines use form and content to wonder what poetry is in any case. *The Strange Case of Mr Fortague's Disappointment* takes **Yeats**' sublime *The Lake Isle of Innisfree* to make its dreamy yearning sound impractical and ridiculous.

His targets could be easier. He had writers of well-meaning doggerel clearly in his sights. *First Child ... Second Child* dashes a bubbly apostrophe of a new-born babe to the ground with the response to a second: "Is it a boy, or quite the reverse?/You can call in the morning and ask the nurse." Sometimes the nonsense can seem like pure sound effects, as if

to parody other studiedly noisy poets such as Vachall Lindsey or Edith Sitwell, but often Nash's purpose is higher. *In The Private Dining Room* four lines about two genteel women become garbled beyond sense until we realise that Miss Rafferty and Miss Cavendish are becoming as drunk as the verse. If this is art for art's sake, he could also be satirically relevant, writing during the Cuban Missile Crisis: "Maybe I couldn't be dafter./But I keep wondering if this time we couldn't settle our differences before a war instead of after."

MAJOR WORKS

Free Wheeling (1931)

Hard Lines (1931)

I'm a Stranger Here Myself (1938)

Parents Keep Out: Elderly Poems for Youngerly Readers (1951)

The Private Dining Room (1953)

You Can't Get There from Here (1957)

Boy is a Boy (1960)

Novalis

born Wiederstadt 1772; died Weissenfels 1801

Already the vibrancy

flickers through us, the mystery

of an echo in the sky,

resonating in the gulf.

Those we miss are signalling

with their breath; it's time to go.

HYMNS TO THE NIGHT, VI,
TR. JEREMY REED

NOVALIS WAS THE ADOPTED name of the German poet Friedrich von Hardenberg. He was writing in the purest vein of European poetry. He had the same preoccupation with light as did **Goethe** and **Dante**. For him too it had a divine source: like the former, he could approach light with a scientific interest, and like the latter, it was something to be attained through love.

In fact, Novalis' progress towards the light had a beginning similar to Dante's. He too fell in love with a young girl, in this case a 13-year-old, Sophie von Kühn, who was 10 years his junior. The couple became engaged, but she died two years later, in 1797. The story is told in Penelope Fitzgerald's novel, *The Blue Flower*. Novalis' craving for the light, while still rooted in Christianity (he had written hymns for church use), then took an alternative form of expression. He wanted to die and looked to death as his salvation. Five years later his prayers were answered when he died of tuberculosis. He felt death's presence most strongly at night, which he came to see as a seductive, mysterious entity.

Novalis rhapsodises night in six hymns, mixing prose-poems with verse. He vividly describes the colours he discerns in darkness, and addresses night with the imagination, the inner vision, in which he had such a firm romantic faith. His regard is Platonic: he presents himself as having existed before night, but able to recognise inner truths as signified by the outer signs night provides. He expounded these ideas in essays, published beside those by Schlegel, and in unfinished novels: it is in his poetry that he expresses it most purely.

Oates

JOYCE CAROL

born Millersport, New York State 1938

He said aloud, staring at his reflection in the bathroom mirror, the ruddy skin, the quizzical eyes, turning his head from side to side, slowly, pondering, admiring, 'This is the way it was meant to be.'

'SURF CITY', IN RAVEN'S WING

JOYCE CAROL OATES IS an incredibly prolific novelist, as well as the author of poems, plays and short stories. The speed at which her work appears has led critics to assume there must be more faults to find than actually exist. But Oates has mastered a large range of techniques, maintaining great diversity, even within the same genre, and brings this variety to bear upon the contemporary American situation.

There she finds much violent crime and domestic brutality. Often this has a family setting, as in the book that secured her reputation, *them*, which centres on the inhabitants of Detroit's rougher areas over three generations. Although the work's realism highlights modern problems, elsewhere the causes are shown to have deeper roots. In a series of Gothic-style novels – *Bellefleur*, *A Bloodsmoor Romance* and *The Mysteries of Winterthurn* – she uses a more traditional form to renew discussion of timeless issues, such as good and evil.

Another family chronicle, *You Must Remember This*, takes pains to recreate the atmosphere in 50s America, invoking nostalgia in order to shock with an unsentimental view of post-war society.

Her gifts of characterisation take her as deep into the male psyche as into the female. She has made an intimate study of boxing, which she can present as a codified, disciplined manifestation of force far removed from crimes outside the ring. Boxers reappear throughout her stories, as do other masculine characters whose conventional interests emerge without narrative comment. In fact, Oates is so adept at darting in and out of her creations' thoughts and feelings that we can begin to forget that we are in the hands of a detached, third-person storyteller.

O'Casey

SEAN

born Dublin 1884; died Torquay, Devon 1964

It's me's the sorry soul for listening to you. You promised a quiet hour of poetry, but we were hardly here when you began to move. Yeats's poems soon flew out of your head and hand. You got as far as 'I will arise and go now, and go to Innisfree'; then before the echo of the line was hushed, you had me clapped down on your knee.

BEDTIME STORY

SEAN O'CASEY BELONGS to a tradition of Irish writers and artists who felt misunderstood in their own country. Like **Wilde**, he moved to England, embracing not so much his adopted home as his status as an exile – he declined a CBE. Like J.M. Synge's work some 15 years before, his plays were capable of causing riots in Dublin and **W.B. Yeats** vigorously defended both to the crowds.

But Yeats was also to feud with O'Casey when he rejected *The Silver Tassie* at the Abbey Theatre in Dublin because it departed from the realism of earlier plays. Although the two men were later reconciled, this dispute, and his love for the London-based actress Eileen Carey, kept O'Casey out of Ireland permanently. In the end, he discouraged performance of his plays there.

What disturbed his audiences were his open Marxism, attacks on the clergy and particularly the appearance of an Irish Tricolour in an on-stage pub scene. These issues called his patriotism into question, but for all his pacifism, he played his own part in the Irish Revolution. His plays are strong on dialect and his spelling reflects pronunciation more than orthography. He writes dialogue with great musicality, with characters building up patterns of rhetoric and echoes between one another; this dignifies O'Casey's world of suffering workers and strong women. If he tends to idolise the latter, he still has much fun at the expense of repressed men and their panic-stricken sexuality.

O'Hara

FRANK

born Baltimore 1926; died New York 1966

an invitation to lunch

HOW DO YOU LIKE THAT?

when I only have 16 cents and 2

packages of yogurt

there's a lesson in that, isn't there

like in Chinese poetry when a leaf falls?

hold off on the yogurt till the very

last, when everything may improve

FROM FIVE POEMS, IN LUNCH POEMS

FRANK O'HARA WROTE many of his poems during his lunch breaks, while working as an assistant curator at the Museum of Modern Art in New York. His descriptions of street scenes fix on the ephemeral, block by block, as he walks to and from his midday meal. In these contexts, he can divulge his thoughts. Although these seldom lie far beneath the level of stimulus response, sometimes the fugitive nature of that response works its own poetry.

His most famous poem is an exception that demonstrates this. It is *The Day Lady Died*, with the poem dithering over a literary present and pausing at a tobacconist's: his poem commemorates where he was when he discovered Billie Holiday had died. He concludes "…and I stopped breathing".

This kind of cadence leaps out of his work. Other epiphanies glint more briefly from the same laid-back verse style. When the sun wakes him up in the morning, it is for a chat about poetry – nothing heavy. O'Hara's description of the technique is best: a poem called *Poetry* begins, "The only way to be

quiet/is to be quick, so I scare/you clumsily, or surprise/you with a stab." He could write at length, as in his pamphlet-sized opus *Second Avenue*, and in a number of plays he wrote for Off-Off Broadway; but his pieces tend to be short. Whether his lines are luxuriant or staccato, crammed with metaphor or just taking in the scene, his tone is always talky, even when he's hectoring.

Ever the art critic, the poet relied on his eye as much as his ear and must account for it in *Why I Am Not a Painter*. His eyes are at their widest when he's at the cinema: like his own poetry, it has an immediate effect, but repays frequent revisits.

'Omar Khayyám

born Nishapur c. 1048; died Nishapur c. 1122

You rising Moon that looks for us again –
How oft hereafter will she wax and
wane;
How oft hereafter rising look for us
Through this same Garden – and for
one in vain!

THE RUBÁIYÁT OF 'OMAR KHAYYÁM, TR
EDWARD FITZGERALD

'OMAR KHAYYÁM WAS a Persian astronomer, mathematician and poet, who was summoned to Court in 1074, where he helped enquire into time-keeping. He also published works on algebra, but is best known in the West for his *Rubáiyát*.

This is the collective name for the distinctive form of quatrain called the *rubái*, imitated in the famous translation of Edward Fitzgerald. It is through this version that the work attributed to 'Omar Khayyám is best known (much of the work's authorship has been disputed). The translator admitted to taking liberties with the original and later attempts strove to capture a grittier quality in the original where Fitzgerald favours lyricism. Still, Fitzgerald's offering is still treasured as a miraculous achievement of what Salman Rushdie has called in his novel *Shame*, whose hero is named after the poet, "carrying across".

The original poet drew on the mystical Sufi traditions flourishing around his native Nishapur and shares their theme of intoxication. But whereas in Sufism this invokes heady spirituality, for 'Omar Khayyám, wine is a defence against the brevity of life and the austerity of religion. The poet asks why God has allowed the vine to exist, if it is so forbidden. Drink becomes a metaphor for the human condition. In one sequence, jugs in a shed talk to one another, wondering why they have been made in so many different ways. God is cast as the potter, Time as a crusher of grapes, people as vessels and the wine-cup as bearing the soul.

Throughout, the poetry perfectly evokes the evanescence of life. Even the stanza form suggests it: one rhyme will always slip away uncapped. In expressing an Eastern mistrust of reality, such verse advocates wine "to drug the memory" while facing a future in which the only certainty is death.

O'Neill

EUGENE

born New York 1888; died Boston 1953

The makings of a poet. No, I'm afraid I'm like the guy who is always panhandling for a smoke... I couldn't touch what I tried to tell you just now. I just stammered. That's the best I'll ever do. I mean, if I live. Well, it will be faithful to realism, at least. Stammering is the native eloquence of us fog people.

LONG DAY'S JOURNEY
INTO NIGHT

EUGENE O'NEILL IS the first great name in American theatre. His interest in the stage must have been fired in boyhood – his father was an actor – but survived his professions as sailor and journalist, just as he survived tuberculosis. He pored over plays on his sick bed and when he recovered joined a theatre workshop in Harvard. He began as he would end (in *Long Day's Journey Into Night*), with writing strongly reflective of his own experience, especially of his family, and his early plays recall his times at sea.

His early work absorbed many of the current European trends in drama. Many of his pieces would draw on symbolism or expressionism to make his points, which were often profoundly psychological. His plays were regularly on Broadway, although he refused to allow any of his work to be performed between 1934 and 1946. He was awarded the Pulitzer Prize four times, the last time posthumously, and won the Nobel Prize for Literature in 1936.

His writing shows breathtaking ambition. His dramas are reliably lengthy and make enormous demands of the performers, almost to the point of stifling interpretation. Still, there are very different ways of staging O'Neill: directors can treat him with **Shakespeare**an reverence, or else be less daunted by his rhetoric, which can provide some magnificent speeches poeticising a heart-felt, Freudian view of human relationships. His trilogy *Mourning Becomes Electra* does this with **Aeschylus'** *Oresteia*, dispensing with deities and a chorus to give a more realistic view of guilt. It is set in the American South immediately after the Civil War.

Orwell

GEORGE

born Montihari, Bengal 1903; died London 1950

In the public wards of a hospital you see horrors that you don't seem to meet with among people who manage to die in their own homes, as though certain diseases only attacked people at the lower income levels.

HOW THE POOR DIE

GEORGE ORWELL DECLARED that he wrote every word toward the establishment of democratic socialism.

He won a scholarship to Eton, where the difference between his background and those of his fee-paying classmates provided him with an early understanding of social disparities. When he left, he saw the situation in a starker, more global light: he joined the Imperial Police Force in Burma, taught English in France, experienced great poverty there and in England, and encountered politics more formal than guilt alone could have given him when fighting with the Republicans in the Spanish Civil War. From these experiences came the memoirs *Down and Out in Paris and London*, chronicling his struggle to survive down to the last centimes, and *Homage to Catalonia*, which contains glimpses of the widely divergent factions of left-wing thought and action, through which he tried to find his own personal vision.

Further evils abroad made this harder still. The threat of Fascism convinced him that Britain could only confront it by reforming itself totally and Stalinism drove him to explore what form socialism could take without the threat of totalitarianism. To this end he wrote his two most famous books, *Animal Farm* and *Nineteen Eighty-Four*.

The former is an allegory of the Russian Revolution and its failures in the most pathetic and human terms (all the more so because its characters are animals), while the latter shows a society in which the state's power extends to its subjects' innermost thoughts. Orwell's examination of those thoughts as they range from defiance to submission show him to be a writer of great psychological subtlety, able to demonstrate the motivations behind apparently evil acts as much as instinctively human ones. With Newspeak, a jargon-ridden tongue that rehashes ideas into pellet-like form for the "proles" to swallow, he exposes power's abuse of language. His own plain English did much to counter it.

Ossian

Perhaps thou art like me, at times strong, feeble at times; our years descending from the sky, and hastening together towards their end. Rejoice, O sun! as thou advancest in the vigour of thy youth.

OSSIAN'S ADDRESS TO THE RISING SUN

A poet, in his closet, could no more compose like Ossian, than he could act like him in the field or in the mountain.

HUGH AND JOHN MCCALLUM, IN THEIR 1816 EDITION OF OSSIAN'S POEMS

OISIN IS THE GAELIC name for this bard and warrior from the Highlands, who might have lived in the second or third century AD. In 1760, James Macpherson claimed to have recorded poems often about him and usually attributed to him and produced a modest sample of Gaelic to lend his translation authority. **Dr Johnson** expressed doubts as to the work's authenticity in his *Journey to the Western Isles of Scotland* and Macpherson proved unable to procure the sources of his *Fragments of Ancient Poetry Collected in the Highlands of Scotland, and Translated from the Gaelic or Erse Language*. After his death, an enquiry decided Macpherson had found ancient poems, but extemporised so freely on their themes that it was almost a different work.

The English could now dismiss these productions as forgeries, comforted that the Scots had no **Homer** after all. But by 1816, the Highland Society had collected enough material to publish *Ossian's Poems*. The editors' ability to cite their originals and their damning ripostes to Johnson make the neglect of this volume bizarre. Much of it is fragmentary, with less of the plot Macpherson tried to impose, and perhaps transcribed from what the remaining clan-like bards could recite.

What England could ignore now had Europe aflame. Ossian had captured the romantic spirit. **Goethe** and Napoleon were enchanted. Earthier epic had emerged to rival Homer and the refined **Virgil**. The high-pitched rhetoric, the epithets and translationese of the work delivered just what readers wanted. The neat match of supply and demand still seems to many more than a coincidence, but the similarity between the Scottish and Greek oral traditions provides a revealing study of how stories get told, in whatever culture.

Ovid

born Sulmo, the Abruzzi 43 BC; died Tomis, on the Black Sea c.17 AD

We, yield, and take this passion with a fight?

We yield: a burden gladly borne is light.

LOVES

OVID WROTE THAT to produce good poetry, you need "ars" and "ingenium" — knack and luck. Ovid's poetry is so clever and sharp that it seems all artistry. Even in exile by the Black Sea, he never sounds like the tortured genius we meet in **Propertius** – which is not to deny that he was genuinely miserable. For Ovid, everything looks too easy: in the very first lines of his corpus, he demonstrates how Cupid rigged his metre, and then makes it his own. He wrote elegy according to stricter rules than anyone had attempted before and yet made it more immediate: his jokes are still funny and quite rude.

But he was a unique figure, not happy simply to perfect the work of others. He was the author of some completely original poems. Other poets had written wondering why women spent so long on their make-up: it took Ovid to begin it as a treatise in mock-epic language. Even in jest, he wants to enlighten as well as enliven. When guiding the reader through the mysteries of love, he is a more hands-on instructor than other elegists, especially in *The Art of Love*. He suggests you take your date to the circus, where sand gets in awkward places, and obliges you to brush it off.

Other poems aim to provide less erotic information. His work on Roman feast days provides the most complete view we have of contemporary religion, and intrigued the anthropologist James Fraser. Ovid's masterpiece, *Metamorphoses*, is more ambitious still. It is an encyclopedic presentation of myths in which people turn into things. The subject matter is no limit to his imagination and his only attempt at epic shows him varying his material with the same consummate balance of his love poems, introducing contrasting episodes and pacing their narration with a care that never seems precious. As ever, it is as though the theme found him, rather than the other way round – he had as much luck as knack after all.

Owen

WILFRED **born Oswestry 1893; died on the Western Front, France 1918**

...Behold,

A ram, caught in a thicket by its horns;

Offer the Ram of Pride instead of him.

But the old man would not so, but slew

his son –

And half the seed of Europe, one by one.

THE PARABLE OF THE OLD MEN
AND THE YOUNG

MAJOR WORKS

Poems, edited by Siegfried Sassoon (1920)

"MY SUBJECT IS War, and the pity of War", wrote Wilfred Owen, and except for a few early poems, it was to be his only subject. These first works show a young teacher in France trying out new metres and rhyme-schemes in verses showing facility, but which read as exercises. This is partly because his experiments with poetry were daring enough to need some practice. His style and themes at the time showed his deep love of **Keats**. It was not the language of horror.

He joined the army in 1915. Although less seduced by events than Rupert Brooke, he began the war in a similar spirit, feeling something like heroism. Throughout the hostilities, he showed immense courage and was awarded the Military Cross. But in 1917 his nerves failed and he was sent to recover at Craiglockhart psychiatric hospital.

There he met Siegfried Sassoon, a poet and soldier who was by then actively campaigning against the war. Owen showed him his poems in all humility and received some encouragement. The technical effects he had nearly mastered before the war had now become a successful way of imitating the sheer noise of the trenches and his sudden changes of pace within potentially static sonnets and quatrains could suggest life-or-death panics. He wrote, "I don't want to write anything to which a soldier would say No Compris!" From Sassoon, he learned to adopt a more direct, speech-like voice. Sassoon sometimes used this for brusque and brutal satire, while in Owen's hands this conversational approach let him animate a ghost-world: in *Strange Meeting*, the chilling exchange takes place between dead soldiers.

Here characters reflect on what might have been, if it hadn't been for the war. We know Owen could be given to happiness, but that he would never be able to forget this pity. Today, poets are still indebted to his innovations in rhyme, but we cannot know what he might have done. He was killed one week before the war ended.

Parker

DOROTHY   born West End, New York State 1893; died New York 1967

DOROTHY   born West End, New York State 1893; died New York 1967

Razors pain you;

Rivers are damp;

Acids stain you;

And drugs cause cramp.

Guns aren't lawful;

Nooses give;

Gas smells awful;

You might as well live.

RÉSUMÉ

DOROTHY PARKER IS remembered for her wit. Wit can be put to any number of uses – for her, it was peculiarly functional. She was a member of a circle (a Round Table, in fact, which would convene sporadically at the Algonquin Hotel in New York) whose members made a living from their wits. The cheques for Parker's came first from *Vogue*, then from *Vanity Fair*, where, often under the pseudonym of Constant Reader, she became renowned for her damning reviews of plays and books – **Sinclair Lewis**, in particular, came in for brutal drubbings.

But money was not the only object. She had to survive mentally as well. She was the only woman of this circle (**Edna Ferber** would pop in, but even she was too gushy for Parker) and was often stigmatised for wanting to be a man. She later confessed that if the age had demanded cuteness, she would have been cute. But she was the harshest of them all. It is hard to smile at a Parker quip without simultaneously pitying its victim.

Ultimately Parker has a strong claim on our sympathies. Even in her comic verse (which she refused to call poems), she addresses the issue of suicide and the fallibility of relationships. The latter theme came to characterise her short stories. If the public manifestation of failed romances and a disturbed childhood was well-worded impatience, their private expressions were worse amorous entanglements, alcoholism, drug abuse and several suicide attempts. She survived these, too, but remained constantly aware that some things are not proper subjects for humour.

Pasternak

BORIS

born Moscow 1890; died Peredelkino 1960

He both feared and loved that future and was secretly proud of it, and, as though for the last time, as if saying goodbye, was avidly aware of the trees and clouds and of the people walking in the streets of the great Russian city struggling through misfortune – and he was ready to sacrifice himself to make things better but was powerless to do anything.

DOCTOR ZHIVAGO,
TR. MAX HAYWARD AND MANYA HARAI

BORIS PASTERNAK LOVED his country. He was a poet sensitive enough to understand at once its need for change and the suffering much of that change inflicted. From World War One onwards, he was in trouble with the authorities and unable to publish anything for 10 years. When the Stalin era ended, the "thaw" under Khrushchev, which benefitted so many other writers, did nothing for Pasternak. It was then that he wrote his masterpiece, *Doctor Zhivago*. He had worked on it since 1946 and it appeared in print 11 years later in Italy. The book was banned in the Soviet Union and the author's rulers forbade him to accept the Nobel Prize it was awarded.

He had not meant to criticise the regime. He had welcomed the Bolshevik Revolution with modernist poems written in the same vein as his friend **Mayakovsky**, but his sensitivity to the more perennial truths he divined in nature dominated subsequent work. His apparent disregard for historical movements attracted the authorities' attention, particularly with the line, "What century is it out there?" in *About These Poems*.

The poet-hero Doctor Zhivago cannot remain so indifferent. By then Pasternak had suffered his own griefs in the Soviet Union and no longer felt able to address human concerns: his mistress had been sent to a labour camp. His prose shows a lyric poet's leaning toward short episodes, contrasting voices and word music. The hero's own poems are appended to the text, showing the author's continued faith in Christian imagery and complete identification with his central character.

Pavese

CESARE

born San Stefano Belbo 1908; died Turin 1950

I could understand if they talked about brushes, colours, turpentine – the things they use – but no, these people talk obscurely because they like to and sometimes no-one knows what certain words mean and there's always somebody else who suddenly begins to argue, says no, that it means such and such and everything's upside down. They are words like those in the newspapers when they talk about paintings.

AMONG WOMEN ONLY

CESARE PAVESE WAS A POET and novelist who brought to Italian letters a passion for American and English writers, as well as an interest in modernism. His writing is in some ways exemplary of the realism prevalent in the Italy of his day, but there is the strong influence of **Joyce** and **Melville** – Pavese translated *Moby-Dick* into Italian in 1932.

His own prose is more accessible than that of his masters. He avoids rhetorical flourishes, but the construction of scenes and chapters show him to be a natural poet. *Among Women Only* has a narrator who tunes in and out of the socialite babble of surrounding Turin. The whole effect shows Pavese's ear for cadence (the book's last line is stunning), while only a few of his characters are of any consequence to the story.

This quest for a meaning in life occupies characters elsewhere in his work. They typically seek it in their history or sexuality. Failure in the search can bring out their suicidal tendencies, or extreme violence. For all the realism of a work like his last, *The Moon and the Bonfires*, the farmer who murders his incestuous lover does so after so little provocation that his motives can barely exist outside him.

Pavese seems to have shared this extreme form of loneliness. Like several of his characters, facing the choice of accepting life or refusing to take part in it, he chose death. After producing a flurry of instantly-acclaimed work and prizes, he committed suicide.

Paz

OCTAVIO

born Mexico City 1914

Between what I see and what I say,

between what I say and what

* I keep silent,*

between what I keep silent and what

* I dream,*

between what I dream and what

* I forget, poetry.*

SHEAF, TR. ELIOT WEINBERGER

OCTAVIO PAZ IS the leading poet working in Spanish today. His public life has extended well beyond poetry – he has worked as a diplomat and teacher – but his commitment to poetry is particularly single-minded. He has always avoided dogmatism: when **Neruda** made it possible for him to witness the Spanish Civil War, the left-leaning Paz found much the same mess of political objectives that **Orwell** encountered and he was not completely convinced by the Republican cause. Still more upsetting for many on the left was his insistence on speaking up about the atrocities of Stalin and the Soviet labour camps. His continued refusal to represent beliefs that are not his own culminated in his resignation in 1968 from the post of Mexican ambassador to India, when his government's troops fired on student demonstrators during the Olympic Games.

His poetry is avowedly free of political creeds and celebrates the purity of the form. "Every poem is time, and burns," he has written; his lines show care over each syllable that composes them. His haiku prove this most succinctly: "The whole world fits in-/to seventeen syllables,/and you in this hut." His verse, meanwhile, found a kind of freedom through the surrealism of **Breton**, but his sensitivity to his language's unique way of evoking the erotic properties of sun and landscape fills *Sun Stone*.

His memories of that sun and of Mexico illumine his subsequent work. His poetry from India notes a similar dryness: in fact, the poems in *East Slope* balance reflections on the gardens of Delhi with recollections of his own country in a time of trouble. The result is an insight into the poet's sense of isolation: "The writer should be a sniper, he should endure solitude, he should know himself to be a marginal being."

Peake

MERVYN   **born Kuling, Kiangsi Province, China 1911; died Burcot, Oxon 1968**

'What have you brought with you?' she said. Mr Pye turned his gaze upon her. 'Love,' he said. 'Just... Love...' and then he transferred the fruit-drop from one cheek to the other with a flick of his experienced tongue.

MR PYE

MERVYN PEAKE WAS a writer of alarming imaginative powers. He was as much a visual artist as a verbal one and would draw his characters before describing them. He illustrated his own books, such as *Mr Pye*, his volumes of verse and he provided images for other texts. **C.S. Lewis** praised those that accompany *The Rime of the Ancient Mariner* for their rendering of terror in purely formal designs and his pictures for *Bleak House* are stunning.

The atmosphere and characterisation (including the names) in the *Gormenghast Trilogy* show the continuing importance of **Dickens** to Peake. He has the same propensity for bursting into blank verse (at which he excelled) and while Gormenghast seems like a fantastical creation, its absurdities are grounded in a Dickensian kind of realism. There events advance slowly, with a formal precision. In this dilapidated family seat, everything happens strictly according to order and precedent long-established: Titus Groan is the 77th Earl. The pile itself is skirted by slums: so apparently remote and changeless a world is vulnerable to the charismatic boy-rebel Steerpike, who provides a peerlessly plotted portrait of moral collapse as he menaces the place with destruction.

Peake worked on the book during World War Two while recovering from the nervous breakdown he suffered in 1943. He remained active in wartime as an artist and was one of the first to witness the death camps at Belsen. What he depicted there moved him to extraordinary poetry, which strove to express the horror of trying to represent a consumptive woman there: "If such can be a painter's ecstasy... Then where is mercy?" His words and lines always contrived to make his bleak vision real, but at the last he concluded, "To live at all is miracle enough", and left it as his epitaph.

Perec

GEORGES

born Paris 1936; died Paris 1982

Let us imagine... a man of exceptional arrogance who wishes to fix, to describe, and to exhaust not the whole world... but a constituted fragment of the world: in the face of the inextricable incoherence of things, he will set out to execute a (necessarily limited) programme right the way through, in all its irreducible, intact entirety.

LIFE: A USER'S MANUAL, TR. DAVID BELLOS

PEREC WROTE a 300-page novel without the letter "e"; a shorter book (*Les Revenentes*) without "a", "i", "o", or "u"; a palindrome 500 words long; an inventory of everything he ate in 1974; works in autobiography with deliberately misremembered facts; symmetrical texts which negate themselves; and the unbelievable *Life: A User's Manual*.

These might seem like arid exercises with no point and no soul, but work so moving can never be pointless. Even his driest lists can be dreamy or hilarious, poems even, full of soul. His first book, *Things*, presents a young couple in the 1960s who want material proof that they've "arrived", attain it, but start craving "things" simply for their own sake. Their lives become "frankly insipid". Other Perec characters can anticipate this realisation; in *Life: A User's Manual*, they dedicate themselves to projects they often know will come to nothing. Even the "e-less" *A Void* shows a world in which first a vowel vanishes,

then the hero Anton Vowl, then anyone who looks for him. And the Paris block housing the apartments of *Life...* will hardly survive its inhabitants.

This can reflect the author's tragedy. His father died in battle, moments before Paris fell in 1940, while his mother "disappeared" at Auschwitz. Much of Perec's writing points towards guilt and loss. But what he has achieved in *Life...* , in glimpses of often empty flats at a moment fixed in time, where artefacts occasion stories leading to other stories, with jokes, teasers, tearful histories, parodies, hidden quotes, all fitting – jigsaw-like – into a purposely-flawed system, is the most perfect, most joyous account of the novel, and of life, imaginable.

Perelman

S.J.   **born New York 1904; died New York 1979**

*There aren't any humorists any more,
except for Perelman... Perelman must be
very lonely.*

DOROTHY PARKER

*Love flies out the door when money
comes innuendo.*

MONKEY BUSINESS

WHEN GROUCHO MARX said, "From the moment I picked up your book to the moment I laid it down, I was convulsed with laughter. Some day I intend reading it," he was talking about S.J. Perelman's first collection of sketches. This was meant to commend the book rather than condemn it, and appeared as blurb. Still, Perelman felt that he was remembered only as the co-writer of the Marx Brothers' films *Monkey Business* and *Horse Feathers*. In turn, Groucho felt Perelman's brand of joke could be too literary to reach a wider audience.

Perelman worked as a cartoonist and sketch-writer, appearing regularly in *The New Yorker*. There he pioneered his parodic and punning prose: the most regular butt of his wit was himself. These pieces are considered to be his best writing. He had a technique that seemed impromptu, similar to the best Marx Brothers moments, when sheer pace let his verbal schtick lead to more without us having to spot the connections. But this gift did not transfer well to the stage: however fine the lines were, they did not cohere as whole shows. As with his film work, he wrote for the theatre collaboratively, both with his wife, (the sister of **Nathanael West**), and with **Ogden Nash**. His pace dialogue, balanced by Nash's comic verse skills, went into the musical *One Touch of Venus*, with a score by Kurt Weill.

His acute eye for the absurd focussed on his compatriots, though few could take offence: if he was describing human folly, he involved himself in it fully. Still, few of his fellow fools had so reliable a knack with language.

Petrarch

FRANCESCO

born Arezzo 1304; died Arquà 1374

And cowarde Love, then, to the hart apace

Taketh his flight, wher he doth lurke

   and playne

His purpose lost, and dare not

   shew his face.

For my lordes gilt thus fawtles

   byde I payine;

Yet from my lorde shall not my

   foote remove:

Sweete is the death that taketh end by love.

RIME 140, TR HENRY HOWARD,
THE EARL OF SURREY

PETRARCH'S GREAT LEARNING and poetic skill anticipated the literary concerns of the Renaissance and contributed enormously to the later interest in expressing classical themes in new, lyrical forms. His scholarship began with legal studies and then a training for the priesthood, although he never took full orders. He distinguished himself at the court of Robert of Naples, whose clothes he wore when becoming poet laureate at Rome in 1341 and through whom he became a friend of **Boccaccio**.

It was Petrarch who advised Boccaccio not to renounce his life's work and become a priest; yet the poet's own work displays qualms about the same issues. He repudiated his famous lyric poetry later in life and would have preferred recognition of his contemplative Latin writings, most notably the *Secretum Meum*, an imaginary conversation with St Augustine on this dilemma.

Although his poetry is remarkably pure, celebrating his unrequited love for a married woman many think to be Laure (Laura) de Noves, it has the same paradoxical spirit. His theme of freedom in servitude is as classical as it is Christian; his imagery and rhetoric are straight from the Roman erotic elegists (he owned a now-famous manuscript of **Propertius**) and echoes **Catullus**'s sentiment, 'I love, I hate – perhaps you wonder why…' He refined his expression of these ideas in sonnets and provided the model of that verse form. His methods of listing symptoms or states of mind throughout a poem, to subvert them at the end and of using 14 lines to explore an image only to point out how ill it fits his own case, established a genre that dominated the Renaissance and that **Shakespeare** later perfected, in adapted form, in English.

MAJOR WORKS

IN ITALIAN
Canzoniere

Triumphs

IN LATIN
On Famous Men

Africa

On the Solitary Life

On Religious Study

Bucolics

Letters

My Secret

Against a Certain Doctor

Petronius

Roman, 1st Century AD

The Satyricon, including
Trimalchio's Feast

'And no-one taught him. I refined him
myself by sending him to the tramps. So
he has no equal in imitating muleteers or
tramps. He's madly clever: he's as much a
cobbler, cook and fisherman as property
of all the muses. He has two weaknesses,
without which he'd be all there: he's
circumcised and snores. As for his
squiffey eyes, incurable: that's how Venus
sees.'

TRIMALCHIO'S FEAST

PETRONIUS MAY HAVE been the "Judge of Taste" in Nero's court – a stoic whose suicide was made famous in the film *Quo Vadis?* – or he may have been someone else who just happened to be called Judge (*Arbiter*). The work attributed to him is an equally unknown quantity. Only fragments survive of what might have been a long work called the *Satyricon*. The name derives from satyrs – half-men and half-goats, whose lewdness would round off the Dionysian play festivals (see **Harrison**), but might be punning on the Latin *satura*, meaning a ragout or hotchpotch. The work is just that, incorporating snatches of verse and parodies of epic in slangy and immediate Latin prose. It is appropriate that the surviving excerpt gives an account of a lavish feast, with delicacies from all over the world served in relentless mixtures by Trimalchio, a loud-mouthed host eager to display his wealth. Even faced with this plenitude, his guests don't mind talking exhaustively about other meals they've eaten recently and telling stories that spin off from those.

We see it all from the point of view of two slaves who have gate-crashed. They are on the run and the banquet is just one adventure on the way. There is much satire: Petronius shares **Juvenal**'s target of the *gauche parvenu* and makes fun of Trimalchio's much-vaunted love of his slaves. The slaves themselves are silent witnesses to the extravagance around them, but do not emerge sympathetically from other fragments. In showing us the extremes of Roman decadence (especially if he was writing during Nero's reign), Petronius leaves us to contemplate a society in which these abundant depravities are even imaginable, let alone likely. Fellini's film embraces this chaos and takes it further still.

Pinter

HAROLD

born London 1930

In Düsseldorf about two years ago I took, as is the Continental custom, a bow with the German cast of The Caretaker at the end of the play on the first night… we took 34 curtain calls, all to boos. By the 34th there were only two people left in the house, still booing. I was strangely warmed by all this, and now, whenever I sense a tremor of the old apprehension or expectation, I remember Düsseldorf, and am cured.

WRITING FOR THE THEATRE

IT WOULD BE EASY to call Harold Pinter's plays experimental – his method of composition involves putting characters in a room and seeing what happens – but through all his innovation, he seems to know exactly what he's doing. From the age of 20, he acted in many plays and occasionally performs in his own; his stagecraft is matched by an ear honed by writing a lot of poetry, only a little of which he has published.

His subject matter and language is prosaic, but as his characters interact, they attain the rhythms of verse. They play with words and transform their registers: in Pinter "succulent" can become taboo, or "Sidcup" talismanic. In *The Birthday Party* two men in suits who come from nowhere harass a jobbing pianist as much with clichés as with violence. We don't always discover why characters find certain phrases so threatening, but during a good performance, we come to share their sense of dread. The relationships that form between them can be more convincing than those in plays with fuller plots.

Pinter avoids writing plays with a moral purpose, although human dignity emerges as a major concern. He campaigns for human rights and has written a play for Amnesty International, *Mountain Language*. He keeps his own passions for offstage, including his love of cricket and dislike of America.

Pirandello

LUIGI   **born Agrigento, Sicily 1867; died Rome 1936**

I persist in giving audience every Sunday morning to the characters of my future short stories.

Three hours, from seven to 10.

I almost always find myself in bad company.

A CHARACTER'S TRAGEDY,
TR. STANLEY APPLEBAUM

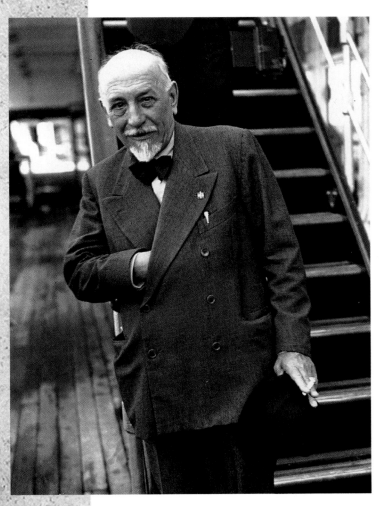

PIRANDELLO TRANSFORMED theatre to express an extraordinary state of mind: the feeling that we are not in control of our actions. In his work, this is not so much because we are puppets of fate or the gods; we just feel like puppets. There is no philosophical accounting for this sensation. Its roots lie in rootlessness, or an inner madness.

Pirandello knew about both of these first-hand, from his efforts to raise a family in his native Sicily. His wife became dangerously insane, accusing him of sleeping with their daughter; when she was institutionalised, he felt free but homeless. He began reworking his stories into what became his 40 or so plays. The most famous of these shows a family incapable of acting out its own story. That the memories of their tragedy are too painful is not their only problem. *Six Characters in Search of an Author* is a play within a play, whose actors protest that they aren't proper actors; if anything, they are ghosts of an author's ideas, much like **Ibsen**'s ghosts. The two plays are comparable as landmarks in the development of drama.

The idea that the self is a composite of how we interact with others, rather than something fixed within us like a personality, continues in Pirandello's most admired play, *Henry IV*, which takes the idea into the realms of madness. This kind of expression eventually brought him into conflict with the Fascist regime with which he had previously enjoyed good relations: he wanted social change and Mussolini wanted progressive art. His country was naturally proud of his Nobel Prize in 1934, but by then he no longer wished to be buried in Italian soil. He wanted to be cremated, and his ashes scattered to the air around his childhood home.

Plath

SYLVIA   **born Boston, Massachusetts 1932; died London 1963**

Love set you going like a fat gold watch.

The midwife slapped your footsoles, and

   your cry

Took its place among the elements.

MORNING SONG

SYLVIA PLATH'S SUICIDE cut short a career that produced forceful and immediate poetry. Much of it is hard to read without thinking of her early death, but this tends to obscure the range of her work, which can be ecstatic as well as bleak. Throughout her life she suffered from manic depression, which may account for the violent swings in mood. Towards the end she was writing at speed – sometimes up to two or three poems a day – a rate that would seem to indicate extreme emotional activity. This contrasts with her earlier output, which she wrote methodically, often with a thesaurus, and includes sonnets and several villanelles, a form requiring the discipline that served her well.

This part of her poetic training was complemented by classes with **Robert Lowell**, whose confessional style suited Plath's mode of self-expression. But both before and after, Plath's emotional pitch remained high and her themes constant. In early work she used classical myths to explore herself – Persephone's dual personality reflects her own experience – and later poems are just as subjective. They dwell increasingly on the clinical institutions she had come to know through mental illness and childbirth: her short, sparing lines and quickly captured images convey a terrifying cleanliness, sterility even.

Her only novel, *The Bell Jar*, explores this sense autobiographically, telling of her education both in the US and at Cambridge, and ultimately of her breakdowns and an early attempt at suicide. It examines the protagonist's youth in well-to-do America, and expresses anger at the strictures and the demands made of women. These do not disappear in England, although she is happier there for a time. Plath settled in London and married Ted Hughes. She was becoming increasingly established as a leading poet, especially through radio broadcasts, when she took her own life. Posthumous publications of her work have confirmed this reputation, won by the vivid representation of otherwise unimaginable terror in verse that seldom loses control.

Plato

born Athens c. 429 BC; died Athens c. 347 BC

But my point is that what they call love isn't love of a half, or of a whole, my friend, so much as of whatever strikes them as being good, since men really want to cut off their own feet and hands if they reckon there's disease in them. You see, I don't think people embrace what is theirs, unless one can call something that seems good one's own, and something bad someone else's.

DIOTIMA, IN THE SYMPOSIUM

PLATO WROTE the finest prose in Greek. All the peculiarities of the language serve his turn, down to the tiny words that can spring a sentence's rhythm or swing an argument completely.

But he preferred interaction and speech to writing, which he felt could not stand up for itself. This is why his writing is so conversational. His dialogues present his teacher Socrates hailing people in the street and teasing out of them definitions of words he would query through compelling dialectic. To some, such as **Aristophanes**, this seemed like sophistry. Plato defended Socrates' reputation, losing his faith in a political system that sentenced his hero to death.

Plato's ideal state would have been ruled by philosophers; but even the severe constitution he proposes emerges from another attempt to define one word: justice. The whole *Republic* aims to show it in action. Other works follow such enquiries to less definite conclusions and a discourse leads typically to a state of *aporia*, or cluelessness. This might seem like a sophist's technique; but in Plato's thinking, we cannot understand real truths with language, or the senses. They existed before we were born and await our contemplation when we die.

Plato is his own best critic, even of this most dearly cherished belief: his dialogue *The Sophist* attacks it directly. Throughout his career, he recreated this *aporia*. The most sublime single example of this is *The Symposium*, in which party guests try to describe Eros. Even when Socrates argues that the exercise is misguided and convinces us with another view, his drunken admirer Alcibiades crashes in to subvert the whole process. Elusive as ever, Plato never tells us what love really is. But then, whoever did?

Plautus

born Sarsina, Umbria c. 250 BC; died Rome 184 BC

From what I hear this writing to be
*   saying,*

unless it makes you cry out silver coins,

you'll no more get the thing you want
*   with tears*

than you could catch a rainfall in a sieve.

I won't leave you, now you're in love;
*   don't worry.*

PSEUDOLUS

PLAUTUS DID MORE than anyone to bring comic drama to Rome. Of some 130 plays, 20 survive complete. These are usually taken from earlier Greek sources, which he acknowledges, without indicating how much he has adapted or simply lifted from his originals. These originals were most notably Menander and Diphilus, who represented the "new" Athenian comedy, as opposed to the older style of **Aristophanes**. It was from there that Plautus drew the character types that were to dominate the theatre for centuries afterwards: the braggart soldier, the love-sick youth (a figure who influenced lyric poetry as much as drama) and the slave who knows more than his employers about life and the plot.

Plautus' achievement was to translate these tales for an audience he knew well. The presentation was always in Greek dress, but the language was distinctly Latin. Not only did this accommodate more word-play; it also allowed fun at the expense of Greek names, which could become ludicrously long. He was a practical man of the theatre and only took to writing after spells as a stage-hand and actor. He learned how to take a Greek scene as a starting point for his own comic invention, or dispense with the original plots according to his own dramatic requirements. His scenes advance in pace verse styles and songs can break up the action. His own plays have become the model for later dramatists, especially **Molière** and **Shakespeare**: the latter turns the plot of *The Brothers*, with its two sets of identical twins, into *A Comedy of Errors*. Three Plautus plays were conflated to produce the musical *A Funny Thing Happened on the Way to the Forum*.

Po

LI   **born Szechuan Province, now China 701; died 762**

Her robe is a cloud, her face a flower;

Her balcony, glimmering with the bright

  spring dew,

Is either the tip of the earth's Jade

  mountain

Or a moon-edged roof of paradise.

A SONG OF PURE HAPPINESS,
TR. WITTER BYNNER

IN THE WEST, Li Po is known through **Ezra Pound**'s inventive but gorgeous versions (Pound gives his name in Japanese, as Rihaku); through Mahler's settings of German translations in *The Song of the Earth*; through the punning name of the Paris-based literary workshop OuLiPo (see **Queneau**); and, more in his proper context, through the work of the orientalist Arthur Waley (*The Poetry and Career of Li Po*, 1958).

In China he is better known as the reckless, drunken counterpart to the language's other best-loved poet, Tu Fu. While Tu Fu shows restraint and observes the constraints Chinese tones impose on its poetry, Li Po is more spontaneous and famed for producing eloquent formal verse for the emperor at a moment's notice and in an alcoholic stupor. Legends about him abound, as if they are measures of his popularity: he is said to have died either drunk in a boat, trying to grasp the moon's reflection, or else by being carried to heaven on the back of a dolphin. The idea that he was divine and immortal was one that Li Po was only too pleased to confirm.

He grew up in exile, in what is now Sinkiang province (then outside the empire). As a young man, he travelled around performing good deeds. In his dealings with the establishment, he showed scant regard for Confucian precepts, as did his early poetry, whose promise led the authorities to indulge him, without ever giving him any official position. In *The Bridge at Ten-Shin* he casts a dispassionate eye over court jostling. His skills won him a pleasant enough existence – he had four wives. His work celebrates wine and women in song, while in his treatment of youth and beauty, death is ever absent: even in his cups, he was contemplating the moon.

Poe

EDGAR ALLEN

born Boston, Mass. 1809; died Maryland 1849

---

*We stand upon the brink of a precipice.
We peer into the abyss. We grow sick
and dizzy. Our first impulse is to
shrink from the danger, and yet,
unaccountably, we remain.*

THE IMP OF THE PERVERSE

POE WROTE OF POETRY'S PURITY in his criticism, while writing theatre reviews that would shift copies for their ruthlessness. He began his literary career with verse that would charm readers with its musicality, and became famous for later stories of imponderable bleakness.

In his short, turbulent life, he had known such bleakness. He was orphaned at the age of three. He gambled as a student, and was expelled from military academy; he became an alcoholic, and was regularly fired from periodicals. When he was 24, he secretly married a 13-year-old girl, who died when she was 25. He died in circumstances that have never been explained, his memory was vilified by his agent and friend, and true details of a life-story he had largely invented for himself were long in emerging.

In his fiction, he would explore apparently motiveless crimes, with the recurring theme of entombment. The horror is intensified by Poe's presentation of apparently sane people, who chronicle their own mania coolly, until the hypersensitivity induced by intolerable guilt takes over. But this is not the usual structure of cause and effect; it is as though crimes are waiting to happen. In his criticism, Poe would explore how elements in a story should contribute equally to one another, rather than that one should be of primary significance, to create a unified work of art. It is the same with the coherent sound-world his poems summon; he would consciously produce work that could be read whole in one sitting.

He can obsess readers, while some English-speaking critics have shrugged him off. His influence on the literature of other languages has been colossal: **Baudelaire** produced definitive French translations, **Mallarmé** would emulate his awareness of the inexpressible in decadent themes, and **Dostoyevsky** acknowledged his own debt to Poe.

Pope

ALEXANDER

born London 1688; died London 1744

The vulgar thus through imitation err;

As oft the learn'd by being singular;

So much they scorn the crowd, that if the throng

By chance go right, they purposely go wrong.

AN ESSAY ON CRITICISM

AS A CATHOLIC, Pope could not receive a school education, hold a public office, or even live in London for part of his childhood. Physically, he was a peculiar figure in an awkward age, but his poetry had a robustness that the age demanded. When his critics became personal about his faith or frailty, he trounced them in *The Dunciad*, a lengthy skit that he updated as his rivals varied.

The best introduction to Pope is his *Essay on Criticism*, more for its technique than its precepts. He writes in rhyming, "heroic" couplets and shares with us the dos and don'ts of composing them. He not only parodies bad poetry, but shows the reader how to achieve the best effects – as if his imitators could produce lines as harmonious.

He used the form to translate **Homer**, as **Dryden** had done with **Virgil**: his *Iliad* and *Odyssey* did as much for English verse as his original works. One commentator remarked of his efforts, "It is a pretty poem, Mr. Pope, but it is not Homer…" For all Pope's luxuriance, his version, where every line has a strong finish and repeated phrases echo for longer with the rhymes, comes as close to Homer's tone as English has yet managed.

This work was crucial to his own poetry. He was the master of an epic style he could now parody better than his rivals and he used it in his most polished poem, *The Rape of the Lock*. Figures that in Homer would have been agents of the gods are now skulking in boudoirs, waiting for some heroic action to sway: but the stakes are no higher than a lock of hair (although this reaches the heavens) and the work's climactic event is a sneeze.

Pound

EZRA   **born Hailey, Idaho 1885; died Venice 1972**

There is no end of things in the heart.

I call in the boy,

Have him sit on his knees here

   To seal this,

And send it a thousand miles, thinking.

EXILE'S LETTER

IT IS TOO EASY to pass over Ezra Pound's poetry. To open *The Cantos* is to confront a text decorated by Chinese ideographs, Greek script and transcriptions of French or German texts, sitting beside banking letters from Renaissance Italy. The work of his beneficiaries is less intimidating: He encouraged writers as diverse as **Robert Frost**, **T.S. Eliot**, **H D** and **Ford Madox Ford**. Even **W.B. Yeats** was indebted to him. He could recognise others' talents and weaknesses without imposing his own artistic agendas. His extensive and often unacknowledged advice on *The Waste Land* shows Pound's expert ear for the types of verse Eliot could and couldn't write.

He was more dominant in organising the Imagist group of poets and persuading a large number of authors to share his faith in poems with an oriental economy, presenting images rather then expounding ideas. Again, all of these poets pursued their own artistic goals afterwards, but were nonetheless involved in his prophetic vision of literature, which he described as "news that stays news".

His own work followed this vision further than his contemporaries. His poetry is always at least one step ahead of cultural developments, seeking to rebuild what he calls in *Hugh Selwyn Mauberley* "a botched civilisation", most doggedly in *The Cantos*. This huge assembly of verse attempts to tell "the tale of the tribe" from *The Odyssey* onwards. His idiosyncratic understanding of history nearly cost him his life, when his anti-semitic, pro-Mussolini broadcasts brought him accusations of treason from the advancing Americans during the war. He was not executed; instead he spent a third of his working life in a mental institution. He recanted his Fascistic rantings, but not the questionable Cantos, which he claimed were misunderstood: he continued revising his masterpiece until the end. For the richer passages, Hugh Kenner has credited Pound with an ear to rival **Shakespeare**'s in *Twelfth Night*.

MAJOR WORKS

A lume spento (1908)

The Spirit of Romance (1910)

Ripostes (1912)

Cathay (1915)

Homage to Sextus Propertius (1917)

Hugh Selwyn Mauberly (1920)

The Cantos (1925, 1928, 1930, 1934, 1937, 1940)

The ABC of Reading (1934)

Make It New (1934)

Guide to Kulchur (1938)

Patria Mia (1950)

The Classic Anthology Defined by Confucius (1954)

Powell

ANTHONY

born London 1905

'*Seeing the world broadens the outlook. You can learn a lot abroad. They're a funny lot, foreigners. I always go abroad for my holidays. I like it over there.*'

VENUSBERG

ANTHONY POWELL IS AN English novelist best known for the 12 novels which make up the series called *A Dance to the Music of Time*. The title comes from a painting by Poussin, and refers to the unpredictable rhythms of life. The source of these rhythms becomes less identifiable the more characters crowd the drama and interact, and ultimately it is time itself which determines the action.

There is a Powell-like novelist figure throughout the work, called Nicholas Jenkins. His story spans from his childhood before the War to his situation in the early 1970s. This is the period of Powell's own development, from his school-days at Eton, his time as a student at Oxford, through his service in the Second World War (in the Intelligence Corps) to his life among fellow aesthetes. The lushness of the books' language, and their focus on the plights of the privileged, make it seem like the product of a **Proust**ian age rather than British post-war austerity, particularly with its introspection. But it follows the social fragmentation of the times, and responds to the age's new-found pragmatism with the manipulative new man, Kenneth Widmerpool. He makes the narrator long for a lost age with the wistfulness of **Evelyn Waugh**'s *Brideshead Revisited*.

Like Evelyn Waugh, Powell began his career with satirical novels, and retains the humour throughout his *magnum opus*. Readers have tried to find the identities of his friends depicted within, and have found clues in Powell's similarly cyclical memoirs beguiling, as if the fictionalised account is more informative than what passes for autobiography.

Priestley

J.B.   **born Bradford 1894; died Alveston, Warwickshire 1984**

We can find many excuses, however, for those foreign visitors, and especially the Frenchmen, who have come so quickly to the conclusion that we are forever morose and melancholy. England is the land of privacy, and therefore, the stranger who comes here is at a disadvantage. He sees the high walls, but not the gardens they enclose.

ENGLISH HUMOUR

J.B. PRIESTLEY WAS an extremely prolific writer, whose work is imbued at once with a love of England and a strong social commitment. This meant, as Winston Churchill said, that the government found him useful in World War Two (he had fought in the Great War), but his social criticism was always able to rile the establishment. Between the wars he wrote long and gritty novels. The first of these, *The Good Companions*, drew on his theatrical experience, which was also invaluable for the lucrative playwriting career he pursued later.

In his plays he displayed the journalist's instinct for what people wanted, but remained faithful to his own purpose. *An Inspector Calls* combines the metaphysical elements of his earlier pieces (he was interested in the tricks time can play on the mind) with the slippery detective story, to take a direct aim at his audience's conscience. *Three Men in New Suits* address the vexed issue of rebuilding the country after the war and was written for the 1951 Festival of Britain.

In his essays and memoirs, he displays himself as a dour Yorkshireman, full of good advice and canniness. He once said a writer should be a rebel, not a revolutionary. He was certainly a gadfly, but also a connoisseur of traditional Englishness. He declined a knighthood but accepted the Order of Merit, with its less imperial connotations.

Pritchett

V.S.

born Ipswich 1900; died London 1997

Human beings are simply archaic, ivy-covered ruins, preserved by the connoisseur, and they stand out oddly in the new world of the masses.

THE FUTURE OF FICTION

SIR VICTOR PRITCHETT — known familiarly as VSP — was primarily a story-teller who became as highly regarded for his criticism. He would never over-complicate or intellectualise writing, relying instead on wide reading and breadth of vision; he never regretted not attending university, while finding books and life vital to each other: "books have always seemed to me a form of life, and not a distraction from it."

He was born in a toy shop in Ipswich, gaining from his father an insight into personalities that can become unhinged by minutiae, and from his mother an ear for the way natural speech can carry narrative. These combined to make his short stories have something of the air of **Dickens**; for Pritchett, the oddities of speech could convey a whole world lying hidden behind them.

He considered his novels less successful. They often draw on his travels. He left his family for Paris when he was 20, and travelled as a journalist to Ireland and Spain. His natural gift for languages (he was fluent in French, German and Spanish) gave him a feel for cultural differences, which his fiction would explore. His more home-grown products would focus on undistinguished but quietly extraordinary figures. He would write by pretending to be them, seeking to "unself" himself.

In his critical writing, he discusses his influences, and his preferences reveal much about his own literary ambitions. He wrote biographies of **Balzac** and **Chekhov**, and has drawn comparisons with the latter. In turn he has influenced younger writers, including **Raymond Carver.** He lectured in American and British universities, which came to honour him; students and readers have cherished him for his great humanity untrammelled by any kind of dogma or nonsense.

Propertius

SEXTUS | **born Assisi c. 48 BC; died Rome shortly after 16 BC**

Let well-read girls praise me because I
please,
and tolerate their frequent raileries;
henceforth let the neglected lover read me,
and my known problems help him should
he need me.

ELEGIES, I. 7.

NO POET HAS SUFFERED as much from misprints as Propertius. Early scholars tried correcting what they thought to be mistakes, to be corrected in turn by later scholars… now there is confusion about whether he wrote four books of verse or five, even about where one poem ends and another begins.

He wrote Latin elegy. Propertius was its first real master, bringing to his verse form such conventional discussions of love as a state of servitude, or a state of warfare. He describes the rapture of first love, the sadism of sustained love and the pain of parting: ultimately not even death separates the poet from his beloved Cynthia. After Propertius, the language of elegy froze. This has led scholars who have asked what he actually wrote to assume he is more boring than he is.

In fact, his treatment of his themes and sources is strikingly individual. His most important influence is **Callimachus**, whom most of his earlier commentators cannot have read. His later work is often dated by how much of **Horace**'s poetry he appears to have absorbed: Horace had no time for him, although they both had the same patron (Maecenas), as did **Virgil**. Propertius provides a link between Horace and **Ovid**, an obvious admirer, but Propertius' handling of elegiac couplets is more flexible and his material more prone to a lover's waywardness.

He introduced to Latin verse questions such as "Is poetry the proper activity for a young man?" and "Does it impress girls?" He is unembarrassed by his immense knowledge of mythology, which he parades when looking for a conceit or when explaining how a town acquired its name. But even then, he shows heroes at their frailest, as when he describes Hercules confessing that he dressed as a slave-girl ("a gentle girdle bound my shaggy chest") before being turned away from a women-only drinking fountain.

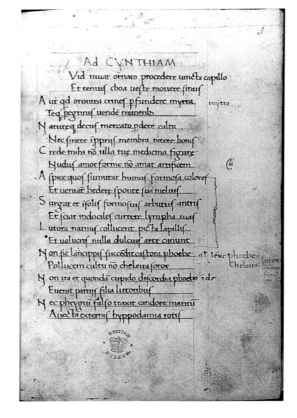

Proulx

E. ANNIE

born Vermont 1935

MAJOR WORKS

Heart Songs and Other Stories (1988)

Postcards (1991)

The Shipping News (1993)

Accordion Crimes (1996)

Dear Sirs: I recently saw your advertisement in The Globe and Mail for a research assistant. Although I do not speak Japanese I am willing to learn...

Dear Sirs: I recently saw your advertisement in The Globe and Mail for a position in brokerage operations. Although my training is in marine traffic control I am willing to learn...

THE SHIPPING NEWS

E ANNIE PROULX'S WRITING embraces the sense of alienation central to her view of America, which she perceives beneath a façade of instant remedies. But rather than leave her characters stranded in the urban soullessness of, say, **Saul Bellow**'s world, she lets them explore their loneliness in matching terrain. Her first novel, *Postcards*, introduces Lloyd Blood, whose feelings of guilt force him to live as a wanderer. It shares with her earlier stories an emphasis on the need to survive – a theme dear to the heart of the American novel with its frequent evocation of the pioneering spirit.

The book that secured Proulx's international reputation takes an isolated soul back to his roots beyond the United States, to Newfoundland. The achievement of *The Shipping News* is in its painstaking account of life there, recording its dialects and remoteness with such faith and warmth that it makes those who have never visited the area want to, and those who have want to return. It describes small communities whose over-fishing has created aching unemployment and that try patiently to adopt new industries. But at heart the story is a personal one, telling of an individual's battles with the elements and ultimately his search for love.

She had already been hailed as the author of something like the Great American Novel before the publication of *Accordion Crimes*, which seems a more direct attempt at it. Generations of immigrant life are made real to us through the presence of a green accordion, which changes hands many times throughout the book: its varying strains summon traditions and memories of the cultures that have formed the United States, recalling and reviving the nation's claim to be built as One from Many.

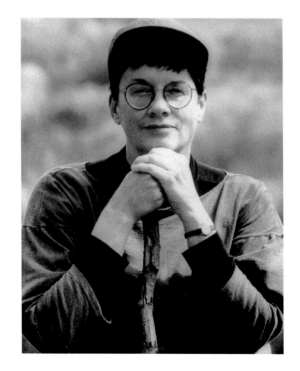

Proust

MARCEL

born Auteuil 1871; died Paris 1922

Moreover, pained to reflect, at the moment [the phrase of Vintueil's sonata] passed at once so near and so linked to the infinite, that as long as it was directed at them, it did not know them, he almost regretted that it had any meaning, any fixed and intrinsic beauty, foreign to them, as in jewels that are gifts, or even in letters written by a beloved woman, where we find the water of the gem, or the words of language, wanting, because they are not formed uniquely by the essence of a fleeting liaison and a particular being.

SWANN'S WAY

MARCEL PROUST IS A colossal figure in literature, remembered as the author of the mighty, multi-volumed work, *In Search of Lost Time*. He wrote it in bed, in a pollen-proof room, over the last 10 years of his life.

It is a testament both to the times and to the individual genius. Proust spent his youth in Paris during the early Third Republic, and so moved in circles more concerned with aesthetics than anything else. The account he gives of his impressions of the world shows a profound subjectivity displaying his deep admiration of figures such as John Ruskin.

While his prose examines these sensibilities in his unique style (for Proust style bore the stamp of personality and so was everything to a work of art), it analyses sensations such as love and loneliness as though they were scientific phenomena, striving to find objective ways of describing them.

This is what makes the project an attempt at the complete novel, a book that might somehow account for the whole of a life's experience. It seeks its wholeness by trying to chart inner realities rather than external ones, and attempts this through memory. The narrator's inability to remember and recapture everything right up until the work's end begins to explain the work's shape. Sections the length of whole novels can appear only as digressions within still larger enquiries; but themes and characters recur and develop in ways that reveal an almost perfectly constructed piece of art.

Pushkin

ALEKSANDER

born Moscow 1799; died St. Petersburg 1837

*Love passed, the Muse appeared, the
  weather*

of mind got clarity new-found;

now free, I once more weave together

emotion, thought, and magic sound...

EUGENE ONEGIN, TR. JOHNSTON

BEFORE PUSHKIN, Russians considered French a better language than their own for their literature: what writing there was in Russian was earnest and worthy. Pushkin read European literature widely – he was especially fond of **Byron** and in fact had Byron's range. He made a more liberated treatment of almost every genre possible in Russian, making even tragedy and heroic epic less daunting to his audiences.

In his masterpiece, the verse novel *Eugene Onegin*, he lets all his talents loose at once. He displays his gift for love lyric, with insights culled from strings of his own romances, as well as the descriptive powers of his folk poetry. He adds to this a dramatist's ear for speech, especially pace dialogue, and a novelist's sensitivity to a character's inner feelings, when novel-writing was still a relatively new craft. It is at this form that he excels. Critics since (notably Bakhtin) have marvelled at the way the poet is present at every stage of the story, sounding like his characters or having his characters sound like him. They must all talk in a strict but addictive sonnet form: this never stifles Pushkin's vitality. He is constantly commenting on his own technique and his knack for parody leaves us wondering how seriously we should be taking even his most moving passages.

But *Onegin* is more than just an entertainment. The hero has a kind of world-weariness that was the poet's own. Pushkin had been exiled for his friendships with revolutionaries and finished up writing under the patronage and surveillance of Tsar Nicholas I. The death of the posturing bard Lensky in the poem prefigures his own death: he was shot in a duel that may have been orchestrated by the authorities. **Lermontov** was exiled for writing a poem publicising this theory.

Pynchon

THOMAS

born Glen Cove, New York State 1937

If they can get you asking the wrong questions, they don't have to worry about the answers.

PROVERBS FOR PARANOIDS,
GRAVITY'S RAINBOW

THOMAS PYNCHON is a famously reclusive writer. His novels appear after varying periods of total silence. In the absence of biographical information about him, readers have scoured his texts for personal references.

There seem to be so many clues. The work is so hugely inventive that any character's name could be concealing something: Oedipa Maas, Dr. Hilarius, Isaiah Two Four (named by hippies after Biblical chapter and verse) and Genghis Cohen might be leading anywhere. Such figures can appear anywhere in Pynchon's multi-layered narratives, and disappear without warning. They are experts on the minutiae of life, often at the expense of a bigger picture. An ability to date any film exactly, or to discuss anything from plastics to plastering, can lead to a jumbled world-view, abounding with international conspiracies. The result is a modern mythology: in a book like *Gravity's Rainbow* (his most famous work, which scandalised the Pulitzer Prize committee), this can include the ever-lasting light bulb, the Schwarzkommando (a crack troop of African Nazis), and a hero whose penis can predict air-raids.

The style devours all other styles, and has become distinctively Pynchon's own. Fairy-tales, songs, science fiction, hysterical rants and all-too-plausible bands or B-movies pile into narratives that have abandoned any traditional ideas of structure. If he inherited this freedom from the Beats, he owes an unstoppable sense of adventure to John Buchan, with whom he shares an addiction to chase sequences. The element of political thriller introduces forces of darkness sometimes absurd enough to make the characters susceptible to them seem merely paranoid; but Pynchon's feat is to present a world which makes such warped sense on its own terms that the readers feel paranoid too.

Recently he has published his largest book yet, *Mason & Dixon*, a novel about the creators of the eponymous line dividing North and South. It seems to have occupied him for many years, during work on other projects. Again, it follows a spell of silence; as with his other books, it seems to have come from nowhere.

MAJOR WORKS

V (1963)

The Crying of Lot 49 (1966)

Gravity's Rainbow (1973)

Slow Learner (1985 collected short stories)

Vineland (1990)

Mason & Dixon (1997)

Rhys

JEAN   **born Roseau, Dominica, West Indies 1894; died Exeter 1979**

There were two children under the big mango tree, a boy and a little girl, and she waved to them and called 'Hello' but they didn't answer her or turn their heads. Very fair children, as Europeans born in the West Indies so often are: as if the white blood is asserting itself against all odds.

I USED TO LIVE HERE ONCE

JEAN RHYS WAS BORN in Dominica, the daughter of a Welsh doctor and a Creole woman. Some of her short stories recall the landscape of her childhood and the tone of an outsider pervades her work. Much of it drew on her experiences of wandering in and out of jobs in Paris and London: she worked as an artist's model, a film extra, a mannequin and a chorus girl, just like the heroine of *A Voyage in the Dark*. Her first book, *The Left Bank*, was a collection of short stories published with an introduction by **Ford Madox Ford**, who did much to promote her work. In this work she began her examination of superficial coteries and the vulnerable existence of women in the arts world, where they are prey to exploitation.

In spite of her early promise, she published nothing for 37 years. In 1958 she was discovered living reclusively in Cornwall and in 1966 she produced her most famous work, *Wide Sargasso Sea*. The narrative takes up the few leads **Charlotte Brontë** gives us about Mr Rochester's first wife (in *Jane Eyre*), who had been brought over from the West Indies. In a markedly different style, Rhys begins with Antoinette Cosway relating her plight as a mulatto, looking after a wayward mother, before being given in marriage to Mr Rochester to redeem a debt. The narrative continues from Rochester's point of view: Rhys' even-handedness lets us feel some sympathy for him even when he is behaving irresponsibly. The principal characters feel the loneliness and alienation that Rhys would study in her later work.

Richardson

SAMUEL   born Mackworth, Derbyshire 1689; died Parson's Green, nr. London 1761

Will you, good Sir, allow me to mention, that I could wish that the Air of Genuineness had been kept up, tho' I want not the letters to be thought genuine; only so far kept up, I mean, as that they should not prefatically be owned not to be genuine...

LETTER TO WILLIAM WARBURTON,
ON THE PREFACE OF CLARISSA

RICHARDSON WROTE SOME of the earliest novels and in *Clarissa* one of the longest (it is considerably longer than the Bible). If his work's dimensions were not ambitious enough, the form was extremely adventurous. His books are called "epistolary novels", being composed entirely from exchanges of letters. The chief advantage of this narrative technique is that the length of time between action and reaction (action often happens almost while a character is writing about it) is long enough to ensure suspense and keep the reader turning the page.

Richardson had developed the idea after producing a book of model letters on a variety of "common concerns in human life": it occurred to him to shape a story he remembered in the same form. His purpose was to teach: for many readers, he seemed to provide too ideally moral a world-view. **Fielding** was quick to parody *Pamela*, but considered *Clarissa* a work of great genius, as did **Dr Johnson**. Nowadays, Richardson seems odder for his presentation than his precepts. The letter form demands that we suspend disbelief and it has been suggested that Clarissa must have spent up to eight hours a day writing – leaving precious little time for anything to happen to her. One cannot deny the genre's potential, however, especially as perfected by **Laclos**, and by Woody Allen in *The Gossage-Vardebedian Papers*.

Sand

GEORGE

born Paris 1804; died Nohant 1876

I'm setting sail on the stormy sea of literature. I must live. I am not rich at the moment.

LETTER TO JULES BEUCOIRAN

LIKE **George Eliot**, George Sand was a woman. She freed herself from an aristocratic marriage to Baron Casimir Dudevant in 1831, rebelling against the social strictures that confined her. She would spend a lifetime as a prolific novelist railing against social *mores*, and would live out her precepts of freedom too. She had a trail of distinguished lovers, including Jules Sandeau (with whom she collaborated, and from whom she derived her pseudonym), the obsessive **Alfred de Musset**, and the composer Chopin. This last liaison lasted nine years; in a painting of Sand's coterie, he is depicted as the colourful budgerigar on her wrist.

Her sympathies were completely Romantic. She rushed to Paris in 1848 to support the revolutionaries, but condemned the bloodshed as an outrage in the name of fraternity and equality. These were profoundly her own goals — she proclaimed herself a friend of the people. The spirit of the age is evident throughout her writings, strongly championing the passions of the individual in the face of society's constraints, to which suicide can be a just response: in *Mauprat*, Edmée famously declares: "We cannot tear a single page out of our lives, but we can throw the book into the fire."

As **Mme de Staël** before her, she found conventions especially repressive towards women, since "men make the rules and apply them." Her early work found marriage to be the instrument of this humiliation, and although her attitude towards marriage mellowed later in her career, she never relented in a call for freedom that echoed **Rousseau**'s. Although her late, pastoral novels are less read now, they were much loved by **Proust** and **Flaubert**, who was desolated by Sand's death and wrote *A Simple Heart* in his friend's memory.

Sappho

born Lesbos c. 612 BC; died Mytilene

To me, that man, whoever he is sitting

opposite you seems equal to the gods who

listening near responsively to your sweet

utterances, your

laughter so lovely that it makes my heart go

fluttering in my ribs, for when I see you

all ablur, then there's nothing left of any

utterance in me,

rather my tongue solidifies, a subtle

undercurrent of flame upon my skin comes,

to the eyes, nothing, everything I hear is

out of proportion,

and a sweat comes in patters, and a shivering

over me whole, I'm pallider than grass and

faltering I appear to be approaching

dying a little.

TO A GIRL

MAJOR WORKS

Fragments from nine books of poetry

WHEN THE THEMES and images of lyric poetry start seeming tired, as they might in the duller moments of Latin love elegy, it does us good to recall how they got there. **Gertrude Stein** talks about a time when a poet "could say "O moon", "O sea", "O love", and the moon and the sea and love were really there." Something of this feeling comes with reading Sappho.

This is partly because we have her work in fragments only: just one poem, to Aphrodite, seems intact. Later ancients, especially **Catullus**, who translated her sublimely, would have known more poems and complete ones. For them, she would have belonged more firmly within a tradition and her themes of marriage, hopeless love and the night skies would have seemed as much their territory as hers.

This territory existed before Sappho. But we still have the sense that she found it. When she names things or actions, she can do so in long, compounded Greek words that seem (and often are) invented for her metre. That metre was hers, too: lines end with a distinctive "tum-ti tum-ti tum tum" made smoother by flowing into the next line.

Senses run into other senses as well and can dissolve into non-sense. Where previous poets praise the stature of a bride-groom, Sappho wonders how so grand a man will fit into the hall — "Raise high the roof-beam, carpenters!" Where **Homer**'s sunrise has rosy fingers, in Sappho it is the moon.

Sarraute

NATHALIE   **born Ivanovno-Voznesenk, Russia 1902**

And the word is there, completely ready, the word 'love', open, blessing... and what was drifting everywhere, whirling, engulfs itself stronger and stronger, immediately condenses, fills it wholly, founds, confounds itself with it, inseparable from it, they are just one thing.

'THE WORD LOVE' IN THE USAGE OF SPEECH

NATHALIE SARRAUTE was born in Russia but writes in French. Her parents settled in France, where she trained as a lawyer at the Sorbonne. she continued her studies at Oxford.

There is something forensic about her writing. She analyses a character's inner motivations thoroughly, even clinically, before turning the narrative's attention to actions or dialogue. Her first novel best exemplifies this technique. It takes its name, *Tropisms*, from the unseen shifts of auxin from cells on one side of a plant to the other, causing the organism to incline towards the sun. What makes people behave as they do is thus depicted here as invisible and barely explicable, while anything they say is incapable of justifying it. In Sarraute, the narrator can address the reader in an immediate style, sharing vivid images in a conversational-enough way – while actual conversation itself must remain stifled by clichés.

She examines this beautifully in her pieces on language, *The Usage of Speech*. She takes phrases and strives to name the impossibilities they invoke; at one point she points out that words, in all their lightness, are incapable of describing their source.

Still, much of Sarraute's narrative takes place nearer that source than most writing comes. She uses interior monologues, and can shift from the thoughts of one character to another without warning the reader. In the 1950s, she was a chief exponent of the *nouveau roman*, the new novel, a genre seeking to unite such diversely-collected impressions in a single work of art. Like **Simone de Beauvoir**, the substance of her novels often deals with educated characters, whose involvement with literature enables them to discuss the kinds of texts which include them (as in *The Fruits of Gold*).

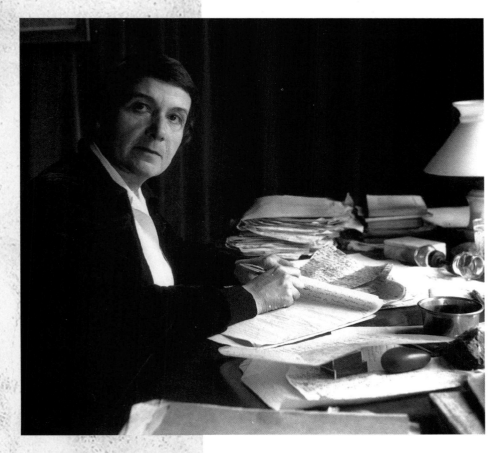

Sartre

JEAN-PAUL   **born Paris 1905; died Paris 1980**

I have understood the autodidact's method: he is teaching himself in alphabetical order... Today he has reached 'L'. 'K' after 'J', 'L' after 'K'. He has passed abruptly from the study of coleopterae to that of quantum theory, from a work on Tamerlane to a Catholic pamphlet against Darwinism... Behind him, before him, there is a universe. And the day approaches when, closing the last book on the last shelf on the far left, he will say to himself: 'And now what?'

NAUSEA, TR. ROBERT BALDICK

SARTRE WAS A PHILOSOPHER for whom people could only be justified by their actions, rather than their personalities (for example, being a coward should not prevent you from doing something brave). He embodied this principle when he joined the army in 1939, was imprisoned, then fought for the Resistance on his release in 1941.

But his writings were actions too, and the characters of his plays and novels had to act on his philosophy. This is why the books can be read autobiographically: *Nausea* is the diary of an academic who frequents cafés. He begins with an inability to doubt and is prone to the kind of malaise that gives Sartre's philosophical work its subjectivity; he finishes intending to write a novel.

Sartre wrote more novels: the *Roads to Freedom* trilogy has a young man facing domestic and political crises as World War Two begins. The second volume, *The Reprieve,* becomes as fragmented as Europe during the "appeasement" period, before it finds a note of deluded hope. Here, as in his treatment of tragedy (*Les Mouches* takes on **Euripides**' *Electra*), events that seem to have no immediate consequence reveal themselves as meaningful by the conclusion, as if to question the effects an existential way of life can have on the surroundings of the person living that life.

Sartre's reflection on what the times demanded led him and his partner **Simone de Beauvoir** to support Communism, Chairman Mao and the Paris student uprising of May 1968. He declined the Nobel Prize for Literature in 1964.

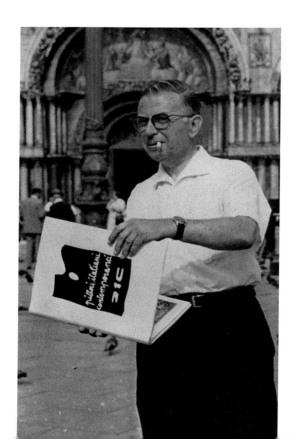

MAJOR WORKS

FICTION
Nausea (1938)
The Wall and Other Stories (1938)
The Age of Reason (1945)
The Reprieve (1945)
Iron in the Soul (1949)

PLAYS
The Flies (1943)
No Way Out (1944)
Crime Passionel (1948)
Loser Wins (1949)
Lucifer and the Lord (1951)

PHILOSOPHY
Sketch for a Theory of Emotions (1939)
Being and Nothingness (1943)
Existentialism and Humanism (1946)
Portrait of an Anti-Semite (1948)
The Problem of Method (1960)
Words (autobiography, 1963)
The Family Idiot (on Flaubert, 1971)

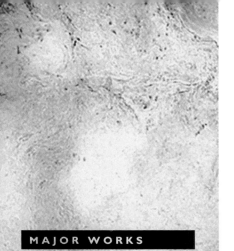

Schiller

FRIEDRICH VON **born Marbach a. Neckar 1759; died Weimar 1805**

Give him the nectar!

Pour out for the poet,

Hebe! Pour free!

Quicken his eyes with celestial dew,

That Styx the detested no more may he view,

And like one of us Gods may conceit him to be!

Thanks, Hebe! I quaff it! Io Paean, I cry!

The wine of the Immortals Forbids me to die!

THE VISIT OF THE GODS, TR. COLERIDGE

SCHILLER WAS PROFOUNDLY influenced by the spirit of **Rousseau**, and a strong zeal for freedom emerges from his plays and poems. He was one of the leading figures of the *Sturm und Drang* movement (storm and stress, a robust expression of Romanticism), and as such, drew inevitable comparisons with **Goethe.** They were friends, especially when Schiller was Professor of History at Jena, and when Goethe was asked to judge between them, he said, "Germany is lucky to have two such boys."

In both drama and historical texts, Schiller portrayed free spirits at odds with their rulers. In *Don Carlos* and *William Tell*, he presented oppression in Spain and Switzerland respectively, in pieces which, as operas, would serve Italy in its own struggle. In *Mary Stuart*, the freedom is more spiritual: the hero-ine's joy at being even briefly out of prison, and on the ultimate liberation of her soul, finds lyrical expression worthy of *Faust*. Such a work shows the influence of the hugely Graecophile spirit pervading Germany at the time; although Schiller's drama is not as classical as **Racine** thought it, the way characters can put their cases, as if disputing in court, certainly echoes **Euripides.**

His poetry too can emulate Greek lyric, both in subject matter and in form, as his *Ode to Joy*, so famous from Beethoven's Choral Symphony. But its influence depends more on its heady response to an age of revolution. While much of this might seem overblown to readers in English these days, Schiller can convey his passion with a persuasive urgency, just as his characters do onstage.

Schnitzler

ARTHUR   **born Vienna 1862; died Vienna 1931**

The human ear is so formed that it can
sleep at the sound but wake at the echo.

BOOK OF SAYINGS AND REFLECTIONS

ARTHUR SCHNITZLER MADE his name principally as a dramatist. He worked in *fin-de-siècle* Vienna, that great moment in cultural history when Jewish artists and thinkers secured such freedoms of expression in the face of intolerance. It was a city under the grip of the mayor Karl Luger, who managed to maintain the support of the intellectual classes while relying on anti-semitic journalism and propaganda. Schnitzler was keenly aware of these apparent disparities, feeling that of all people, liberals treated Jews the worst. He would approach anti-semitism in his work, dramatically in the hospital politics of *Doctor Bernardi*. (He lost his own job as a medical orderly for publishing the novella *Lieutenant Gustl*, ridiculing the military figures around him.) He suffered the same persecution as Freud, Mahler, Schoënberg and his friend Hugo von Hofmannsthal. He stayed in Vienna throughout his life.

He trained as a physician, and followed keenly the development of psychiatry. As with **Robert Musil**, his work is so contemporaneous with Freud's that it becomes hard to say who anticipated whom. They all share an interest in the unconscious. Schnitzler's plays particularly raise the question of what we are really thinking: mostly about decadent forms of sexual pleasure. In *Paracelsus* we are told that life is a dream, and that nothing is certain; throughout Schnitzler's dramas, characters enact their dreams, providing manifesta-

tions of aristocratic fantasies in an age of decadence.

He presents these often in one-act plays consisting of short, sketch-like themes. *Anatol* is the most famous example, and introduces character-types much like those found in **Plautus** and New Comedy, notably the lovelorn rich boy and his wilier factotum. Scenes are linked, with characters reappearing; in *Merry-go-round*, this is systematic, with one partner in each duet surviving into the next one, until the ensemble forms five couplings in a tight circle.

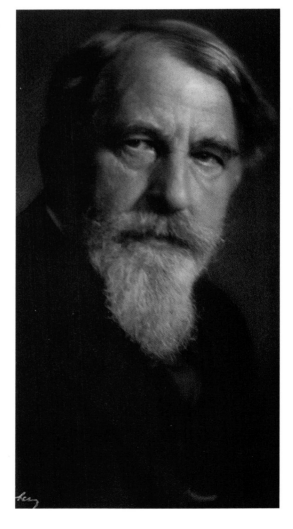

MAJOR WORKS

PLAYS
Anatol (1893)

Playing With Love (1895)

Paracelsus (1897)

The Green Cockatoo (1899)

Merry-go-round (1900)

Intermezzo (1905)

Professor Bernardi (1912)

NOVELLAS
Lieutenant Gustl (1901)

Flight into Darkness (1926).

The Road to the Open
  (novel, 1908)

Scott

SIR WALTER

born Edinburgh 1771; died Abbotsford 1832

To aching eyes each landscape lowers,

To feverish pulse each gale blows chill;

And Araby's and Eden's bowers

Were barren as this moorland hill.

THE DREARY CHANGE

FOR MANY PEOPLE, Walter Scott *is* Scotland. He would have liked it that way. He invented clan tartans, as though they were ancient, for the moment when George IV visited Edinburgh, and Scott took

him round the town as representative of all things Scottish. In his Romantic age, when Europe was already in a swoon over the discovery of **Ossian**, his poetry and prose evoked a lost world of Celtic gallantry.

Scott worked hard to restore some idea of that world. It had been destroyed systematically by the English after Culloden, who banned clans from assembling, and sent their leaders into internal exile. Scott has been accused of pandering too much to his neighbours, not least by glamourising the English in *Ivanhoe*, but he was as concerned to reconcile England with Scotland as the Lowlands with the Highlands.

The success he won with his poems enabled him to build a castle at Abbotsford, near the border, where he became a self-styled laird. His poetry was enormously successful – he was offered the post of Poet Laureate in 1813, but recommended Southey. His fame was eclipsed by **Byron**; feeling the need to build an extension to his pile, he turned, anonymously, to prose fiction.

In this, he is credited with the invention of the historical romance. He produced them with an astonishing fluency, making few plans for his first, *Waverley*, and dictating *Ivanhoe* in two weeks. This kind of speed served him well when he fell into immense debt, which he worked ceaselessly to earn the equivalent of £5 million during the last seven years of his life. Such work might seem mass-produced for the tourists it began attracting in his life-time; but his poetry shows that his epic feel for tales of honour were motivated as much by Romanticism as by a benign Scottish Nationalism.

Seth

VIKRAM   **born Calcutta 1942**

She lies asleep, unswiftly breathing;

Her thoughts are not with him, her
dreams

Traverse the solitary streams

Of inward lands, yet her hair, wreathing

The pillow in a mesh of light,

Returns him to the fugitive night.

THE GOLDEN GATE

VIKRAM SETH IS A POET and novelist who delivers breathtaking virtuosity in every form he attempts. He has published several volumes of lyric verse and versions of Chinese poetry, all of which reveal a vast range of interest (he trained as an economist, but his knowledge does not seem to stop anywhere convenient). Still, this did not prepare anyone for *The Golden Gate*.

In Chapter Five, Seth describes the surprise that greeted his decision to write a verse novel, before pointing to the model of **Pushkin**'s *Eugene Onegin*, which was made accessible to English readers by Charles Johnston's miraculous translation. Seth's tale plays the same games with a strict but addictive verse form, to tell the stories of educated young San Franciscans. He crams in their responses to everything from love and death to nuclear war, art, sex, viticulture and pet iguanas; the work is studiedly complete, but completely refreshing.

He is more famous still for *A Suitable Boy*, perhaps the longest novel ever published in English. However, only its size is intimidating. Literary great Salman Rushdie is falsely alleged to have called it a "soap opera": it is nonetheless a symptom of how the adventurous spirit of Seth's enterprises can blind critics to his works' deeper merits. The book is set in India in 1951 (shortly after Partition), in an imaginary town, conceived in the spirit of **R.K. Narayan**'s Malgudi. Narayan's delicate handling of local intrigue also informs the work, especially on faculty politics. But in its romantic theme (the burgeoning relationship between a Hindu girl and a Muslim boy) and the huge cast of characters, it also takes on the 19th-century English novel. It is hard to know what to expect next from Seth: if hints that he is attempting drama prove correct, theatre might never be the same again.

MAJOR WORKS

POETRY
Mappings (1980)

*The Humble
   Administrator's Garden*
   (1985)

All You Who Sleep Tonight
   (1990)

VERSE NOVEL
The Golden Gate (1986)

PROSE FICTION
A Suitable Boy (1993)

Shelley

MARY

born London 1797; died London 1851

And now, once again, I bid my hideous progeny go forth and prosper. I have an affection for it, for it was the offspring of happy days, when death and grief were but words which found no true echo in my heart.

FRANKENSTEIN,
INTRODUCTION TO THE 1831 EDITION

MARY SHELLEY'S NIGHTMARISH imagination was awakened early in her life. Her youth was spent at the very heart of the romantic movement. Her mother was Mary Wollstonecraft, author of *A Vindication of the Rights of Women*, and her father was William Godwin – whose rational but anarchistic philosophy attracted the attention of the young **Shelley**, whom Mary married.

After Shelley's early death, she edited and published his poetry, wrote travel memoirs and fiction set in the future. In this she was always careful to maintain a realistic view of human nature, however fantastical her stories became. *The Last Man*, for example, tells of a plague-ridden British republic in the year 2100, where only one human survives.

Her most famous work is *Frankenstein*. It shares with the later *Lodore* the **Rousseau**-inspired theme: can a creature grow up in a state of innocence? The creature that looms out of the novel cannot: he has been made by a man, who has stolen the vital spark, imparted by a bolt of lightning, that is only God's to impart. The creation is necessarily flawed and evil. This aspect of the tale shares her husband's attraction to the figure of Prometheus, while drawing on his other verse (quoting *Mutability* and invoking Mont Blanc, a view of which inspired one of Percy's most awesome poems). The supernatural theme was suggested by conversations with Shelley, **Byron** and Byron's doctor (with each of them agreeing to undertake the writing of a ghost story): subsequent nightmares helped. Whatever she owed to the latter, she left a profoundly personal vision that expressed her age's tendency to distinguish individual genius from the agencies of God.

Shelley

PERCY BYSSHE   **born Horsham, Sussex 1792; died Livorno 1822**

Strangers have wept to hear his

   passionate notes,

And virgins, as unknown he past, have

   pined

And wasted for fond love of his wild

   eyes.

The fire of those soft orbs has ceased to

   burn,

And Silence, too enamoured of that

   voice,

Locks its mute music in her rugged cell.

ALASTOR

SHELLEY FAMOUSLY CALLED poets "the unacknowledged legislators of the world". He was profoundly unhappy with the acknowledged legislation and his remedies for society's ills involved love and a sensibility to the natural forces of the universe.

In his identification with animals and the elements, he voices his most urgent social theme: his call for freedom. When he was 20, he was distributing pamphlets in Dublin towards the emancipation of Irish Catholics; at the end of his short life, he found in the Greek uprising against the Turks a model for all servitude, by which he felt the English were also bound. For himself, he legislated as he went. At 18 he eloped with Harriet Westbrook, two years his junior, then invited her to live with his new lover and soon-to-be wife **Mary**. In this he denied divine authority (he had been expelled from Oxford for avowed atheism) and railed against the courts, finding morality in love alone.

When he writes against tyranny and inhumanity, love accounts for his abiding optimism. His *Ode to the West Wind* has the wind vivifying the poet; the *Sky-Lark*, too, is made to share the poet's vision of a better world. In all this, he saves himself from the curse of being "morally dead". As nature frees the poet from this fate in the blank verse *Alastor*, so in *Prometheus Unbound* the elements rally round the mythical saviour of humanity in a poem that emulates **Aeschylus** in form and **Milton** in language. Often this **Platonic** notion of the soul's freedom leads Shelley to hope for a better existence after death; his drowning seemed to fulfil the craving his richly wrought verse frequently captured; but his personal generosity and gift of friendship (with **Keats** and **Byron**) bound him as closely to the living.

MAJOR WORKS

Prometheus Unbound (1820)

Epipsychidion (1821)

Adonais (1821)

other works collected and published posthumously

Singer

ISAAC BASHEVIS

born Radzymin, Poland 1904; died New York 1991

He is chiefly remembered for his tales set in the villages of Kreshev, Frampol and Goray, where his first novel is set. *Satan in Goray* is just one of many appearances the devil would make in Singer's work — a figure who might fulfil his role as malignant tempter, but more often is heard complaining and making jokes. In Singer's work, the Devil can present himself as a reject and an outcast and so provides a disturbing analogy with the Jewish experience of exile and persecution. The presence of evil can be felt in more human forms: "The Gentleman of Cracow", for example, offers a starving village a wedding banquet, only to incite an orgy and leave the children charred in their cradles.

But this fantastical and unsentimental world provides Singer with his richest moments of absurd humour. In "The Dead Fiddler", a venerable elder fears an extra-marital pregnancy only to discover that a dead fiddler has taken abode in his daughter's stomach, soon to be joined by a simple girl who died several hundred years before.

Singer was a great admirer of Aesop's Fables; like Aesop's, his writing shows an interest in character types, such as *Gimpel the Fool*, optimistic and lanky, well versed in the Torah and little else. Singer would always avoid over-intellectualising, and he made a natural story-teller for children. He won the Nobel Prize in 1978.

When the writer becomes the center of his attention, he becomes a nudnik. And a nudnik who believes he's profound is even worse than just a plain nudnik.

INTERVIEW WITH RICHARD BURGIN

ISAAC BASHEVIS SINGER IS a demon in a gaberdine. He wrote in Yiddish, which he said "has minerals other languages lack", and was steeped in its tradition: he was born in Poland, the son of a rabbi. His stories range from the Hassidic communities of his youth, with their Messianic mentality, to the esoteric circles of Manhattan. He settled in New York in 1935, to escape European anti-semitism.

MAJOR WORKS

Satan in Goray (1935)

The Family Moskat (1950)

Gimpel the Fool and Other Stories (1957)

The Magician of Lublin (1960)

The Slave (1960)

The Spinoza of Market Street (1961)

Short Friday (1964)

In My Father's Court (autobiography, 1966)

The Manor (1967)

The Séance and Other Stories (1968)

The Estate (1969)

A Friend of Kafka (1970)

Enemies: A Love Story (1972)

A Crown of Feathers (1973)

Schlemiel the First (play, 1974)

Sinyavsky

ANDREI

born Moscow 1925; died Paris 1997

[I advocate a] phantasmagoric art with hypotheses instead of a Purpose, an art in which the grotesque will replace realistic descriptions of ordinary life.

ON SOCIALIST REALISM

IN 1966 THE KGB discovered it was Sinyavsky who, under the name of Abram Tertz, had been publishing work in the West that the authorities thought slandered the Soviet Union and provided propaganda for reactionaries overseas. There was a sort of trial. Sinyavsky pleaded that he loved Russia and that he had published abroad for stylistic reasons rather than political ones: he was told he was attending criminal proceedings, not a literary seminar.

His claim was justified, up to a point. As a budding historian of Russian literature, he had aligned himself with the fantastical work of **Gogol** and **Dostoyevsky**, rather than the socialist realism of **Gorky**. To have claimed this was brave enough even during Khrushchev's thaw. However, as a close friend of **Pasternak** (he was his pall-bearer, and wrote an introduction to his poems), he knew the new leniency was superficial and that his Symbolist, richly imaginative novels based on the Stalinist terrors – during which his father was arrested, but of whose horrors he was only just learning – could not be published in his own country. He had become a political writer in spite of himself.

The Trial Begins described the sense of fear that was everywhere during the Stalin years. The *Makepeace Experiment* criticised Soviet ideals more generally. In subsequent volumes, Sinyavsky followed his own victimisation. The court sentenced him to seven years' hard labour. During his term, he wrote a book in the guise of letters to his wife, *A Voice from the Choir*. He was released in 1971 and in 1973 began teaching Russian literature at the Sorbonne, in Paris. He then wrote autobiography, journalism and criticism, leaving at his death the first completed draft of a new novel.

MAJOR WORKS

On Socialist Realism (1960)

The Trial Begins (1960)

Fantastic Stories (1961)

The Makepeace Experiment (1965)

Thoughts Unawares (1965)

A Voice from the Choir (1973)

In Gogol's Shadow (1975)

Walks With Pushkin (1976)

Goodnight (1989)

Ivan the Simple: Paganism, Magic and Religion of the Russian People (1990)

Snow

C.P.

We talked about personal politics, of which, not only in the college, we had now seen a good deal. One point had struck us both: will, sheer stubborn will, was more effective than cunning or finesse or subtlety. Those could be a help; but the more one saw, the more one was forced to the conclusion that the man you wanted on your side was the man who believed without a shade of doubt that you were right.

THE MASTERS

C.P. SNOW'S REFINED NOVELS document his own distinguished public life, from the varied perspectives of academic, scientist and civil servant. His first works of fiction included a detective story, *Death Under Sail*, and *The Search*, on scientific research. All his novels after 1940 come under the collective title of *Strangers and Brothers*.

The brothers are Lewis and Martin Eliot, the one an academic lawyer, the other a scientist. The former is the narrator, sometimes telling his brother's story, sometimes those of strangers. His knowledge of law gives him an understanding of the corridors of power (Snow's title introduced the phrase into the language), which the author culled from his own time in Whitehall. Snow's own administrative work drew on his scientific knowledge – he was Under-Secretary in the Ministry of Technology, the source of Harold Wilson's "white heat." Consequently his work casts a rare view on the ethical dilemmas at stake when political and scientific power combine. He discussed these themes, and his own treatment of them, in his controversial Rede Lecture of 1959.

His best-known work remains *The Masters*, set in a Cambridge college much like the Christ's of which Snow had been a fellow. In his handling of disparate personalities seeking to succeed a dying Head of House, he displayed a wryness and reverence towards the subject; however, after Tom Sharpe's *Porterhouse Blue*, the former seems more appropriate nowadays.

Solzhenitsyn

ALEKSANDR

born Kislovodsk 1918

Literature is the memory of peoples; it transmits from one generation to the next the irrefutable experiences of men. It preserves and enlivens the flame of a history immune to all deformation, far from every lie.

NOBEL PRIZE LECTURE, 1970

IN HIS NOW CELEBRATED speech on accepting the Nobel Prize for Literature in 1970, Solzhenitsyn spoke of the writer's obligation to bear witness to the truth; for what he called "the lie" allowed violence to flourish.

Solzhenitsyn's courage appears all the greater for the evil he witnessed himself. In 1945, he was arrested for remarks he was supposed to have made against Stalin. He had been fighting in the war, had been twice decorated and attained the rank of captain: now he would be imprisoned for eight years in a labour camp. On his release, he was kept in exile until 1956, when he was rehabilitated under the increased tolerance of the Khruschev régime. But his writings would soon suffer the same backlash as Sinyavsky experienced under Brezhnev. His work was banned in Russia, and he was expelled from the Writers' Union.

His courage had to endure disbelief in the west too. Communists internationally considered Solzhenitsyn's testament a betrayal, especially his three-volume account of Russian history from the implementation of the Soviet Terror in 1918 to 1956, *The Gulag Archipelago.* Commentators scrabbled around for explanations as to why the Gulag system was somehow "not as bad" as the Nazi death camps, and so missed the author's treatment of inhumanity and evil on its own terms.

For all the specific documentation of Stalin's crimes in his work, Solzhenitsyn recognised these injustices as being far from unique to the Soviet Union. Once in the West, he spoke of the cowardice displayed by the United Nations, and campaigned against what he saw as the imperial conflict in Vietnam. By now he had embraced Christianity, and demanded of political systems only that they be founded on love, compassion and the humility of its governors. Literature remains for Solzhenitsyn the means of reflecting "the growing spiritual unity of mankind."

Sophocles

born Colonus c. 496 BC; died Athens 405 BC

All that is mine will go today, and you

will need take no more onerous

  care of me;

it's harsh, children, I know:

  and yet one word

alleviates this kind of suffering.

There is no man than he from

  whom you part

to live out your remaining life, from

  whom

you could have had more love.

OEDIPUS AT COLONUS

SOPHOCLES WAS THE DEFINITIVE author of Greek tragedy. In *Oedipus Rex*, he provided what Aristotle considered the model of what a tragedy should be. The judges of the Dionysian theatre festival thought him the best, too: he wrote some 30 cycles of plays (123 pieces in all), won first prize with 24 of them and second prize with the rest. He stands between **Aeschylus** and **Euripides** chronologically and in the history of drama's development he added a third actor to Aeschylus' format, hugely increasing the possibilities of staging. He also anticipated Euripides' less lyrical, more psychologically economical representation of action.

Sophocles' timing and poetry can make the drama agonisingly tense, even in the one example of weak structure (*Women of Trachis*). His lyric odes, which involve the chorus very emotionally, can praise mankind, or love, or the poet's birthplace. Although he is known to have written non-dramatic verse, it is his ear for the inevitable cadence in the mouth of an actor (and he had been one) that can move us as much as the terrible crisis a character may face.

He gave words their fullest value. Oedipus puns on his name to invoke the theme of self-knowledge (it can sound like the Greek for "I know where..." in this plot of detection), and yet can descend into panicked or alliterative stuttering. The hero in *Philoctetes* must also howl his pain in strict Greek iambics: "Papapapai papai papai papapapai!" This visceral incoherence bursts into a play whose language elsewhere is marked by subtle persuasion and vivid scene-setting. Sophocles was always in control of his effects and the text of his last play is said to have been used as evidence when his relatives thought him of unsound mind.

Soyinka

WOLE   **born Abeokuta, Western Nigeria 1934**

Who does not seek to be remembered?

Memory is the Master of Death, the

   chink

In his armour of conceit. I shall leave

That which makes my going the sheerest

Dream of an afternoon. Should voyagers

Not travel light? Let the considerate

   traveller

Shed, of his excessive load, all

That may benefit the living.

DEATH AND THE KING'S HORSEMAN

WOLE SOYINKA IS a Nigerian writer who has published poems and prose (the latter largely autobiographical), but he remains better known for his theatrical work.

To some extent this shows the influence of **Brecht** and Greek tragedy – he has adapted *The Threepenny Opera* and **Euripides'** *Bacchae*. He studied at Leeds University, then worked reading plays for the Royal Court Theatre in London, but his voice is distinctly African, whatever his detractors there might say. His Brecht treatment attacks dictators such as Idi Amin, Bokassa and Nguema; his version of the *Bacchae* introduces African songs and dances as choric episodes and casts the story, with the death of the king, Pentheus, as an event whose ritual implications can rejuvenate the earth.

This is the theme of *Death and the King's Horseman*, in which a chief must follow his king to the grave, to complete the burial rites. Colonial attempts to intervene can only pervert the natural order as presented in the play, which the drama makes lyrical and real in the face of Western incomprehension. Still, the chief's tragedy is more to do with the human condition than Empire. Soyinka's earlier depictions of a society under the spell of a sham prophet in *The Trials of Brother Jero* and *Jero's Metamorphosis* are as telling about corruption as they are about the potential disaster Christianity can bring to a community with very different traditions.

Soyinka's relationship with Nigeria has always been difficult. He was imprisoned there for two years during the Biafran War, has left in self-imposed exile and has protested loudly against the barbaric actions of General Abacha's present régime. He won the Nobel Prize for Literature in 1986.

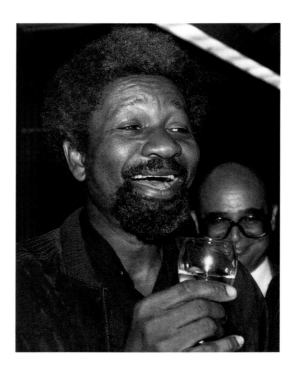

Stein

GERTRUDE   **born Allegheny, Pennsylvania 1874; died Paris 1946**

I am I not any longer when I see. This sentence is at the bottom of all creative activity. It is just the exact opposite of I am I because my little dog knows me.

HENRY JAMES, DUET

GERTRUDE STEIN WAS a writer whose importance to modern literature is immense. She is more often remembered for her influence on younger writers such as **Fitzgerald** and

Hemingway than for her own work, which is often barely comprehensible.

But she was a great experimenter and this inscrutability is part of her adventure with words. As a student at Radcliffe, she was the star pupil of William (brother of **Henry**) **James**, gaining top marks even when she walked out of the exam room. She embraced his notions of the stream of consciousness and of the value of words. Although she did not produce "automatic" writing, she played with parts of speech. Her special concern was with nouns. Sometimes she tried to restore to them their full value (her famous "rose is a rose is a rose" is an attempt to take the word out of the context of its commonplace connotations) and sometimes she tried to do without them altogether.

In Paris (where she lived for 40 years), she was a great collector of paintings and a friend of Picasso. Her writing sometimes aims for a kind of cubism, where her perversely-punctuated sentences can throw up ambiguities that invite reading from different angles. This makes her narratives deceptively simple, and sometimes unstoppable, as she chases up possibilities: *The Making of Americans*, a telling of national history through that of her own family, runs to 900 pages.

During her lifetime, her following was at best cult, with publishers feeling able to send her rejection letters in her own imitable, studiedly repetitive style. The almost besotted **Thornton Wilder** did much to bring her work academic and popular respect, although she barely needed him to remind her of what a great writer she was. Still, although she ranked herself with **Whitman**, **Poe** and James, she had a fine sense of humour.

Steinbeck

JOHN

born Salinas, California 1902; died New York 1968

Tell you what – I use to get the people
jumpin' and talkin' in tongues an' glory
shoutin' till they just fell down an' passed
out. An' some I'd baptise to bring 'em to.
An' then – you know what I'd do? I'd
take one of them girls out in the grass an'
I'd lay with her... Come the nex' time,
them an' me was full of the spirit, I'd do
it again.

THE PREACHER, IN THE GRAPES OF WRATH

JOHN STEINBECK WROTE with real commitment and experimental style, largely about his native California. In *The Grapes of Wrath*, a family is uprooted from a plot they have always farmed. They head west in the dream-like hope of fruit-picking in a land of plenty, only to become disillusioned and to lose innocence in a politicised world. The trek west, always an epic motif in the US, provides the action of *The Wayward Bus*, in which a disparate group of travellers are thrown together on a journey they eventually share.

Steinbeck's is an arid landscape, with characters typically waiting for rain. They live by the land, but this has become corrupted: in *In Dubious Battle*, fruit is left to rot. *Tortilla Flat* again focusses on fruit-pickers and looks beyond immediate economic problems to tell the story of Danny, a libertine who nonetheless attracts a Christ-like following in his community. The recurrent idea of original sin in Steinbeck has attracted

criticism that he is too fond of his intellectual premises for his stories' good. *East of Eden* has him tackling this problem insistently: the Salinas Valley is the setting for his re-telling of the conflict between Cain and Abel and introduces a range of characters in the Old Testament manner. The collected letters he wrote to his editor show what a professional he was: "Today I wrote 3,000 words and built a coffee table."

However difficult his subjects, his language is markedly straightforward, experimental in its juxtapositions perhaps (like his contemporary **Dos Passos**), but direct in its narrative and persuasive in its poetry.

He was awarded the Nobel Prize in 1962.

Stendhal

born Grenoble 1783; died Paris 1842

He was afraid of terrible remorse and eternal ridicule if he deviated from the ideal model he had set himself to follow. In short, what made Julien a superior being was precisely what prevented him from savouring the happiness which came his way. Every inch the young girl of 16 who has delightful colouring, and is foolish enough to put on rouge to go to a ball.

THE RED AND THE BLACK,
TR. CATHERINE SLATER

STENDHAL RECALLED THAT when he was five, he saw a hatter shot in the back on the street outside his home in Grenoble. He considered it the first bloodshed in the Revolution. Even then, he could respond immediately to his times. Later, his career was very public: he was a diplomat in Italy during Napoleon's reign and had been part of the Emperor's military administration. In fact, when he was awarded the *Légion d'Honneur* in 1835, he would have rather had it for statesmanship than literature.

Like Napoleon, he combined a revolutionary spirit with an innate understanding of social niceties. He was an artist working in an atmosphere at once classical and romantic. The aristocratic hero in *Armance*, his first completed novel, was a means of satirising the effusive excesses of **Chateaubriand** and **Hugo**, although Stendhal acknowledged his debt to both. Elsewhere, his heroes consider themselves "superior beings" on the Napoleonic model, before becoming bound up with intrigues that recall an earlier age; but they regularly lack the *sang-froid* to cope with it.

This calls on the irony at the disposal of Stendhal's narrators, as well as pacy narration. He designedly wrote page-turners, which won over **Balzac**, who wrote fulsome praise of *The Charterhouse of Parma*. That book had been written in 53 days – the author is as eager to get on with the story as is the reader. His masterpiece, *The Red and the Black*, often uses the present tense and even shifts in characters' psychology can come across as action.

Sterne

LAURENCE   **born Clonmel, County Tipperary 1713; died London 1768**

The fifteenth chapter is come at last; and brings nothing with it but a sad signature of "How our pleasures slip from under us in this world." For in talking of my digression – I declare before heaven I have made it! What a strange creature is mortal man! said she.

This is very true, said I – but 'twere better to get all these things out of our heads, and return to my uncle Toby.

TRISTRAM SHANDY,
VOL IX, CHAPTER 15 (COMPLETE)

LAURENCE STERNE WAS a sickly parish priest with one of the wildest imaginations in literature. His 18th-century readers scarcely knew how to greet his work: clerics' wives were bitterly offended, urbanites were hugely admiring and **Dr Johnson** wrote the author off as an oddball.

Although his triumphant *Tristram Shandy* glosses the rising novel genre just as *A Sentimental Journey* mocked Smollett's splenetic brand of travel-writing, still the work transcends its place in history. Wayne Booth has compared it to the passage of an hourglass, through which everything before it passes and that fills everything after it.

It is cast as an autobiography, but its narrator isn't born until the end of Volume IV: first we must learn of his conception, his shameful name and why his nose is mis-shapen. Shandy is in no hurry; his digressions are "incontestably the sunshine of the work" and any reader caught skipping is sent back to re-read sections. As if to make the point that such a book is too strange to be bound, we are invited to rip out pages that don't exist, or provide illustrations for blank ones. Sterne is happy to fill other lacunae with marbling or black pages. Even without the in-jokes, the reconstruction of Uncle Toby's part in the Siege of Namur and the inconclusive anecdotes (one of which takes most of the narrative even to begin to emerge), the prose provides a magnificent adventure of its own.

Stevens

WALLACE   **born Pennsylvania 1879; died Hartford, Connecticut 1955**

The leaves cry. It is not a cry of divine attention,

Nor the smoke-drift of puffed out heroes, nor human cry.

It is the cry of leaves that do not transcend themselves,

In the absence of fantasia, without meaning more

Than they are in the final finding of the ear, in the thing

Itself, until, at last, the cry concerns no one at all.

THE COURSE OF A PARTICULAR

WHEN WE HEAR the quiet, assured poetic voice of Wallace Stevens, we begin to forget that he worked in insurance. When a critic came to ask him about his achievements, Stevens walked him around town pointing out the buildings he had insured, before bidding him good day. He never gave up his day job and wrote at nights, but one colleague joked that if they hadn't known he was a poet, the firm would have fired him long before.

And what a poet. He had a modern angle on **Emerson**'s theory that language has a counterpart in the natural order: "words of the world are the life of the world". Stevens would have agreed with his friend **William Carlos Williams**' dictum, "no ideas but in things", and he found these things beautiful on their own terms: "The pears are not seen/ As the observer wills." He drew a **Rilke**-like distinction between the world outside and inside the poet: but the poet offers his productions as things in themselves, which can make their way into other apprehensions.

This means the beauty of his poetry can come from simply naming more things in his restrained and elegant diction and making us feel them. Nothing appears to happen except in the mind. *Sunday Morning* takes place during a church service, but removed from it: it collects the images a woman summons as bearers of a non-religious joy, to preserve them. Elsewhere he writes, "Beauty is momentary in the mind.../ But in the flesh it is immortal./ The body dies; the body's beauty lives."

So Stevens' poetry can be calm, even static in diction, but still celebrate the life force, especially as manifested in music-making, and rejuvenated by the sun and beaches which he so loved.

Stevenson

ROBERT LOUIS   born Edinburgh 1850; died Vailima, Samoa 1894

All the brothers were hurrying to the chapel; the dead in life, at this untimely hour, were already beginning the uncomforted labours of their day... And I blessed God that I was free to wander, free to hope, and free to love.

TRAVELS WITH A DONKEY
IN THE CEVENNES

ROBERT LOUIS STEVENSON was a Scottish novelist and poet, who trained first as a civil engineer and lawyer. His decision to become a writer estranged him from his parents until he was 30. He was always given to wandering. His earliest published work includes travel-writing, of which he was a master. *Travels with a Donkey* provides beautiful examples of sensitive but detached observation and it is impossible to be unmoved by the ultimate parting of man and beast.

Travel-writing (particularly Kingsley's *At Last*) inspired his most widely-read work, *Treasure Island*. It contains the intrigue and buccaneering that characterise much of his work. This guaranteed him eager audiences in his own time and critical respect later for his efficient and compelling technique as a storyteller. He wrote with deep feeling of 18th-century Scotland, scarred by the aftermath of the Battle of Culloden in 1746. This is the spirit that informs *Kidnapped* and *Weir of Hermiston*, an unfinished tale, which many agree to contain his most

accomplished work.

Many of his wanderings were prompted by a search for the climate best-suited to his sickly disposition. Eventually, he settled with his family in Samoa, where his grasp of local affairs provided material for *The Beach of Falesa*; but his quest had previously taken him to the US, where he married, and to Bournemouth, where he befriended **Henry James.** By the end, he was as famous for his travels as his writings, although he considered books "a mighty bloodless substitute for life".

Stoppard

TOM   **born Zlin, Czechoslavakia 1937**

DOCTOR: *Keep saying to yourself, 'I have no orchestra. I have never had an orchestra. I do not want an orchestra.'*

IVANOV: *Absolutely...*

DOCTOR: *Good.*

IVANOV: *There is one thing you can do for me.*

DOCTOR: *Yes?*

IVANOV: *Stop them playing.*

EVERY GOOD BOY DESERVES FAVOUR

TOM STOPPARD'S PLAYS share **Beckett**'s bleakness and humour and they are similarly concerned with the loneliness of being alive. But they have a parodic wit and a sparkle all of their own.

The content can often be densely philosophical, but themes emerge through word-play and teasing paradoxes. This would not make fine theatre on its own and Stoppard's stagecraft is especially evident in *Rosencrantz and Guildenstern Are Dead*, a student production of which on the Edinburgh Fringe brought him rapid fame. The two nobodies are disposable to the greater characters of *Hamlet*. They while away their numbered days by tossing a coin, at once speculating on probability and pacing their own tragedy.

Stoppard's play takes place behind the scenes of **Shakespeare**'s; elsewhere he extrapolates the lives of historical characters, such as **Byron** in *Arcadia*, or the meeting of Lenin, Tristan Tzara and **Joyce** in Zürich, where they will be involved in staging *The Importance of Being Earnest*. This calls for several layers of parody. In *The Real Inspector Hound*, the humour is at the expense of blatant stage mysteries of the *Ladies in Retirement* kind.

Stoppard asks many questions, many about theatre itself, but he is committed to answers, too. In *Jumpers*, a relativist thinker expresses satisfaction that not as many people suffer these days as used to. Elsewhere the drama's purpose is idealistic and there is a belief in absolute values such as universal human rights. Stoppard's work has campaigned for freedoms in his birthplace, Czechoslovakia, and he has worked hard to draw attention to **Václav Havel**'s plight. He has translated Havel's work, adapted farce from German and collaborated with Terry Gilliam on the marvellous screenplay for *Brazil*.

Stowe

HARRIET BEECHER   **born Connecticut 1811; died Connecticut 1896**

*His idea of a fugitive was only an idea of
the letters that spell the word; or at the
most, the image of a little newspaper
picture of a man with a stick and bundle,
with 'Ran away from the subscriber'
under it. The magic of the real presence
of distress, the imploring human eye, the
frail, trembling human hand, the
despairing appeal of helpless agony; these
he had never tried.*

UNCLE TOM'S CABIN

HARRIET BEECHER STOWE'S family left New England to take their Christian mission to the frontier town of Cincinnati. It was there that her values were first affronted by the inhumanity of the slave trade. She was in a position to help runaway slaves and was in on the secret of an "underground railway" that conveyed people to Canada.

When the anti-fugitive laws were tightened, Stowe reacted with *Uncle Tom's Cabin*, which chronicles the slave Tom's plight at the hands of a series of owners. Throughout, the hero is called "property", which seems like irony now, but at the time this reminded readers that they were discussing sentient beings. The author has been criticised for her melodramatic style, but when she takes us aside and preaches, we can feel that she addresses us with little more than the conviction required by the age.

The success of the book can be judged by its sales (300,000 in the first six months) and by the feelings it inspired in the build-up to the American Civil War. **Emerson**, who was campaigning for the same cause, wrote that it was read "in the parlour, in the kitchen, and in the nursery of every house".

Stowe later wrote on other subjects – her native Connecticut and Lady Byron, whom she met on one of several trips to Britain. She created a scandal by publishing Lady Byron's account of the incestuous relationship her husband had had with Augusta Leigh, only to be vindicated as further evidence appeared. Still, **Byron** had been an early influence, as had **Shakespeare** and **Chateaubriand**'s *Atala*, with its similar sense of the American landscape. She also wrote more anti-slavery fiction and danced in the streets when Lincoln declared slaves free in 1863.

Swift

JONATHAN   born Dublin 1667; died Dublin 1745

As for his works in verse and prose,

I own myself no judge of those;

Nor can I tell what critics thought 'em:

But this I know, all people bought 'em,

As with a moral view designed

To cure the vices of mankind.

VERSES ON THE DEATH OF DR SWIFT

SWIFT THOUGHT SATIRE had its limits and famously called it a "glass, wherein beholders do generally discover everybody's face but their own." But he believed that through it humans could be brought to see sense and so set about achieving this by all the means at his disposal.

He was born to English parents in Dublin, became a Protestant priest and, after seeking the favour of Whig grandees in England, became disillusioned and co-founded the Tory-sympathetic Scriblerus Club. His political shift reflects his anger at the Whigs' refusal to tolerate Catholics, as well as his more conservative mode of thinking. He returned to Ireland on the death of Queen Anne, where he eventually became Dean of St Patrick's Cathedral in Dublin. There, his pamphlets argued for religious understanding and defended the Irish poor. He always published anonymously. The English Parliament and Irish Senate offered rewards to any who would betray his identity, but no-one did.

A Modest Proposal… demonstrates the savagery of his "satiric touch:/ No nation wanted it so much."

Drapier's Letters, meanwhile, showed it worked, preventing a corrupt minter's coins from entering Ireland. A bleak view of mankind emerges from his poems, which transmogrify classical idylls with contemporary slants (squirm at *A Beautiful Young Nymph Going to Bed*). His prose works allow a more comprehensive view of humanity. *A Tale of a Tub* shows with astonishing psychological acuity how one person's devotion is another's delusion, while *Gulliver's Travels* blends topical references and playfulness with a profounder regard for our fallibility.

He was a fount of wit and the soul of generosity, giving away two-thirds of his earnings to good causes. The brilliance of his writing earned him £200 in his lifetime and, for all his bitterness, a conscience without blemish.

Tagore

RABINDRANATH

born Calcutta 1861; died Calcutta 1941

Only when waves fall on the shore do

they make a harmonious sound;

Only when breezes shake the woods do

we hear a rustling in the leaves.

Only from a marriage of two forces does

music arise in the world.

Where there is no love, where listeners

are dumb, there can never be song.

BROKEN SONG, TR. WILLIAM RADICE

RABINDRANATH TAGORE LIVED a life of breathtaking achievement. He wrote some 1,000 poems, 24 plays, eight novels (besides shorter fiction), composed 2,000 songs (including the Indian National Anthem) and from his late 60s executed 3,000 paintings. He founded his own pioneering educational institution at Santiniketan; he campaigned for Indian self-rule and against the partition of Bengal, while repudiating nationalism; he was often at odds with Gandhi, a dear friend with whom he was ultimately reconciled.

He is India's most revered poet of modern times. His work became known in the West through the efforts of **Yeats** and **Pound** (the former helped touch up Rabindranath's English versions) and he won the Nobel Prize for Literature in 1913. His work has a musician's love of rhythm and enjoys Bengali's capacity for sound effects. His poetic range is enormous, from love lyrics heart-rending in their oratory, to powerful hymns in the manner of the *Upanishads*. His verse has a strong urge to tell stories It shares with his fiction a concern for India's poor: the poem *A Half-Acre of Land* is bitterly ironic about a tenant's eviction and the story *Four Acres of Land* documents similar exploitation and was made into an acclaimed film by Balraj Sahni.

Rabindranath travelled extensively around the world and was at first allured by the West. He admired the British temperament, but deplored its Raj. He returned his knighthood in 1919, after General Dyer's atrocity against the unarmed citizens of Amritsar. In speeches everywhere he championed Asia as the mother culture. His work combines a Hindu awareness of all-pervading spirituality with the playfulness of that tradition's myths.

Tennyson

ALFRED, LORD

born Lincolnshire 1809; died Surrey 1892

Behold, ye speak an idle thing;

Ye never knew the sacred dust.

I do but sing because I must,

And pipe but as the linnets sing:

And one is glad; her note is gay,

For now her little ones have ranged;

And one is sad; her note is changed,

Because her brood is stolen away.

IN MEMORIAM

TENNYSON WAS THE BEST-LOVED poet of his day. He succeeded **Wordsworth** as Poet Laureate in 1850 and to this day remains one of the most quoted writers in English. Rather than stifling him, the large readership Tennyson enjoyed during his lifetime gave him the authority to say whatever he wanted. Although much of this was undoubtedly public, he remained able to explore personal ideas. *The Idylls of the King*, for example, is an epic on the theme of King Arthur, a subject **Milton** had wanted to undertake. Like Milton, Tennyson found in the story a way of expressing his own view of human destiny.

Still, poems such as *The Charge of the Light Brigade* have done much to overshadow his more intimate work, even while displaying his work's virtue. **Eliot** and **Auden** both praised his ear for rhythm, although many have thought this led Tennyson to write lines for their sound effects alone. Although we can see his virtuosity everywhere, with words or phrases echoing as they disappear, or lengthening to lull us (as with *The Lotos-Eaters*), his word music (which has suggested song to many composers) is often so suited to his subject that we can allow its wizardry to work on us unconsciously: *Maud* provides a showcase for metre matching mood. But Tennyson is able to draw attention to his devices, as in a poem where he explains that he is using a metre of **Catullus**, or, in *Northern Farmer*, where the language is more emphatically suggestive for the broad Yorkshire accent.

His best work remains *In Memoriam*, written over 17 years to lament his dear friend Arthur Hallam. Although fairly long, it has economical episodes in a tight stanza form, chronicling grief that we start to share. At its more hopeful close, Tennyson finds plain language that profoundly reflects the aesthetic thinking of his age while reaching a conclusion echoing **Dante**'s.

Thackeray

WILLIAM MAKEPEACE

born Calcutta 1811; died London 1863

Fifty years ago, and when the present writer, being an interesting little boy, was ordered out of the room with the ladies after dinner, I remember quite well that their talk was chiefly about their ailments; and putting this question directly to two or three since, I have always got from them the acknowledgement that times are not changed. Let my fair readers remark for themselves this very evening when they quit the dessert-table, and assemble to celebrate the drawing-room mysteries.

VANITY FAIR

LIKE **DICKENS**, THACKERAY developed his fiction from sketches he had been producing as a journalist. He wrote for *Punch* and *The Times* and became known for satire that systematically skewered bombast wherever he found it.

His contemporary writers were not safe from his mocking either – writers such as Bulwer-Lytton, producing sensational novels based on prison records, were outdone by *Catherine*, in which Thackeray takes the lurid to parodic extremes. Here we see society at its worst and although she can meet saintly characters (Thackeray's purest creations were based on his wife, Isabella who went mad after

the death of their second child), the heroine is at the heart of the darkness.

His most famous work, *Vanity Fair*, has a similarly calculating heroine in Becky Sharp, who manipulates her way around the London of the Napoleonic Wars in a way that provided a model for Scarlett O'Hara in *Gone With the Wind*.

We begin to see how Thackeray gained his intimate knowledge of society from top to bottom in his novel *The History of Pendennis*, which charts "a Rake's Progress". Through the book's eponymous hero, Arthur Pendennis, who – as Thackeray did – gambles away his education and time at Cambridge, the author sought to present a realistic picture of the complete man.

More often than not, Thackeray's humour found historical settings, as in *Henry Esmond* and its sequel *The Virginians*, both set in the 17th century. But he still created worlds that were unsettlingly familiar to his readers.

Thomas

DYLAN

My one and noble heart has witnesses
In all love's countries, that will grope
*   awake;*
And when blind sleep drops on the
*   spying senses,*
The heart is sensual, though five eyes
*   break.*

WHEN ALL MY FIVE AND COUNTRY SENSES

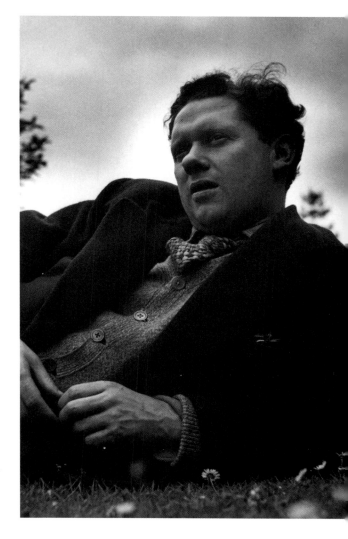

DYLAN THOMAS DIED SUDDENLY in New York, thanks to the ruinous lifestyle that had become as famous as his public readings. His reputation has wavered between the poles of tormented prophet and obscene drunkard. In productions of *Under Milk Wood*, the former can lead to a preciousness that makes one wonder if performers have noticed how the name of the play's fictional Welsh village, Llareggub, reads backwards.

As recordings attest, he was an inspiring lecturer and reader of others' verse. He was particularly fond of **Hardy**, with whom he shared a great inventiveness in stanza form and refrains. In **Hopkins** he saw the possibilities of sprung lines bouncing with internal rhymes.

But it is possible to over-emphasise Thomas' reliance on devices. His phrase "dogs in the wet-nosed yards" is much-quoted as an example of "transferred epithet", but elsewhere it becomes clear that his perceptions can become jumbled to induce a more total experience. This gives his work that robust sense of life that makes the poet respect death all the more. Even death becomes inextricable from the knowledge of death: this fills the poems with a resonance that Thomas' own early end can make deafening. Such work is obviously passionate, but in a poem such as *A Refusal to Mourn the Death, by Fire, of a Child in London*, there is an acceptance of the inescapable life cycle, and an awareness of what a poet can and cannot say by way of comfort, that is worthy of **Yeats.**

Thoreau

HENRY DAVID   **born Concord, Mass. 1817; Concord Mass. 1862**

Poet. See those clouds; how they hang! That's the greatest thing I have seen today. There's nothing like it in old paintings, nothing like it in foreign lands – unless when we were off the coast of Spain... I thought, as I have my living to get, and have not eaten today, that I might go a-fishing. That's the true industry for poets. It is the only trade I have learned. Come, let's along.

WALDEN

IT WAS **EMERSON** who made Concord, Massachusetts, the home of transcendentalism, but of all the movement's prophets, only Thoreau was born there. He also lived the philosophy more completely than any of his fellows. He campaigned against war and slavery; he went to prison in 1845 for refusing to pay taxes towards the war with Mexico; he advocated civil disobedience in an essay that later had an impact on Gandhi and Martin Luther King; he helped runaway slaves escape; and by championing John Brown, backed violent intervention against slavery.

He embodied the individual at odds with society. He said he could be sociable, but coined phrases such as "the majority of one" and "different drummer" to indicate that truth often resides in those who stand alone. In his masterpiece, *Walden*, he does just that. He built a cabin beside Walden Pond, on Emerson's land, where he lived self-sufficiently for two years. Like his earlier book, *A Week on the Concord and Merrimack Rivers* it is written in the journal form that Emerson encouraged him to pursue (Thoreau's journals proper have been published posthumously), offering us a detailed description of the forest with wisdom-studded essays alongside. The work abounds with his intimate knowledge of botany and wildlife and with the calls of birds, in which he found literary echoes.

He also had a taste for puns and felt etymology and word-play revealed language's deeper meanings. Thus Walden becomes "Walled-in", although throughout that great book, the author finds everything but confinement there. Sharing Emerson's pantheism, Thoreau sensed the presence of the divine as much in the soil as he did in the sky.

Tolstoy

LEO

born Yasnaya Polyana 1828; died Astapovo 1910

If he had any feeling for his brother at that moment, it was rather one of envy for the knowledge the dying man now possessed that was denied him.

ANNA KARENINA

COMMENTATORS OFTEN REMARK on how much Tolstoy had in common with Levin, the hero of *Anna Karenina*. They were alike in details – both were landowners, deeply concerned by the plight of their serfs, and both compelled their future wives to read diaries of their sexual exploits. They were also alike in spirit: they approached everything in life with a painstaking enthusiasm, bringing insight and huge knowledge to bear on whatever issue they discussed.

But Tolstoy's strength lies in identifying completely with all his characters, women as much as men (and even dogs) and not just those he resembles. He began his career with memoirs and his observations of war from the Crimean campaign, before producing the two novels which, for many readers, vie to be the best ever written. *War and Peace* is a chronological account of Napoleon's invasion of Russia and an attempt at a completeness that the author admits, in a lengthy postscript, to be impossible. *Anna Karenina*, meanwhile, applies the same absorption of detail to the plight of its unhappily-married heroine, with numerous interior monologues documenting psychological minutiae.

Shortly after its publication, Tolstoy turned increasingly to the spiritual. He denounced private property (while maintaining his) and declared that the public owned his work after 1881. He wrote to

the Tsar warning of imminent social upheaval and urging him to yield power to the people. But his pacifism led him to argue against violent revolution. His political legacy was acknowledged by Lenin and Gandhi.

Ultimately he repudiated his luxurious texts, preferring a simpler, more moral tone, but everywhere in his work the veneer of sophistication cannot stifle his characters' real passions for long (*The Kreutzer Sonata* is an extreme example). His *oeuvre*, which fills 90 large volumes, includes tragedies and comedies for the stage, as well as stories that vary widely in length and subject.

Trollope

ANTHONY

born London 1815; died London 1882

He loved to sit silent in a corner of his club and listen to the loud chattering of politicians, and to think how they all were in his power; how he could smite the loudest of them, were it worth his while to raise his pen for such a purpose.

THE WARDEN

ANTHONY TROLLOPE WROTE 47 books – 21 of them as a man of letters when he was still working for the Post Office, where, as a valued employee, he devised the red pillar box. He unashamedly wrote for money (his mother Frances had raised him by doing the same, nursing his dying father and scribbling frantically in the next room) and in his autobiography he documents his industry, explaining how he trained himself to produce, reliably, a fixed number of words an hour, usually between 5.30 am and breakfast every day. He also tells us how much he earned for his work and that he wishes it were more.

His methods make his novels through – composed and there is a stronger sense of time passing in his work than there is of a plot developing. Consequently, he is best known for his characters, who reappear throughout series of novels. He began his Barsetshire books with *The Warden*, introducing early on his gently – stated theme, progress versus tradition, the town of Barsetshire, an intimately – realised conflation of Salisbury (where *The Warden* suggested itself to him) and Winchester, of which he harboured miserable memories as a schoolboy flogged (or "tunded") by everyone, including his brother.

Later came his "Palliser" novels, which replaced Barsetshire's high-church/low-church intrigues with affairs of state. Trollope stood for Parliament in 1868 and used his books to air his political views (which were far from radical). The recently – ousted Conservative Premier John Major was an admirer, even before the dilemma at the heart of *The Prime Minister* – in which a politician leads a vulnerable minority government longer than anyone expected – became so like his own.

Tsvetayeva

MARINA

born Moscow 1892; died Yelabuga 1941

MAJOR WORKS

The Swans' Encampment
 (1917–1922)

Versts (1922)

A Poem of the End (1924)

The Ratcatcher (1925)

Poems to Czechoslovakia
 (1938)

for the path of comets

is the path of poets: they burn without

> *warming,*

pick without cultivating. They are: an

> *explosion, a breaking in –*

and the mane of their path makes the

> *curve of a graph*

cannot be foretold by the calendar.

THE POET, TR. ELAINE FEINSTEIN

TSVETAYEVA'S WORK has an immediate appeal to Western readers, thanks to Elaine Feinstein's universally acclaimed translations. These present us with a fresh, almost epigrammatic compactness on the subjects about which it is hardest to be concise: love, loss, poetry, displacement and death.

For a Russian poet of her time, these are inextricable. To explore personal feelings at the expense of public commitment was to be at odds with the Bolshevik agenda, which she thought "satanic". She left Russia in 1922 and her husband fought as a counter-revolutionary. In Europe she had a number of intense love affairs, which contributed greatly to her work: in her poetry, the end of love and the end of life are barely distinguishable from one another.

Poetry proved to be equally vital. She was able to endure poverty while creating and would sublimate all other concerns to it. This absolute integrity led to her being outcast by the Paris literati after she refused to join other Russian émigrés and sign a document belittling **Mayakovsky**'s achievement. She eventually returned to Russia in 1939. The war forced her to leave her beloved Moscow (she offered the city paeans as classical as **Mandelshtam** reserved for St Petersburg) and she hanged herself in 1941.

It is hard to avoid sharing something of this great sorrow when reading *A Poem of the End*. It picks up on the tiniest details of lovers' meeting and parting, to deduce the profoundest truths. The things the poet sees, even in passing, are so much a part of her experience that they seem like symbols. She also looks at words as though they must represent her point of view simply by being there, notably the one that appears as "sep   arating". But even this points to a pain the verse can scarcely bear to acknowledge: "In what language is it, when the meaning itself doesn't exist?"

Tucholsky

KURT

born Berlin 1890; died Hindäs, Sweden 1935

From time to time women don't have it easy either. But we men have to shave.

SCRAPS

KURT TUCHOLSKY WAS a novelist, satirist, journalist, critic, poet and songwriter. He worked in Germany from just before World War One and then during the Weimar Republic. He became known for his cabaret pieces, being part of a tradition that had included Joachim Ringelnatz before him and that Kurt Weill and **Bertolt Brecht** made world-famous. Tucholsky was one of the first critics to bring Brecht and **Kafka** to prominence.

Of the two, he identified more with Kafka. His material obliged him to write under a number of pseudonyms, such as Theobald Tiger, Peter Panter, and Kaspar Hauser. Kafka declared he felt more lonely than Kaspar Hauser, the guilt-ridden wanderer whose appearance in **Verlaine** is revealing about Tucholsky: "Although I had no king and country/ And am hardly brave/ I wanted to die at war/ But death did not want me."

Although Tucholsky survived World War One, the experience left him feeling stateless and he lived in Paris from 1924 and Sweden from 1929. The horrors of the war gave his work focus and his writing is full of attacks on innate German militarism, while his satire aimed to promote the fragile democracy of the Weimar Republic. With the rise of the Nazis, his statelessness was officially endorsed, while in the land he had once called home, his books were either banned or burned. He wrote little or nothing from 1932 and killed himself in 1935.

His work includes love stories (one of which may derive from a real liaison in Sweden) and verse. But he is best remembered for his epigrammatic wit, in pieces that explore the differences between the nations (particularly German and French) and the sexes. His irony shows he had more sympathy for non-Germans and non-men.

Turgenev

IVAN

born Oryol 1818; died Bougival, nr. Paris 1883

First love is like a revolution; the uniformly correct ordering of life is smashed and destroyed in an instant, youth takes to the barricades, its bright banner raised on high, and no matter what awaits it in the future – death or a new life – it sends to all things its ecstatic greeting.

THE TORRENTS OF SPRING,
TR. RICHARD FREEBORN

IVAN TURGENEV WAS a Russian writer who began to attract attention in the late 1840s. Some of this was from the police, who arrested him in 1852, after an obituary of **Gogol**.

At that time in Russia, opinion was divided between "Slavophiles", who felt the world spirit (as described by Hegel) would pass to the East, and those who saw themselves as a marginal people. Turgenev had sympathy with the Slavophiles but, as he had studied in Berlin, considered himself a Westernised writer. Consequently, he has perhaps enjoyed more success in Europe than in his own country.

He left Russia in 1856 and made for Baden-Baden, where **Dostoyevsky** later visited him. Despite their friendship – Turgenev helped Dostoyevsky's with his gambling debts – Dostoyevsky attacked him as a traitor, considering *Smoke* the work of someone who barely knew or cared about Russia.

Still, Dostoyevsky recognised the perfection in Turgenev's work and his elegantly-structured tales of love. Not that Turgenev was a writer given to lyrical tenderness. He had a life-long wish to see the abolition of serfdom and had firm political convictions that were radical at first. When *Fathers and Sons* first appeared, the Senate summoned him to justify the book. In the end, the police realised its critique of nihilists favoured the *status quo*. What he faults in a character such as Bazarov is the unwillingness to recognise the power of love, a force from which no wanderer can flee.

Twain

MARK   born Florida, Missouri 1835; died Redding, Connecticut 1910

Very often, of course, the rambling and disjointed humorous story finishes with a nub, point, snapper, or whatever you like to call it. Then the listener must be alert, for in many cases the teller will divert attention from that nub by dropping it in a casual and indifferent way, in the pretence that he does not know it is a nub.

HOW TO TELL A STORY

MARK TWAIN'S OFTEN FUNNY, often compassionate writing does much to preserve the innocence of the American South. However, it is not a naïve project; his work is always aware of the evils that threaten the South – as when *The Gilded Age* shows it being industrialised.

His hope was to restore the unheroic charm of **Cervantes**, as eroded by the romantic myth-making of **Sir Walter Scott**. He went so far as blaming Scott for the Civil War, in which Twain briefly took part.

In much of his fiction, he tries to imagine an American South in which the conflict never happened but is already disfigured by the evils of slavery. Huck Finn grows up with it, but he is marginalised enough in his society to use his conscience and so appeal to ours.

The Eden of this lost world is the Mississippi. Twain lamented the decline of its slang, whose rhythms and cadences he froze in time with his masterpieces, *Tom Sawyer* and *Huckleberry Finn*. He was apprenticed to a printer and became a pilot on the Mississippi, where he gained the nickname Mark Twain (an expression meaning literally "mark twice", calling on the sailor to measure the draught of water with a plumbline). His real name was Samuel Langhorne Clemens.

A humorous style had always characterised his narrative structures, right from his first success, *The Celebrated Jumping Frog*. But in later years, as Twain's fortunes declined and he suffered a series of family bereavements, his work, particularly his aphorisms, developed an unaccustomed gravity. Despite this, he never lost his ability to tell a joke.

MAJOR WORKS

The Celebrated Jumping Frog of Calaveras County (1865)

The Innocents Abroad (1869)

Roughing It (1872)

The Gilded Age (1873)

The Adventures of Tom Sawyer (1875)

The Adventures of Huckleberry Finn (1885)

A Connecticut Yankee in King Arthur's Court (1889)

Verlaine

PAUL

born Metz 1844; died Paris 1896

May your verse become a splendid spree

Sprinkled on the morning's crispy wind

Flowering as it goes the thyme and

*   mint...*

Everything that's left is literary.

POETIC ART

PAUL VERLAINE WAS associated with the Parnassian movement in French poetry, a group responding to the less-honed romantic effusions of the likes of **de Musset** by saying "Passion is no excuse for writing bad verse." His own verse was always sonorous, experimenting more and more with rhythm. It is harder to be convinced by his own passions.

He seldom seemed to be sure of them himself. In his refined expressions of decadence, he followed **Baudelaire** too slavishly for some. In his quest for a poet's purity and experience, he vacillated between his young wife and the even younger **Rimbaud**, who was less timid in exploring extremes. The two set up together in Camden, advertising a French course in what must have been a revelatory teaching environment. During a two-year prison sentence for shooting Rimbaud in the wrist, he turned briefly to Catholicism. This was still not the answer for Verlaine: out of subsequent confusions came his famous essays on the "cursed poet", as he saw **Mallarmé**, Rimbaud and himself. Tempestuous creators have vied for the epithet ever since.

Still, in Verlaine's best poetry, there is little to shock. Its most unsettling aspect is the metre. Even this works entirely in keeping with its own rules and beats beneath delicately placed internal rhymes and half-rhymes. But his ear was entranced by lines with odd numbers of syllables. His deployment of them meant that in order to be read smoothly to the end, each line starts with a jolt, as if the first syllable were missing. This leads to a disruption of the sense and shifts attention to the verbal music of a poem. His extraordinary achievement is keeping poetry that was so based on sound sensible. Where such instincts led **Apollinaire** into surrealism, in Verlaine's work they sometimes yield exquisite phrases, and in *Poetic Art*, quoted in the metrical translation above, it even begins to account for them.

Verne

JULES

born Nantes 1828; died Amiens 1905

His teaching was what the German philosophers would call 'subjective': that is to say it was for himself and not for others.

JOURNEY TO THE CENTRE
OF THE EARTH

JULES VERNE'S WRITING has so engaging a charm, so playful a use of the intellect, so boundless an energy, so adventurous an imagination and such enduring characters that he has directly influenced the most diverse of subsequent authors.

His way of stretching science to just beyond the possible had an immediate effect on **H.G. Wells**; **Raymond Roussel** met him and confessed to worshipping him (emulating the great man's passion for yachting); **Georges Perec** was as hooked as generations of French schoolboys have been, and has paid the master innumerable tributes in his own work, including the use of puzzles and scholarship; and for sheer adventure, as well as locations, **Edgar Rice Burroughs** is deeply indebted to him. Even to pick up a novel by Michael Crichton is to see his enduring legacy, with computer print-outs where Verne would have shared codes and lists with us.

His reputation suffers in that his career was a commercial one; he speculated on the Paris stock exchange and began his literary life writing opera libretti. He could not remain indifferent to the success of **Dumas**' romances and loved travel. Once he had found his *métier* as a mentor of science fiction and fantasy, he wrote at least one novel a

year. His first adventure story, *Five Weeks in a Balloon*, told of a fantastic journey – a motif that recurred throughout his work, most famously in *Around the World in Eighty Days*.

Characters also reappeared, in the manner of **Balzac**'s *Comédie Humaine*: Captain Nemo goes *Twenty Thousand Leagues Under the Sea* and his confessions in *The Children of Captain Grant* resurface in a trunk on *The Mysterious Island*.

His appeal was universal in his lifetime. He was a Companion of the *Légion d'Honneur*, and fêted in society, with a global audience eagerly awaiting new translations.

MAJOR WORKS

Five Weeks in a Balloon (1862)

Journey to the Centre of the Earth (1864)

From the Earth to the Moon (1865)

Twenty Thousand Leagues under the Sea (1869)

Around the World in Eighty Days (1872)

Vidal

GORE

born West Point 1925

Cynthia is a very serious woman and ceramicist, with a sense of the sacredness of all life. Naturally, she eats only macrobiotic vegetables and tofu and, of course, nothing that has ever had a face except cauliflower.

LIVE FROM GOLGOTHA

GORE VIDAL IS A WRITER so experienced at provoking controversy that he is as much a part of the American landscape as the institutions he attacks. He is a consummate talker, whose life has afforded him extraordinary insights into how his country really works.

He was born at West Point Military Academy, where his father was an aeronautical instructor, and he became the first child to cross the Atlantic in a plane. His early knowledge of the political process came from his grandfather, who was a senator. In 1960 Vidal ran for office as a Democrat, intending to spend more on education and less on defence.

He commands most consistent respect for his fictionalised examinations of American history's turning points — Alexander Hamilton's death in a duel in *Burr*, Lincoln's presidency, or the scandals threatening to emerge during the Constitution's centenary in *1876*. This book appeared during the Constitution's bi-centenary and provided an opportunity to reflect on the recent Watergate affair. Although his stories might seem all too real, he sometimes broaches great "what ifs" — such as, in *Hollywood*, the possibility of **Shaw** or **Maeterlinck** working there in 1917.

He has rewritten much of early Christian history, including *Julian* — the confessional memoirs of the liberal Roman Emperor Julian the Apostate — and *Live From Golgotha*, in which Christ's passion takes place in an age of mass communication. He portrays a modern kind of decadence and an obese Messiah in a prose distinguished by Vidal's tasty brand of camp.

People have claimed his *The City and the Pillar* as America's first gay novel, although Vidal has argued that the distinctions between sexualities are so blurred as to be meaningless. If his characters' speech seems fey elsewhere, this early novel has been praised for refusing to stereotype homosexuals.

Virgil

born Mantua 70 BC; died Brundisium 19 BC

I sang about maintaining flocks and fields

and about trees, while Caesar storms the

  deep

Euphrates in the war, and winning, gives

compliant peoples laws, heads for Olympus.

Then sweet Parthenope sustained me,

  Virgil,

blooming with zeal for genteel scholarship,

who played at shepherds' songs and, bold

  in youth,

sang Tityrus, beneath a beech tree, you.

GEORGICS, LAST LINES

VIRGIL WROTE THE MOST PERFECT poetry in Latin. He wrote three works and in each he introduced different strands of Greek culture, in their most polished forms, to Rome, which was emerging from lengthy civil wars into an empire under Augustus.

His adaptations were always applicable to his native Italy and, some have thought, to himself — many have sought a hidden, anti-imperial agenda in his writing. He grew up in Mantua at a time when Augustus (then Octavian) was responsible for reallocating land — like Meliboeus in *The Eclogues*, Virgil's father was one of the losers. *The Eclogues* present the rural charm of the Greek poet Theocritus, but with some updates, including a piece on an imminent imperial baby so Messianic that many in the Middle Ages took Virgil for a Christian before his time.

The *Georgics* likewise use the Greek poet Hesiod's technique of versifying practical advice and apply them to Italian farming. Virgil's guide blends praise of hands-on graft with a pious respect for the earth as a living thing and **Dryden** rightly called it "the best poem by the best poet" in Latin. No Latin verse betters the work's concluding myth.

Homer provides the sources for Virgil's epic, *The Aeneid*. In telling the story of how the Trojans founded Rome, Virgil draws on *The Odyssey* to describe how they arrived and *The Iliad* to depict them battling for it. The work echoes, adapts and even translates Homer. It was nearly finished on his death and, because it wasn't sufficiently polished, the poet asked that it be burned. Virgil agonised over the project, thinking he must have been mad to undertake it and certainly there was madness in his obsessiveness. His technique involved working and reworking drafts, settling on about a line a day "licking them into shape" according to his biographer, "as a mother wolf does her cubs" — an appropriate image for a poet whose greatest work anticipates the birth of Romulus.

MAJOR WORKS

The Eclogues (42–37 BC)
The Georgics (29 BC)
The Aeneid (19 BC)

Voltaire

FRANÇOIS-MARIE AROUET

born Paris 1694; died Paris 1778

VOLTAIRE EMBODIED the Age of Enlightenment. He was a man of many excellent parts: his *oeuvre* consists of plays (tragedy and comedy), poetry (including the epic), pamphlets, letters, essays on any number of subjects and, most famously, his fable-like stories. He was committed to reason, order and tolerance, using his unfaltering wit to condemn any kind of political or religious tyranny, as well as the uneven distribution of wealth in society. In much of this, he resembled his friend **Rousseau**, although the two fell out. His chief hatred was "infamy", as he called the Church's corruption and hypocrisy – and in turn the Church did all it could to portray him as a demonic figure.

In fact, his was a faith made stronger by his capacity to doubt and to ask questions. He stayed a while in England – he was exiled for lampooning the winner of a poetry prize he had expected to win – where he met **Pope** and **Gay** and became deeply attracted to Newton's way of viewing the world. Back in France, he advocated the British political system and was again exiled, finding refuge with Frederick the Great of Prussia.

His wanderings make him seem like the eponymous hero of his story *Candide*, who travels around Europe during a period of war. Candide's travelling companion is his tutor, Dr Pangloss – a man with such a Utopian view of society that when Candide recoils at the increasing carnage they encounter his teacher reassures him that "All is for the best in the best of all possible worlds."

The work's much-discussed ending, "We must cultivate our garden", is optimistic, but not glibly so. The whole is a bitter attack on complacency and is typical of Voltaire's longing for change. He was considered a hero of the Revolution he did not live to see and in 1791 his body was brought back to Paris to be buried in the Panthéon, where Charles de la Villette proclaimed, "The Glorious Revolution was the fruit of his works."

Vonnegut Jr

KURT

There's another clear moral to this tale now that I think about it. When you're dead you're dead. And yet another moral occurs to me now. Make love when you can. It's good for you.

MOTHER NIGHT

KURT VONNEGUT IS ONE of the most effective experimental writers working today, not least because of his accessible, chatty style. This apparent simplicity welcomes readers into his complex and often personal view of the world.

He is a satirist with a mission. There is a shock that resounds through his work, deriving from his own experience of war. In 1944, he witnessed the bombing of Dresden, with its unprecedented number of victims. He recalls the event in many of his books, most famously in *Slaughterhouse Five*.

There Vonnegut identifies himself strongly with his hero, Billy Pilgrim. In other books, the author interacts with his characters, advising them on how to bear their "lot" before abandoning them; but we learn that Billy's experience is Vonnegut's. That is, before he is abducted by aliens who enable him to see all of time, including his own future, making him feel powerless to change anything. The narrative is capable of responding to the horrors of the past and the future with nothing more than the shrugging refrain, "So it goes." Its insistence makes the author's voice a surprisingly loud one, railing at our indifference.

Characters travel from book to book, culminating in *Breakfast of Champions*, which Vonnegut wrote as a 50th birthday present to himself. Regular readers again encounter Mr Rosewater, whose philanthropy is so random that its beneficiaries find him deeply suspicious, and Rosewater's favourite writer ever, Kilgore Trout, who seems to have come up with many of Vonnegut's ideas. But Trout can't help being one of those ideas himself. He is stuck in a world where authors vie for a divine kind of omnipotence, and are unhappy to accept it in its present guilty state.

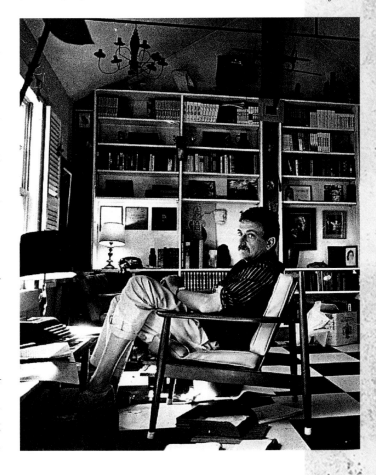

MAJOR WORKS

Player Piano (1960)

The Sirens of Titan (1961)

Cat's Cradle (1963)

God Bless You, Mr Rosewater, or Pearls before Swine (1965)

Slaughterhouse Five (1969)

Breakfast of Champions (1973)

Jailbird (1979)

Wharton

EDITH   **born New York c. 1861; died St. Brice-sous-Forêt 1937**

One of your great-grandfathers signed the Declaration, and another was a general on Washington's staff... These are things to be proud of, but they have nothing to do with rank or class. New York has always been a commercial community, and there are not more than three families in it who can claim an aristocratic origin in the real sense of the word.

THE AGE OF INNOCENCE

EDITH WHARTON WAS A novelist born into a privileged family, wealthy enough to flee the war-torn American South and return to settle in New York without too much discomfort. Her writing shows she was well-placed to record the city at its most opulent, but her background gives readers cause to be grateful that she wrote at all – to her family it would have seemed too much like working for a living. Still, she narrated the harsher fates of those around her.

The scenery for her drama is much like that of her friend and mentor, **Henry James**. Both have an ear for society's often oppressive niceties and an interest in the contrast between America and Europe. They share themes, too, both writing about an America that is coming of age and its emerging class system. In an atmosphere of new wealth, people become commodities. Wharton's heroines are as collectable art works as Isabel Archer in *The Portrait of a Lady* and in *The House of Mirth*, her first successful novel, Lily Bart is even more trapped by social convention than Daisy Miller. But Wharton suffers from the comparison. While she was fond of her intimate's "elaborate hesitancies", she favoured more direct language, once waiting for him to finish a lengthy sentence excusing some breach of etiquette before asking him, "Where's the Post Office?"

White

PATRICK

born London 1912; died Sydney 1990

> *It appeared that pure happiness must await the final crumbling, when love would enter into love, becoming an endlessness, blowing at last, indivisible, indistinguishable, over the brown earth.*
>
> VOSS

PATRICK WHITE WAS AN Australian novelist, a mysterious figure who seems to have shared the dogged singularity of the heroes he created. He was born in London and was educated in England, finishing his studies at King's College, Cambridge, but spent much of his childhood in Australia, where he worked on the land. His father was a sheep farmer.

The two novels that have brought him greatest acclaim show solitary heroes battling with land in the outback: Stan Parker in *The Tree of Man* is trying to survive, Johann Voss in *Voss* is trying to explore. But they are not simply tales of pioneers from Australia's past. The narrative finds poetic truths as it realises man's relationship with the earth and the earth is vital to the characters' relationships with one another. Before setting out to cross the continent, Voss meets Laura. What begins as an exercise in monomania becomes a labour of love.

The severe German explorer and the ingénue girl exchange letters, but feel themselves sharing new knowledge without needing to write. They find a love as unbounded as the vast spaces of desert that sustain it: Voss writes, "No ordinary House could have contained my feelings, but this great one in which greater longings are ever free to grow."

Among his men, who crack under the extraordinary strain and stage a chaotic mutiny, Voss is alone, driven on only by his vision. It remains incomprehensible to those around him. So it seemed to White himself sometimes. He was awarded the Nobel Prize for Literature in 1973, but aroused controversy by failing to accept it in person, sending

his friend, the painter Sidney Nolan, to receive it on his behalf. He used the money to fund an award for underestimated older Australian writers, all of this was deemed "ungracious" by the literary world: it is hard to imagine the author being too upset by the rebukes.

Williams

WILLIAM CARLOS   **born New Jersey 1883; died New Jersey 1963**

The poem

　　if it reflects the sea

　　　　reflects only

its dance

　　upon that profound depth

　　　　where

it seems to triumph.

ASPHODEL, THAT GREENY FLOWER

WILLIAM CARLOS WILLIAMS worked as an obstetrician for most of his life to support himself as a poet. Although he would always "Make It New", as his friend **Ezra Pound** asked of all good Modernists, his work never fitted into a particular school of writing.

Still, his poetry appeared in the Imagist collection Pound published in 1914. Like other poets in the book, he favoured economy of expression and short lines. His chief poetic credo was " – say it – no ideas but in things". Imagist poetry assembled such things for the reader to contemplate and Williams retained a similar interest in the visual, as in *Pictures from Breughel*. Still, it is in Williams that one has the strongest sense of a poem being a thing in itself. By far his most famous poem is not really Imagist: it is a note on a fridge door, apologising for eating some plums. Although the words are delicately placed, we can imagine the person who had been saving the plums for breakfast feeling unappeased.

Although his work is experimental, commentators have tried to intellectualise it out of the reach of the readers Williams would most have wanted. Like **Wordsworth**, he wanted to bring ordinary speech into the rhythms of his poetry. *Paterson* is a long poem attempting to achieve this. He called it "a reply to Greek and Latin with the bare hands". Here poetry sheds its ornament to become a way of communicating. Transcripts of a taped interview appear, as does a quote from a scholar explaining how Greek metres can reflect the way people speak.

The piece is a gift to his town in New Jersey, full of population figures, histories, an idyll here and a letter there. The work's joy is that it is composed of small things, but the whole is greater than its parts. The idea takes off from the things at last.

Wodehouse

P.G.   **born Guildford, Surrey 1881; died Southampton, Long Island 1975**

Other men love you. Freddie Threepwood loves you. Just add me to the list. That is all I ask. Muse on me from time to time. Reflect that I may be an acquired taste. You probably did not like olives the first time you tasted them. Now you probably do. Give me the same chance you would an olive.

LEAVE IT TO PSMITH

IN AN EXTREMELY LONG writing career, P.G. Wodehouse wrote some 120 novels, besides plays and the words for many successful Broadway musicals. The latter show their age, while the novels have lost nothing of their freshness, even though they are seldom set any later than the 1920s.

Shortly after leaving school, he began writing stories about the schoolboy Psmith, who would grow up in later stories to become a journalist, before being able to put in appearances at Blandings, the home of Lord Emsworth, itself the scene of many stories…

Indeed, Wodehouse's characters are most at home in luxurious country piles, or at the Drones Club; although some venture to the East End of London, they are quite stranded there. If they are bemused by the intrigues that embroil them and greet them with language to match, the author can find himself in the same fix. The formula that distiguishes the Jeeves and Wooster stories provided him with the perfect solution. For Wooster as narrator he invented a language consisting of half-finished sentences, conflated quotations and images plucked from panic through which Wodehouse could share his protagonist's bewilderment.

He sustains several plots at once, all hinging on seemingly insignificant props – flower-pots, policeman's helmets, umbrellas… ultimately, it is only Jeeves, his inscrutable butler, "the gentleman's personal gentleman", who can make any sense of it all. Beneath Jeeves' façade of compliance lies an evil genius for manipulation, excusable only if it prevents our hero from looking the chump he really is.

MAJOR WORKS

Psmith, Journalist (1915)

The Man With Two Left Feet (1917)

My Man Jeeves (1919)

The Inimitable Jeeves (1923)

Leave it to Psmith (1923)

Carry on, Jeeves (1925)

The Code of the Woosters (1938)

Wordsworth

WILLIAM   **born Cockermouth 1770; died Grasmere 1850**

Our birth is but a sleep and a forgetting:

The soul that rises with us, our life's Star,

Hath elsewhere had its setting,

And cometh from afar.

INTIMATIONS OF IMMORTALITY

WORDSWORTH LIVED MOST of his life in the Lake District, which provided the setting for much of his poetry. He began to write poetry at Cambridge, but it was only after he left and met **Coleridge** that a revolution took place in his work.

The two jointly published *Lyrical Ballads* and Wordsworth's contribution was the more substantial – even more so in the second edition, which included a second volume of poems and Wordsworth's famous preface defending his new mode of poetry. In it he argued that the very ornate poetry of the 18th century was flawed and that true poetry consisted in "the spontaneous overflow" of feeling and should be written in the "real language of men" – the rural, marginalised characters of his area and work.

Almost all of his important poetry was written in the decade that followed. His *Intimations* ode is the most perfect statement of one of his central motifs – the loss of spontaneity and inspiration as we grow older, and the need to re-imagine the world in order to compensate for that loss. *Tintern Abbey* is a similar example.

During these years Wordsworth all but completed his greatest work, the autobiographical epic *The Prelude*. He considered it only part of a larger project, which was never completed – *The Prelude* was not published until after Wordsworth's death, when the final title was agreed, and it describes the poet's development from his love of books and nature to sympathy with all mankind. It includes a description of events surrounding the French Revolution as its backdrop, but omits big moments in the poet's personal life, most notably the birth of a daughter to a mistress he never married.

His later achievement was his criticism and a number of impressive sonnet collections. In 1843 he succeeded Southey as Poet Laureate and died seven years later, like **Shakespeare**, on St George's Day. He has been, with **Milton**, the greatest literary influence on all subsequent English poetry.

Yeats

W.B.   **born Sandymount 1865; died Roquebrune 1939**

But naught they heard, for they are ever
listening,
the dewdrops, for the sound of their own
dropping.

MISERRIMUS

YEATS IS ONE OF poetry's towering figures. He was the greatest Irish poet to write in English and perhaps the greatest poet writing in English in his day. His verse seems simple and direct. He wrote that it should be that way: "I said, 'A line will take us hours maybe/ Yet if it does not seem a moment's thought/ Our stitching and unstitching has been naught.'"

It is hard to believe that even those lines occasioned toil. Yeats' expressed poetic goals often seem strange. He was an expert in the occult, on a quest for both Irish and Eastern spirituality, forming "Celtic Dawn" as a student, investigating Noh plays and the poetry of **Tagore**. Throughout his life he balanced pragmatism with dreaminess, quite in command of the Abbey Theatre's day-to-day running, yet easily duped (and doped) into watching for leprechauns; consistently attractive to women, yet allured by what he thought was his beloved Maud Gonne's chastity; avidly wanting to form a new Irish poetry, yet unable to master Irish, and uncomprehending when the experimental plays he produced in Dublin occasioned rioting.

Finally, he believed his writing had the power to change things. Here he was less deluded. He expressed some guilt that a play of his might have sent viewers to their deaths in the Easter Rising of 1916. It was thanks to his poetry that he became a figure of national importance, a senator, charged with the Republic's coinage. For all his life's complexities, his poetry succeeded with a direct simplicity that became clearer still over 50 years of writing. The poet's rages or yearnings are felt immediately. His half-rhymes and slackening metres seem to be buckling under the weight of passion, however often he stitched and unstitched them.

Zola

ÉMILE   **born Paris 1840; died Paris 1902**

*The mechanic shrugged. He despised
people with the gift of the gab, who take
up politics as others go in for the law, to
make big money out of phraseology.*

GERMINAL, TR. LEONARD TANTOCK

ÉMILE ZOLA DESCRIBED himself as an experimental novelist. He settled in Paris to lead the professional life of a writer, which he pursued with uncommon vigour, producing a number of studiedly "naturalist" texts. He filled his prose with details so meticulously researched that he was almost writing up a laboratory test. A problem with his legacy is that he anticipated the results. His readers are told they will enter a world where a character's fate is determined by his genetic make-up and physiology.

The result is that events seem inevitable and so all the more tragic. Zola's artistry outdid his social purpose. When Napoleon III lost power, he was able to express his socialist views openly, even though his famous letter beginning "J'accuse!" exposing a military cover-up in the Dreyfus case, landed him a spell in prison and on the run.

Most of his novels follow the fortunes of a family during Napoleon III's reign and were published after it, so that it was too late to implement the reforms he advocated, and his claims to absolute naturalism were impossible to prove. But he remains read for the sheer scope of his project, covering French life in all its aspects from bishops to call-girls.

Ibsen charged Zola with going into the sewer to bathe in it rather than to cleanse it; and although it is

true Zola was unsparing in his ribald dialogue and textual innuendo, he is left with the defence that he is portraying people as a dehumanising, industrial society has made them, rather than concluding that human beings are necessarily beasts.

Index

SORTING THINGS OUT

Everything is made of some kind of material. Materials can be **solids, liquids,** or **gases**.

THINK about different materials.

- A drinking glass is a solid. It has a specific shape.
- **Water** is a liquid. It flows into the shape of whatever is holding it.
- Air is a mixture of gases. A gas has no shape and you cannot see it.

Can you think of other solids, liquids, and gases?

Solid	Liquid	Gas

YOU WILL NEED

A pencil and a ruler

A piece of paper

WHICH MATERIAL IS WHICH

1 Use the pencil and ruler to divide your paper into three equal columns. Label the columns as shown above.

2 Look at all the things around you. What would you say each one is? Are they solids, liquids, or gases?

3 Look in a book or online to discover which gases make up air. Write the names of three solids, three liquids, and three gases in the three columns.

4 Underneath each list, describe what solids, liquids, and gases are like. For example, some solids are hard.

BECAUSE...

Solids are things that you can pick up because they always have a shape. They can be hard, such as wood, bouncy, such as rubber, or soft, such as wool. Liquids are runny and have no shape of their own. They flow into the shape of the container they are poured into. Most gases are invisible, although you can smell some of them. They have no shape and spread out to fill the space they are in. For example, you use the gases in air to blow up a balloon.

WHAT ARE SOLIDS?

Solids are materials that change their shape only when something else forces them to change.

THINK about how you can change the shape of a solid.
• An apple may be cut into slices.
• A piece of wood can be carved into a toy.
How can you change the shape of solids?

YOU WILL NEED
Some solids (e.g. a piece of cloth, modeling clay, coins, cheese, a ball, a plastic ruler, wooden sticks, paper, margarine, grapes, peas)
Tools to change your solids (e.g. scissors, a plastic knife, a large stone)
A pencil and paper

WHAT CAN SOLIDS DO?

1   Test your solids to find out how many ways you can change their shape. Try folding, squashing, stretching, bending, cutting, squeezing, and breaking them.

"BECAUSE...

The shape of some solids is easy to change because the solids are soft or bendy. Other solids are difficult to change because the material they are made from is very hard, so they cannot easily be cut or broken. "

Grape Pea	Squashing

3 Make a list of your solids and the ways in which each one can be changed.

2 Which solids are difficult to change and which are easy? Why do you think this is?

LIQUIDS AND SOLIDS

Liquids and solids can sometimes behave in similar ways.

THINK about what happens when you move milk from a bottle to a glass.
• The milk can be poured.
• It takes the shape of the container that holds it.
Can a solid behave like a liquid?

YOU WILL NEED
A glass of water
A large bowl
A jar of syrup
A spoon
Little plates containing solids of different sizes (e.g. tomatoes, flour, pebbles, peas)

CAN YOU POUR A SOLID?

1 Pour the glass of water into the bowl. What happens?

2 Clean and dry the bowl. Pour a spoonful of syrup into it. How is it different from the water?

3 Pour each plate of solids into the bowl one at a time. Clean the bowl after each use.

4 How do the solids compare with the water and syrup?

" BECAUSE...

The tomatoes do not pour because each tomato is a single lump of material. The pebbles, peas and flour look as if they are pouring but only because each small piece is falling at the same time as the other pieces around it. None of the pieces change shape when they hit the bowl. When liquids are poured, even thick liquids such as syrup, they spread out to form a level surface within the container. "

CHANGING LIQUIDS

Liquids can turn into solids.

YOU WILL NEED
Small, empty yogurt containers
A carton of juice
Aluminum foil
Scissors
Popsicle sticks

THINK about how water **freezes** in the winter.

- When it is very cold, the water in puddles and ponds turns to ice.
- When the **temperature** is low enough, drops of water in the sky turn to snow.

What makes a liquid change into a solid?

HOW CAN YOU MAKE A LIQUID INTO A SOLID?

1 Fill the yogurt containers two-thirds full of juice.

2 Cut a square of foil and fold it over the top of each container like a lid.

3 Carefully use the scissors to make a small hole in the center of each foil lid. Gently push a popsicle stick through the hole into the container.

4 Leave your containers in the freezer for a few hours. Make sure they are upright. What does the juice look like when you take the containers out?

BECAUSE...

The juice turns into a solid because the freezer makes the juice very cold. All liquids will turn into solids if they get cold enough. The point at which a liquid becomes solid is called its **freezing point.** Different liquids have different freezing points.

MELTING SOLIDS

Solids can turn into liquids.

THINK about how solids **melt** to become liquids.

- A popsicle melts when it is taken out of a freezer.
- Chocolate melts when you hold it in your hand.

What makes a solid change into a liquid?

YOU WILL NEED

A pencil and a ruler
A piece of paper
Some solids to test
(e.g. an ice cube,
a square of butter,
a piece of chocolate,
a candle)
4 little plates

1 **HOW CAN YOU MAKE A SOLID INTO A LIQUID?**

Make a chart like the one shown below.

	Ice	Butter	Chocolate	Candle
10 mins				
20 mins				
30 mins				
40 mins				

" BECAUSE...

The ice cube melts quickly because it has a low **melting point**, or the temperature at which a solid turns into a liquid. Butter and chocolate have higher melting points so they take longer to melt. The candle does not melt because it is not hot enough. Ask an adult to light the candle and watch what happens.

"

2 Put the ice cube, butter, chocolate, and candle on separate plates.

3 Leave the plates in a warm place, such as a sunny windowsill.

4 Check the plates every 10 minutes for the next 30 to 40 minutes. Every time you check the plates, record on your chart how the solids look.

MIXING SOLIDS

Solids can be mixed together.

THINK about food made from a mixture of solids.
- Oats, nuts, and raisins are mixed together to make muesli.
- Tomatoes, cucumber, and lettuce can be mixed to make salad.

Can mixed solids be separated?

YOU WILL NEED
2 large bowls
A cup each of dried pasta, dried beans, oats, raisins, sugar, and flour
A colander
A flour sieve

HOW CAN YOU SEPARATE SOLIDS?

1 Put all the solids in a bowl and mix them together. How does the mixture look? Can you see the separate pieces?

2 Pour the mixture through the colander into the other bowl. What happens?

3 Remove the colander and whatever is in it and pour the second bowl through the sieve into the empty bowl. What happens?

4 Which solids are left in the colander? Which solids are left in the sieve? Which are left in the final bowl?

" BECAUSE...

When you pour the mixture through the colander some of the solids are left behind. This is because they are too big to pass through the holes. When you pour the remaining mixture through the sieve, only the flour and sugar are small enough to pass through the sieve holes. If you had a very fine sieve you could separate the sugar from the flour, too.

"

MIXING SOLIDS AND LIQUIDS

Solids can behave differently when they are added to a liquid.

YOU WILL NEED
A large bowl
A cup of flour
A jug of water
A spoon
A fork

THINK about what happens when solids mix with liquids.
- When soil mixes with water it makes mud.
- If you mix powder paint with water it makes liquid paint.

What other changes can liquids make to solids?

HOW DOES A LIQUID CHANGE A SOLID?

1 Pour the flour into the bowl. Can you build the flour into a shape, such as a cube?

> ## BECAUSE...
>
> When they are dry, powders such as flour are difficult to shape. The tiny pieces in them slip and slide around each other. When the flour is damp, all the little pieces stick together. They can then be pressed into a shape. When more water is added, the shape collapses. The individual pieces separate from each other and float around in whatever shape the liquid takes.

2 Add two or three spoonfuls of water to the flour and stir it in thoroughly with a fork. What happens to the flour? Can you make a shape with it now?

3 Add more water and keep on mixing. Now what happens?

19

DISSOLVING SOLIDS

Some solids mix so well with liquids that it looks as if the solid has disappeared. When this happens, we say that the solid has **dissolved.**

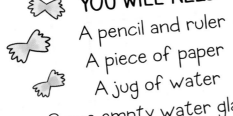

YOU WILL NEED

A pencil and ruler

A piece of paper

A jug of water

Some empty water glasses

Some test materials (e.g. salt, peas, pasta shapes, soil, powder paint, sugar, instant coffee, sand, flour)

A spoon

THINK about adding sugar to a drink.

• If you stir sugar into a hot drink, the sugar dissolves and seems to disappear. The sugar is **soluble.**

What other solids are soluble?

WHICH SOLIDS DISSOLVE?

1 Use the pencil and ruler to divide your paper into three columns. Label the columns: material, guess, and result.

Material	Guess	Result
Salt	✓	
Peas	✗	

2 Make a list of your test materials in the first column. In the second column, checkmark the test materials that you think will dissolve.

3 Fill each glass about halfway with water. Stir a spoonful of a different test material into each one.

4 What happens to the solid in each glass? In the results column, tick the test materials that did dissolve. How many did you get right?

BECAUSE...

"Some of the solids dissolve in the water. They have broken up into such tiny pieces that you can no longer see them.

Some of the other solids spread through the water and make it look cloudy. These solids have not dissolved. They are so light that they float in the liquid for a while. Eventually they settle on the bottom of the glass, leaving the water above them clear. We call these materials **insoluble**.

The larger, heavier solids sink straight to the bottom of the glass. They do not mix with the water at all. These solids are also insoluble."

21

SEPARATING SOLIDS AND LIQUIDS

Some solids are harder to separate from liquid than others.

THINK about what happens when you cook pasta.

• When the pasta is ready, it is poured through a colander to drain away the water before you eat it. Pasta is insoluble, so it can be separated by straining.

How are dissolved solids separated from water?

YOU WILL NEED
A tbsp (15 ml) of warm water
A glass or bowl
A tsp (5 ml) of salt

HOW CAN YOU SEPARATE A DISSOLVED SOLID?

1 Pour the warm water into the glass or bowl.

2 Add the salt to the water and stir until the salt dissolves.

3 Leave the glass or bowl somewhere warm or sunny for several hours to a few days. Look at it again. What has happened?

" BECAUSE...

The water in the glass or bowl slowly disappears and only small, solid bits of salt are left. This is because the water has **evaporated**. The heat from the warm room or Sun has turned the water into a gas. The gas then rose into the air. Dissolved solids can be separated from liquids by the process of evaporation. "

THINK about how laundry dries outside on a sunny day. The sunshine warms the wet laundry and evaporates the water in the material, drying the laundry.

HEATING AND COOLING

YOU WILL NEED

Waxed paper
A baking sheet
Silicone ice cube tray
or small baking cups
Chocolate pieces
A glass container
Colored candies
A helpful adult

THINK about how chocolate shapes are made.

- Chocolate is heated until it becomes liquid.
- When it is liquid, the chocolate can be poured into a mold.
- When it cools, the chocolate will take the shape of the mold.

Can you change the shape of solid chocolate by heating and cooling it?

HOW CAN HEAT CHANGE THE SHAPE OF A SOLID?

1 Cover the baking sheet with waxed paper. Place the ice cube tray or baking cups on the baking sheet.

2 Put the pieces of chocolate in a container and ask an adult to melt the pieces in a microwave or on the stove until the chocolate is runny.

3 Pour the chocolate into the ice cube tray or baking cups.

4 Put the baking sheet in the fridge until the chocolate has nearly set. Then decorate the chocolate shapes with candy and put the baking sheet back in the fridge.

5 When the chocolate has set, gently push the shapes out of the ice cube tray or baking cups. What shape is the chocolate now?

" BECAUSE...

When chocolate is heated, it melts into a liquid. Liquid chocolate can be poured into a mold. When the liquid cools, the chocolate becomes solid again. But the chocolate squares do not go back to their old shape. Instead they take the shape of the mold. "

CHANGED FOREVER

Some materials can melt and solidify over and over again. This is known as a **reversible change.** Others can be changed only once.

YOU WILL NEED

An adult to help you
3/4 cup (150 g) soft butter
3/4 cup (150 g) superfine sugar
A mixing bowl
A wooden spoon
1 tbsp milk
1 tbsp corn syrup
1 tsp baking soda
3/4 cup (150 g) plain flour
1/2 cup (125 g) rolled oats
A greased baking sheet

THINK about how solids and liquids change.

- Butter is solid at room temperature. It melts when it is heated and then cools to a solid again.
- A raw egg is liquid at room temperature. It becomes solid when heated. It does not become liquid again when it cools.

How does heating change some solids forever?

HOW CAN HEAT CHANGE THE SHAPE OF A SOLID?

1. Ask an adult to preheat the oven to 300 °F (150°C). Mix the butter and sugar in the bowl until they are creamy and fluffy. Then stir in the milk, syrup, and baking soda.

"BECAUSE...

When the mixture is heated in the oven, all the ingredients melt and mix together so well that they cannot be separated again. The mixture has become a new solid. This is called an **irreversible change.**"

4 Ask an adult to put the cookies in the oven. Bake them for 20-25 minutes or until they are golden brown, then let them cool.

3 Roll lumps of dough into small balls and put them on the baking sheet, spaced well apart.

2 Mix in the flour and the oats to make a dough.

GLOSSARY

Dissolving
happens when a solid breaks up into such tiny pieces within a liquid that the pieces can no longer be seen.

Evaporation
happens when a liquid heats up and changes into a gas. When puddles dry up in the sunshine, the water has evaporated.

Freezing
happens when a liquid is so cold that it changes to a solid.

Freezing point
is the temperature at which a liquid becomes a solid. Different liquids have different freezing points. The freezing point of water is 32° Fahrenheit (0°C).

Gases
are materials that have no shape. They spread out to fill as much space as they can. Air is made from a mixture of gases.

Insoluble
solids do not dissolve in liquid. Some liquids are insoluble, too. For example, oil does not dissolve in water.

Irreversible change
is when a material cannot be changed back to its original form.

Liquids
are materials that cannot hold themselves in any particular shape. They flow into the shape of whatever container they are poured into.

Melting

happens when a solid heats up and changes into a liquid. For example, when chocolate becomes hot, it melts and becomes liquid chocolate.

Melting point

is the temperature at which a solid changes to become a liquid.

Reversible change

happens when materials such as water and chocolate melt and solidify over and over again.

Solidify

is when a liquid changes into a solid.

Solids

are materials that have a definite shape of their own. Their shape does not change except by some kind of force.

Soluble

materials are able to dissolve in a liquid so it looks like they have disappeared.

Temperature

is a measure of how hot or cold something is. There are different ways to measure temperature. One way is in degrees Fahrenheit (°F) or Celsius (°C).

Water

can be found as a liquid, a solid, and a gas. When water is a liquid, it can flow into and take the shape of any container. If the liquid water reaches a temperature of 32° Fahrenheit (0°C), it will freeze and turn to solid ice. The ice will melt and change back into liquid water when it reaches a temperature of more than 32° Fahrenheit (0°C). This is its melting point. When water becomes extremely hot, it will boil and turn to steam. Steam is a kind of gas. It is very hot, so do not put your hand over boiling water.

LEARNING MORE

BOOKS
Claybourne, Anna. *Recreate Discoveries about States of Matter.* Crabtree Publishing, 2018.

Field, Jon Eben. *Kitchen Chemistry.* Crabtree Publishing, 2011.

Ives, Rob. *Fun Experiments with Matter.* Hungry Tomato, 2017.

WEBSITES
Go to www.dkfindout.com/us/science/solids-liquids-and-gases/ to discover more about solids, liquids and gases..

Learn about solids, liquids, and gases at www.generationgenius.com/videolessons/solids-liquids-and-gases/

PLACES TO VISIT

The Exploratorium in San Francisco, California, combines science, technology, and the arts in one fascinating museum. You can check out the museum's experiments online on its Explore page. Visit at: www.exploratorium.edu and click on Explore and choose a subject.

NOTE TO PARENTS AND TEACHERS:

Every effort has been made by the publisher to ensure that these websites contain no inappropriate or offensive material. However, because of the nature of the Internet, it is impossible to guarantee that the content of these sites will not be altered. We strongly advise that Internet access is supervised by a responsible adult.

INDEX